New Essays on the History of Autonomy

Kantian autonomy is often thought to be independent of time and place, but J. B. Schneewind in his landmark study *The Invention of Autonomy* has shown that there is much to be learned by setting Kant's moral philosophy in the context of the history of modern moral philosophy.

The distinguished authors in this collection continue Schneewind's project by relating Kant's work to the historical context of his predecessors and to the empirical context of human agency.

This will be a valuable resource for professional and advanced students in philosophy, the history of ideas, and the history of political thought.

Natalie Brender is Policy Advisor to the Minister of Foreign Affairs of Canada.

Larry Krasnoff is Associate Professor of Philosophy at the College of Charleston, South Carolina.

New Essays on the History of Autonomy

A Collection Honoring J. B. Schneewind

Edited by

NATALIE BRENDER
Ministry of Foreign Affairs of Canada

LARRY KRASNOFF
College of Charleston

PUBLISHED BY THE PRESS SYNDICATE OF THE UNIVERSITY OF CAMBRIDGE
The Pitt Building, Trumpington Street, Cambridge, United Kingdom

CAMBRIDGE UNIVERSITY PRESS
The Edinburgh Building, Cambridge CB2 2RU, UK
40 West 20th Street, New York, NY 10011-4211, USA
477 Williamstown Road, Port Melbourne, VIC 3207, Australia
Ruiz de Alarcón 13, 28014 Madrid, Spain
Dock House, The Waterfront, Cape Town 8001, South Africa

http://www.cambridge.org

First published 2004

Printed in the United States of America

Typeface ITC New Baskerville 10/13 pt.   *System* LaTeX 2_ε [TB]

A catalog record for this book is available from the British Library.

Library of Congress Cataloging in Publication Data
New essays on the history of autonomy : a collection honoring J. B. Schneewind / edited by
Natalie Brender, Larry Krasnoff.
p. cm.
Includes bibliographical references.
ISBN 0-521-82835-X
1. Autonomy (Philosophy) – History.   I. Brender, Natalie, 1967–   II. Krasnoff, Larry,
1963–   III. Schneewind, J. B. (Jerome B.), 1930–
B105.A84N49 2004
170–dc22   2003062974

ISBN 0 521 82835 X hardback

Contents

Contributors

Natalie Brender, Policy Advisor, Office of the Minister of Foreign Affairs of Canada

John M. Cooper, Professor of Philosophy, Princeton University

Stephen Darwall, John Dewey Collegiate Professor of Philosophy, University of Michigan

Knud Haakonssen, Professor of Philosophy, Boston University

Jennifer A. Herdt, Associate Professor of Theology, University of Notre Dame

Larry Krasnoff, Associate Professor of Philosophy, College of Charleston

Mark Larrimore, Assistant Professor of Religious Studies and Philosophy, New School University

Onora O'Neill, Principal, Newnham College, Cambridge University

Richard Rorty, Professor of Comparative Literature and Philosophy, Stanford University

Acknowledgments

This collection began as a conference honoring the work of J. B. Schneewind, held at Johns Hopkins University in March 2000. We thank Susan Wolf and John Partridge for their assistance in organizing this conference, and all the participants for their contributions to the discussions.

We thank Terence Moore at Cambridge University Press for his interest in and support of the project, his assistants Matthew Lord and Stephanie Achard for their assistance during the editorial process, and the two anonymous readers for the Press for their comments.

Finally, we thank J. B. Schneewind for all he has given us as a historian of moral philosophy, as a teacher and advisor, and as a friend.

Introduction

Like every academic discipline, philosophy has a history. Unlike the other disciplines, however, philosophy has constantly struggled with and against the fact of its history. In traditional humanistic fields like literature and history, it is well accepted that current understandings are historically specific: today's writers situate themselves against the readings of previous generations, and they openly acknowledge that their own readings are motivated by the specific concerns of their own times. In scientific fields like physics and chemistry, by contrast, it is well accepted that history plays no essential role in contemporary practice: scientists understand their results as independently justified by the natural evidence, regardless of the historical contingencies that may have brought anyone to those results. The two understandings are of course radically opposed, and they may even provoke conflict within the academy. But within the disciplines themselves, there is a broad consensus on the role that the history of the discipline should play.

Philosophy, however, has constantly wavered between these two understandings. For the most part, the dominant view has been the scientific one: philosophical positions exist in the realm of reasons, and those reasons have no essential reference to time and place. But philosophy has never left the humanities, and the history of philosophy has remained a constant part of the field. At times, as in the heyday of logical positivism, it has seemed as if the historians might be banished entirely. But the banishment has never finally happened. The strongly scientific account of philosophy has remained an explicit move within philosophy, not the implicit consensus of the discipline. The logical positivists ultimately needed their historicist opponents: without someone to struggle against on behalf of science, there could be no need for positivism at all. For every philosopher who has tried to leave history for the pure realm of reasons, there has been a historicist critic to argue against, a critic who seeks to return the rationalist to his or her place and time.

In this sense, the ahistorical philosophers, for all their Platonic dominance, are constantly on the defensive, and may even face a special disadvantage. They must struggle not only to defend their views with reasons, but also to establish that those reasons are valid in some ultimate sense. The latter claim is so bold and sweeping that it inevitably provokes a skeptical and often hostile response. And in this skeptical or hostile mood, it is easy to take a criticism of the claim to ultimate justification as a criticism of the philosophical view in question. If we can show that a self-described ahistorical philosopher is finally grounded in history, we can easily take ourselves to have shown that the ahistorical philosopher's substantive views are in fact mistaken.

But nothing of the kind follows. Even if philosophical positions are essentially grounded in history, there is no reason to assume that any particular philosophical position is incorrect, even if it is standardly understood as aspiring to ahistorical truth. For if all philosophical positions are historical, then the fact of their historicity does not distinguish among them. To assume otherwise is to assume that historicizing can only undermine the traditional practice of philosophy, and this seems as dogmatic as the claim that the traditional practice of philosophy should pay no attention to history at all.

The authors in this book take up, as J. B. Schneewind has done in *The Invention of Autonomy*, the historical context and implications of a piece of philosophy that may seem an obvious and especially controversial attempt to leave history: the Kantian theory of autonomy. We of course know Kant took his views about morality to follow from the necessary structure of rational agency. According to his historicist and communitarian critics, Kant was part of something called the "Enlightenment project," the attempt to provide morality with a stable and secular grounding in human reason. But if we are suspicious of this project on historicist grounds, must we therefore be suspicious of Kant? The substantive criticism follows from the historicist premise only if historicizing Kant reveals him to be doing nothing more than struggling against history. But if Kant's thinking is embedded in history in a much more complex and interesting way, then the force of Kantian autonomy will turn out to be much more complex and interesting than the critics of the Enlightenment have thought. Kant may have been the child of his time, but this undermines his thinking only if what it meant for him to be the child of his time was to be crude and dogmatic. And that follows not from any historicist premise, but from the crude and dogmatic history that is itself implied in the sweeping notion of the "Enlightenment project."

The historical reality, J. B. Schneewind has labored hard and well to show, was very different. Kantian autonomy, he has argued, sprang not from a simple and dogmatic wish to transcend religion and community, but from a complex engagement with a set of debates about the nature and possibility of moral community with other human beings and with God. If that is so, then it is difficult to fault Kant for taking leave of history, and difficult to criticize Kantian autonomy on those same grounds. The Kant who emerges from this more complex history may not be the familiar Kant, but he may well be a more interesting and even a more appealing Kant.

This last suggestion has two parts, and they correspond to the two parts of this book. In the first part, the authors seek to explore the complex history of Kantian autonomy, and especially its relation to the theological and religious debates of the seventeenth and eighteenth centuries. Exploring a series of controversies over toleration, theodicy and voluntarism, these papers place Kant in a context far removed from what we may understand as Enlightenment rationalism. In the second part of the book, the authors explore the implications of a Kant freed from this kind of rationalism, a Kant more sympathetic to our empirical nature, to the situated nature of our deliberations, and to the idea of plurality or community of rational agents. In different ways, these papers argue for versions of Kantian autonomy that go beyond the notion of a solitary rational agent, legislating eternally valid laws. Instead they argue for a conception of autonomy consistent with a contextual and historical account of human agency.

The authors in this volume do not always agree with Kant or with one another. They sometimes have very different views about the history that led up to Kant, and about what parts of Kant have survived the history that followed him. But the authors are united in their view that an understanding of Kantian autonomy can only be enhanced by a careful study of its historical context, and by a careful study of what our historical nature means for the idea of Kantian autonomy. Such a study is unlikely to end philosophy's struggle with and against its history, but it may show that struggle to contribute something to philosophy itself.

PART ONE

AUTONOMY IN CONTEXT

Justus Lipsius and the Revival of Stoicism in Late Sixteenth-Century Europe

John M. Cooper

In the history of scholarship and of humanist learning, Justus Lipsius is best known for his editions with annotations of Tacitus and (later) Seneca. Indeed, his was a scholar's and professor's life, devoted primarily to the study and teaching of classical Latin literature and Roman history. He cared about nothing more – or so he repeatedly said – than to live in peace and quiet, devoting himself to his books and his students and the enjoyment of his garden, far away from the bustle of politics – and from the civil disturbances and even wars caused by the passionate religious disputes that were so prominent a feature of Northern Europe, and especially of his own country, the present-day Belgium, during his lifetime (1547–1606). He was born near Leuven into a Catholic household, was a pupil from age thirteen to sixteen at the Jesuit College in Cologne (where he began to learn Greek) and then studied law at the university of Leuven. At nineteen he became Latin secretary to the notorious cardinal Granvelle (archbishop of Malines-Brussels), whom he accompanied to Rome (1567–70), where he began his work on Tacitus. Returning to Belgium briefly, he then went to Vienna, apparently hoping for some imperial academic or scholarly appointment (his first big book of textual studies of Latin classics, *Variae Lectiones*, had been published by Plantin at Antwerp in 1569). In this he was disappointed. On his way back to Belgium through Germany a year or so later, he learned of the confiscation by the Spanish army then occupying Belgium of his family property (on which he had been supporting himself). Thus in need of a source of income, and with the help of some German scholars he had become acquainted with, he was offered by the duke of Saxe-Weimar the chair of History and Eloquence at the newly founded Protestant (i.e.,

Lutheran) University of Jena, which he gladly accepted (along with a shift in religious affiliation).[1]

This was in 1572, when Lipsius was twenty-four years of age. Though he seems to have been a popular teacher, he did not stay long at Jena; his appointment in 1574 as dean of the Faculty of Arts was met with opposition from among his colleagues (on what ground we seem not really to know: suspicion of Catholicism? professional jealousy?), and he felt forced to resign from the University (March 1574). In Cologne, where he repaired for the rest of the calendar year, he married. His wife, a widow, belonged to a Catholic family of Leuven. They returned to Belgium, first to live in Lipsius's home village and then in Leuven itself, presumably supported by her or her family's money. He continued to work on Tacitus and took up Plautus as well, but he also resumed his studies of law at the university, receiving his degree in 1576. The Spanish army interrupted his peaceful life as a private scholar again in 1578, when their advances toward Leuven drove him off to stay with Plantin at Antwerp; when the Spanish took the city of Leuven, soldiers sacked his house and only the intervention of a Jesuit friend resident there (Spanish, to judge by his name), Martin Delrio, saved his books and manuscripts from destruction. Again in need of a livelihood, he looked to Holland. He was offered a professorship of history at the newly founded (Calvinist) University of Leiden in 1579, the year the United Provinces were established, in full revolt from Philip II of Spain – entailing a second switch in religious affiliation away from Catholicism, this time to Calvinism. There he stayed for thirteen years, until his final return to Leuven in 1592 as professor of history and Latin literature in the Catholic University there. He functioned in this position until his death in 1606.

I have related these biographical details because I think they may help us in reading and evaluating Lipsius's works on ancient Stoicism. Even in his earlier years while working largely on Tacitus he had apparently been much taken with Seneca, and with the Stoic philosophy that animates Seneca's *Moral Essays* and *Letters to Lucilius*.[2] His edition of Seneca's *Opera Omnia* was not completed until shortly before his death (it was published by Plantin at Antwerp in 1605). But already while at Leiden, in 1584, Lipsius published what proved to be his most widely read work, his two books *De Constantia (On Constancy)*, in which he presented and defended a Stoic moral and psychological outlook, derived largely from Seneca, upon the civil and religious disorders and the severe and brutally repressive Spanish rule in Belgium of that time; and while working on the Seneca edition he published two works in 1604 offering an introduction to and survey of Stoic philosophy, the *Manuductio ad Stoicam Philosophiam (Guide to the Stoic Philosophy)* and *Physiologia Stoicorum (The Physical Theory of the Stoics).*[3] (A third projected work, on Stoic ethical theory, remained unwritten;[4] in fact, however, the *Manuductio* is already largely devoted to questions of ethics, so taken together the two works do amount to an exposition of the whole Stoic system.) As I mentioned, *On Constancy* relies very heavily on Seneca (not necessarily, and indeed not even very notably, on Seneca's treatise of the same name), and otherwise almost entirely on Latin authors (Cicero, Aulus Gellius); it shows little or no knowledge of what are for modern scholarship the principal, or anyhow most highly regarded, Greek sources for our knowledge of classical Stoic theories – book VII of Diogenes Laertius's *Lives of Eminent Philosophers*, Plutarch's anti-Stoic treatises *On Stoic Self-contradictions* and *Against the Stoics on Common Notions*, the selections from Stoic authors in Stobaeus's *Eclogae* and Sextus Empiricus.[5] The later two works of 1604, however, show extensive and, in a scholarly sense, responsible and insightful use of these Greek sources (mostly, it seems, in the Latin translations that by that time had appeared of them all – but Lipsius does show that he can consult the Greek text when that is necessary or desirable).[6] Lipsius's account of Stoic philosophy in these later works aspires to, and obviously does, go well beyond Seneca and other Latin sources to discover the original form of the Stoic doctrines in the hands of Zeno and Chrysippus and other 'Old' Stoics of the third century B.C., and to deal with important questions about the evolution of these doctrines over the centuries from then to Roman imperial times. The version of Stoicism that Lipsius left in these two works for his successors in the study of the school is remarkably sophisticated and well-informed – much more so, as it seems, than standards and practices of the time would have led one to expect. It was, however, through *On Constancy* that Lipsius's revival of Stoicism as a framework for life and thought in early modern Europe was mostly effected. Hence in discussing Lipsius's Stoicism in what follows, I will concentrate on this very popular and widely read early writing.[7]

On Constancy (in two books) takes the form of a dialogue – like so many works of ancient philosophy. Interestingly, Lipsius's dialogic style in this work is more like that of Plato's dialogues than Cicero's philosophical works (or Seneca's so-called *dialogi*, in which Seneca, as the sole speaker, frequently raises and responds to things that "someone" or an unspecified "he" may say in objection or puzzlement): conversational interchange persists throughout, with no Ciceronian lapse into monologic exposition of doctrine. However, like Cicero, Lipsius is the narrator as well as one of the interlocutors; he begins by setting the scene for the conversation that is to follow. He reports that "a few years past" he was traveling from Leuven to Vienna (as in fact he had done, as we have seen, around 1570) and stopped in Liege to visit friends, among them Charles Langius, "the leader in virtue and learning among the Flemish" (71). Lipsius tells him he is leaving Belgium for other lands in order to distract his mind from the grievous distress caused him by the constant insolence of government functionaries and soldiers (under the sovereignty of the Spanish king), and by all the dislocations consequent upon the civil wars and seditions the country is beset with. No one, he says, could be of so "hard and flinty" a heart as to endure all these evils with equanimity – certainly, *he* has no "plate of steel about his own heart" (72). In addition to distress caused by his personal victimization, Lipsius reports grave distress simply at the constant sight of what the country and his fellow countrymen in general are enduring: once he is finally away from the country altogether, there will be "less grief to hear reports of evils than to be an eye-witness to them" (73).

In response, Langius sets out, in a conversation over that afternoon and the following morning, to disabuse the young Lipsius of the false "opinions" that Langius maintains lie behind Lipsius's grief and distress, and to put in their place "bright beams of reason," which, he says, will cure Lipsius's mind of the illness that makes it possible for, and indeed causes, him to accept those false opinions and suffer the consequent severely disturbed feelings. Traveling elsewhere will do no good, since the illness of the mind that he suffers from now, while in Belgium, is the cause of his troubles – not the events themselves that he has called "evils." Unless that ill mind is corrected it will simply accompany him to Austria, and ruin his life there just as surely as it has been ruining his life at home. The correction needed is to instill constancy of mind, the stable condition of one's mind that results from knowledge about what really is and what really is not actually good or bad: this constancy will prevent him from ever even momentarily falling for the false opinion, say, that some misbehavior of some soldier has actually *harmed* him or (of itself) *harmed* his life – and, consequently, from feeling grief or distress at what has happened.

Now, one might have thought that, despite what Langius implies, even with a cured mind Lipsius would still have found quite decent reasons to leave Belgium, at least until the Spanish army withdrew and some reliable civic order was restored. He has just reported that when working in the city he is interrupted by "trumpets and rattling of armor," but then is driven back to town by the need to keep away from "murderers and soldiers" if he seeks refuge in the country. You might have thought that the reasonable desire to find circumstances in which profitably and pleasantly to pursue his own studies and enjoy the company of his friends could give him enough reason to get away from Belgium (even if his life *could* go on unharmed even there, as Langius says it could). It is perfectly reasonable to want to avoid disruptions and disturbances in one's preferred way of life, if one reasonably can, even if one has a strong and constant enough mind not to be upset by them if one cannot, or simply does not, manage to avoid them. In fact, as we know, the real Lipsius did complete his journey to Vienna – and though the dialogue concludes with the literary Lipsius declaring that in hearing and acquiring Langius's philosophy he has now "escaped the evil and found the good," he does *not* add: "So, armed with it, I'll turn around and go back to Leuven." Still, since the civil and military disturbances besetting Europe – not only the Low Countries – at this time were seemingly unavoidable, it certainly might well have seemed to Lipsius and his contemporaries no small benefit to have learned, through Langius's Stoic analysis, this way of not allowing them to occasion suffering also in one's own mind. Presumably, the very great appeal of this work of Lipsius in his own lifetime and in the following decades must largely be due to its readers' expectation of this benefit.

In his note To the Reader at the end of the work, Lipsius defends himself against a possible charge that in thus reviving in his own Latin the ideas of Seneca or Epictetus, he must be guilty of foolishly and immodestly dealing with matters already dealt with better and more fully by the ancients themselves (207). No, he says: neither of these authors, nor any other of the ancients, has attempted what he has achieved in this treatise, namely, to offer "consolations against public evils." "Who has done it before me?" he asks.[8] Even Seneca's own little treatise *De Constamitia* primarily offers only a demonstration that nothing can injure or offend a truly wise man. A wise man cannot be so much as reached or touched by supposed insults or harms inflicted on him by others; his firmness and steadiness of mind is therefore entirely secure. Seneca refers, rather in passing (10.4), to the things that truly *do* buffet even a wise man. Such things include bodily pain or illness, or the death of friends or children, but also his country's ruin amid the flames of war – a "public evil" in Lipsius's terminology. These he says may wound the wise man – reach him, affect him – as the alleged insults and injuries of his enemies do not (*they* are nothings to him, things only to be smiled at). Nonetheless these "blows" are ones he immediately overcomes and puts right. The wise man does not assent even momentarily to any idea that he has been harmed in any way by them. However, as noted, Seneca's focus is not at all on "public evils" and the wise man's response to them, so Lipsius seems to be correct about the novelty of his work and its objective.

However, Lipsius has a grander objective as well. He does not limit himself simply to popularizing Stoic ideas about the vanity of worldly goods (and evils), the better to help those suffering from the civil unrest and the wars to endure their tribulations with as great equanimity as possible. In his dedication of the work to the Senate of the city of Antwerp, he describes its novelty in different, less limited terms. Referring to his study of ancient philosophy in general, he says that "(if I am not mistaken) I am the first to have attempted to open and clear up this path of Wisdom, so long shut off and overgrown with thorns" (203). He immediately adds: "which certainly is such as (in conjunction with Holy Scriptures) will lead us to tranquillity and peace." One could see this merely as linking his work directly with the aim, announced in the note To the Reader, of offering through the Stoic philosophy helpful consolation in times of war and civil strife. But in fact the claim that the ancient way of Wisdom, opened and cleared up by Lipsius himself, offers the chance of recovering or securing "tranquillity and peace" need not and (especially when addressed to the magistrates of a city) presumably does not refer simply to people's private states of mind. It refers to the elimination as well, and principally, of the external causes of the widespread mental pain and distress to which he and Langius address their conversation: namely, the civil unrest and wars. It is tranquillity and peace in outward affairs, not in inward consciousness, that the Senate of Antwerp must be principally concerned with, and it is this that Lipsius is claiming that his reopening of ancient philosophy (and specifically, of course, Stoicism) will lead us to. How does he suppose it might achieve that?

Lipsius nowhere in the treatise alludes to religious factionalism as the ultimate source of this unrest and these wars. It is easy, of course, to understand why he does not do so. Each of the factions (the Catholics and the various groups of Protestants) was acting in the full conviction that God wanted them to suppress the other religions and their adherents as heretical or heathenishly liturgical, and in either case as disrespectful of the true God. Each must hold that religious factionalism is not responsible for all the public evils that Lipsius decries, but rather the stubborn and sinful refusal of the *other* factions to give up their own religious practices and specific doctrinal statements and return, or go over, to *theirs:* each holds that *it* is no "faction" at all, but simply the true religion, the instrument of the true God at work for the salvation of all. As we will see, the argument of Lipsius's work published five years later, his *Six Books of Politics* (1589), shows him convinced that if people do govern their lives on the basis of their religion, such disorders are well nigh inevitable. At any rate, they will be inevitable if people are made to live in the same community with others who have a different religion. In *On Constancy*, instead of attacking the religions directly as responsible for the evils and suggesting, for example, that God does not in fact *want* these awful things done in his name, Lipsius adopts the delicate position of arguing that we should not live at all on the basis of our religious convictions and practices, but rather on the basis of the reasons that Stoic philosophy gives us as to what is good and bad for us. Only if we do that will we live in tranquillity and peace. The underlying aim of *On Constancy* is to show, through Langius's discourse, what living according to reason itself, alone, will require and what it makes possible. This is what it means to Lipsius to say that he is opening and clearing up the ancient path of Wisdom for the use of his contemporaries: he wants people to come to see good reasons why they should live according to the Stoic philosophy, just as his hero, Seneca, had done – and as a result how they can rid the European world of civil strife and war. And that, though of course he could not openly *say* this, means living *not* according to the – or any – Christian religion.

Lipsius recognizes that one cannot live in the 1580s as a Roman (or a Hellenistic Greek) pagan, and he does not propose that as the ideal. Instead, he argues for a revised Stoicism, one that takes account of the effects of Christianity on the worldview of any educated person of that time. Inevitably, that includes some philosophical ideas deriving not from ancient Stoicism but from its ancient rivals, especially Platonism, simply because Christianity itself adopted so much from Platonism. Lipsius's Stoicism is thus a Christian Stoicism. However, that does not mean a Stoicism in the service of a Christian *religious* commitment, whether a Catholic or any variety of Protestant one; it means merely the sort of Stoicism that could make sense for a person brought up with a basically Christian outlook on the world as part of his "commonsense" view of things. In discussing *On Constancy* in what follows I want to examine the special features of Lipsius's Stoicism in comparison with that of Seneca and the original Greek Stoics of the third century B.C. Just what features of sixteenth-century common sense did Lipsius think needed to be incorporated into a viable modern Stoicism that could, in particular, lead people toward living in peace and tranquillity with their neighbors professing religions

other than their own? How far, in fact, does this Stoicism depart from
that of the ancients?

Lipsius assumes as part of common sense the view of the world as a
world created by the omnipotent Christian God and peopled by humans
possessed of free will, all of whom are sinners, and he also accepts, as part
of this common sense, the central components of the long tradition of
Christian theology and moral psychology. So, early on in his discussion,
Langius urges on Lipsius the need to cure his own mind, rather than
to change where he lives, if he is to rid himself of sorrow at the evils
besetting the Low Countries. In doing so, Langius speaks of Lipsius's
need to restore his mind to control by reason and remove it from control
by passions and affections. The latter, he says, are by rights and by nature
the mind's "servants" (74.27), but in giving way to his sorrow Lipsius is
allowing his "principal and sovereign part," reason, to "let fall the scepter"
of rule so that it "willingly serves its own servants."

It is difficult to be sure, but this does give the impression that Lipsius
is accepting the Platonic or Aristotelian psychological theory (adopted
by the Church Fathers), according to which passions and affections, such
as lust or sorrow or anger, are not themselves products or expressions of
erroneous normative views adopted by one's weak and sick reason, but
are rather independently generated normative feelings that reason has
to "take up the sceptre of rule" in order to moderate and govern.[9] And
later, Langius happily adopts the Aristotelian idea that "virtue keeps to the
mean, not suffering any excess or defect in its actions, because it weighs all
things in the balance of Reason" (79.28). Admittedly, he does not there
apply that idea to the need to moderate the passions, to feel only some
due amount of anger or sorrow rather than to eliminate them altogether,
as his own Stoicism demands.[10] He is discussing instead the fact that the
virtuous person does not have either an inflated conception of his own
worth or the sense that he is worthless and so deserves any mistreatment
that comes his way – but rather some appropriate, intermediate sense
of himself and his value. Langius's point is that if, as he is arguing, the
virtue of constancy is what we need in order not to give way to sorrow
and grief and other passions, that is because constancy implies a noble
and high-minded voluntary sufferance of whatever happens to us – a
sufferance based in "right reason" that tells us correctly and precisely
how to value both ourself and these externals. He contrasts it sharply with
mere "patience" in the face of (alleged) evils, a reaction deriving from
the abject baseness of a cowardly attitude, which itself is due to mere
"opinion." But the free appeal to the Aristotelian stock idea of virtue as

"keeping to the mean" does, I think, show Lipsius's willingness as a Stoic to adopt a by his time deeply engrained or commonsense view about the passions as independent of reason. He is at the least disinclined to fuss over the ancient Stoics' insistence on technical philosophical reasons for its inadequacy.[11]

Indeed, in handling the distinction just noted between right reason and opinion, Lipsius again shows a similar degree of laxity that an ancient Stoic philosopher would never have tolerated. He defines right reason as "a true sense and judgment of things human and divine" and treats opinion as its contrary, being "a false and frivolous conjecture of those things" (79–80).[12] In that case, both right reason and opinion ought to be acts or properties of one's mind, right reason being the condition of the mind in which it judges strongly and correctly, and opinion the condition in which it judges weakly and incorrectly, about ourselves and God and about what in consequence is truly of value for us and what is not. Yet in what follows (chap. 5) in explaining the sources of reason and opinion, Lipsius assigns the former to the soul and the latter to the body: through its opinions the body contends with reason for control over the soul and so over our life, while reason, which is only one part of the soul, fights back with its own proper understanding. In this chapter Lipsius is plainly adopting formulations from Plato's *Phaedo*, where Socrates assigns appetites and desires in some way to the body itself (66b) and emphasizes the affinity of the soul to the eternal, divine forms (80a–b).[13] Imitating Plato, Lipsius calls (right) reason the part of the soul that is "uniform, simple, without mixture, separate from all filth or corruption: in one word, as much [of the soul] as is pure and heavenly" (81.8–11). Yet if reason is only one part of the soul, what is the other part? One might suppose that it would be precisely a part that, in bad people, weakly adopts opinions (false views about what is good and what is bad, views that are favorable to bodily gratifications, say), and so destroys their lives – but that in completely good people is perhaps completely inactive. In that case, Lipsius's language of opinion as itself belonging to the body (to the senses) would be an inaccurate way of saying that the plausibility to the soul of false evaluative views, and the pressure to adopt them, comes from appearances originating in the body, through the senses. These appearances would then not amount to *opinions* but only to representations of things, to which the errant part of the soul would have to assent wrongly in order for an opinion to first come into being.[14] But, as with the Aristotelian doctrine of the mean in the previous chapter, here Lipsius prefers to stick to the familiar Platonic picture and leave all such details to one side. This is dangerous, however, since it leaves his reader with the impression that for a Stoic, virtue consists in controlling and holding in abeyance false opinions that will nonetheless still beset the virtuous person's soul (in one part of itself, or else by being located in the body), instead of getting totally rid of all such false views. A person in such a condition could hardly be called totally tranquil and at peace with himself or herself and the world.

In any event, the thrust of Langius's admonition here and throughout his discourse is to urge the youthful Lipsius to live on the basis of right and sound reason, not through reliance on opinion. If Lipsius does this, he will find himself possessed of just that constancy of mind that will enable him to live happily and well even in the presence of the public evils that he has been lamenting. What does right and sound reason tell us, however? In subsequent chapters Langius progressively reveals it to consist, basically, of the leading ideas of Stoic moral and physical theory (and, as part of the latter, the theological theory of God's relation to the world). Langius mostly does not attempt to give arguments to show that these ideas *do* enjoy the support of reason, when reason is rightly employed. Rather, he presents them simply *as* the contents of right reason. He explains them in detail as they appear in their ancient context, and relates them to various elements of the inherited Christian worldview and defends them in that relation (or alters them to make them conform better to it). Finally, he argues from the resulting theory to various salutary conclusions.

First and foremost among the Stoics' doctrines for Langius's purposes is their theory of all external things and events as neither good nor bad – however much, in opinion, they may be counted as such. In chapter 7 he roundly but briefly declares this Stoic doctrine: false goods and false evils are "such things as are not in us, but about us – which properly do not help or hurt the inner man, that is, the mind" (85.12–15). For example, "riches, honor, authority, health, [and] long life" are not goods but only falsely so regarded, and neither are "poverty, infamy, lack of promotion, sickness and death" evils. To this he appends, quite accurately, the old Stoic conception of all emotions or passions as falling into one or another of four basic types, depending as they do on holding one or another of these false opinions about externals: desire or appetite and joy or elation have regard to some supposed such good, present or in prospect, while fear and sorrow or distress relate to supposed evils.[15] Since to be affected by a passion is to hold such a false opinion, and since people who properly employ their reason would never hold any such false opinion, those who employ their reason properly will never permit themselves to experience any passion or affection: not sorrow, fear, elation, passionate desire, or any of their subvarieties. Thus the public "evils" Lipsius has been lamenting, and other things like them (war, pestilence, famine, tyranny, slaughters and the like), are not evils at all, Langius insists, and it is a serious mistake ever to feel any passionate affection in relation to any of them (86.6–7).

Having laid down the basic Stoic theory and drawn out these consequences, Langius turns to show at length just why the alleged calamities that have befallen the people of the Low Countries really cannot be regarded as evils – and hence should not be grieved over, passionately objected to and so on. In chapter 13 of book I, he lays out a fourfold program for the whole of the remaining discussion. He will argue (1) that, in fact, God himself has imposed all these public evils upon the people of the Low Countries in his providential concern for the whole cosmos – mischance or misfortune (something one *might* have reason to lament over) have nothing to do with it (1.13–14). (2) The evils have come upon them by necessity, as a fated or destined outcome of the whole order of the universe, laid down, as it were, from the beginning of things (1.15–22). (3) In fact there is profit in these evils for those beset by them, through chastisement or just punishment or else to provide contexts in which they can exercise better their good moral qualities; or perhaps, unfathomable though this might be to us, they are adequately explained as being for the ornamentation and beautification of the cosmos itself (11.6–17). (4) Finally, he argues that there is nothing strange or noteworthy in the recent events in the Low Countries, such as might legitimately invite one to pay them special attention; all the lamentations rest upon an exaggerated estimation of these events' qualities and extent (11.19–26).

It is in discussing the first two points – God's providential ordering of everything that occurs in the universe, and fate, which is in Stoic theory very closely bound up with this providence – that Lipsius seems to feel the greatest obstacles in developing a version of ancient Stoic theory that could be found adequate by an educated late-sixteenth-century European. In chapter 5 of book I he has already begun, without blanching, to speak of the human mind as being some fiery material within us that has somehow sprung from God, of which or whom it is a part – thus implying that God too is somehow to be conceived as a fire (a "fiery nature," 81.14).[16] But he is much concerned with Plato's apparently approving quotation at two places in the *Laws* (741a, 818b) of poetical sayings to the effect that not even God can evade necessity (106.19–21). He hears in this the sort of thing Homer speaks of (anyhow as Lipsius interprets it) when he makes Zeus lament (*Iliad* 16.433ff) in seeing that his beloved son Sarpedon's death is impending at Patroclus's hands, since that is Sarpedon's long-established doom (121.10–11). Rather oddly, in fact, Lipsius associates this traditional Greek idea of even Zeus's unwilling subjection to the decrees of fate with the ancient Stoics' conceptions of Zeus and fate: for the ancient Stoics, fate is identical with the sequence of causes that works out Zeus's own providential plan for the development over time of the life-history of the world as a whole; Zeus's reason and plan establish and direct fate, and therefore they could not without serious confusion be regarded as ever *subject* to fate in any way.[17]

Lipsius, however, mentions that the Stoics "are charged with two impieties, that they make God subject to the wheel of Destiny, and also the actions of our will," and he confesses that he cannot firmly acquit them of either of these faults (115.24–30). He thinks we do find such things asserted in some of their writings. On the first point, God's subjection to fate, he immediately cites a passage from Seneca's *On Providence* (5.8) (I quote a bit more of the context than he does):

What then is the part of a good man? To offer himself to fate. It is a great consolation that it is together with the universe that we are swept along; whatever it is that has ordained us so to live, so to die, by the same necessity it binds also the gods. One unchangeable course bears along the affairs of men and gods alike. Although the great creator and ruler of the universe himself wrote the decrees of fate, yet he follows them. He obeys forever, he decreed but once.[18]

However, Lipsius also insists that the "true Stoics [i.e., the Greek founders of the school] never professed such a doctrine," never said or implied that God is subject to constraint by his own decrees once he has enacted them. It is not even true, he adds, on the Stoic view as that was set out by the "true Stoics" that we *humans* are subject to constraint by the fated order of the universe decreed by God: Chrysippus, Lipsius says (though without offering any explanation at this point of how he did this – I come back to this later), clears the Stoics of the charge of "depriving man of free liberty." According to Lipsius, even Seneca in the quoted passage really says only that God is subject to God, not to some external fate constraining him (whether established by himself or not). The fate he is declared to be subject to is just another way of referring to God himself, as several statements Lipsius quotes from Zeno, Chrysippus, Panaetius and Seneca himself elsewhere confirm.[19]

Nonetheless, instead of insisting that he *can* acquit the Stoics of these two impieties or faults (as in fact he could have, at least if he knew the texts he seems to allude to),[20] Lipsius sidesteps the charge by maintaining that if they did go astray in these points, they did so out of a laudable desire to free men from the fears and other distresses caused by the belief that pure chance and good and bad fortune play a role in human life (117.12–17). Once you know that absolutely *nothing* happens by chance or fortune, that everything that happens happens from determinate, ineluctable causes, themselves linked backward in time through an unbroken chain of causes to an ultimate source in the causation of God's own mind in planning the universe, nothing should surprise, nothing should upset you when it does happen. I do not know what author or authors Lipsius is thinking of in recording, and taking so seriously, these charges of impiety. Perhaps these authors had sufficient authority that it would have seemed dangerous to his pro-Stoic cause to provoke them, or others on their behalf, by disputing their charges: perhaps that could have caused a damaging counterattack. Or perhaps Lipsius did not have any specific authors in mind at all. In either case it might simply have seemed to him inappropriate, in a work of this kind, to go into the philological and hermeneutical detail required to make a case for acquittal. In any event, he goes on in chapters 19–22 to drop the discussion of the "opinions and dissensions of the ancients" and to propose on his own behalf an account of the "true" fate (117.21–2) It is this "true fate" that he wishes to propose for adoption as part of the sixteenth-century Stoicism that he himself wants to live by and is urging others likewise to do. As we will see, this doctrine owes a great deal to the ancient Stoics' views (and especially those of Chrysippus). However, Lipsius does see the need to correct the ancient doctrines on two points in order to bring them into line with sixteenth-century common sense. So maybe after all it was at least a good and clarifying tactic to officially leave the ancients aside for this part of his argument – and to allow without dispute the charges of impiety lodged against them.

Fate, Lipsius says in explaining his own "true" conception of fate, is the decree of God from eternity, through his providence, for the order and the unfolding of events in the universe that he has created. It consists in "an unchangeable decree of Providence inherent in changeable things, which firmly brings everything about in its order, place, and time" (118.8–11). Here, if not following then I think clearly in harmony with Chrysippus, he sharply distinguishes fate from providence, on which fate depends and which it expresses. Lipsius makes a point of this because, he says, unnamed "divines of our days" have confounded fate with providence both in name and in nature. But in fact, he maintains, fate refers to something actually present in the changeable things of the world, working within *them* to bring about, with all precision and all certainty, God's plan. God's plan or providence itself, however, is in God, not in the changeable things of the world: it is a "power or faculty in God of seeing, knowing and governing all things," whereas by contrast, fate "seems to descend into the things themselves and to be seen in the particulars of them, being as it were a disposing and bestowing abroad of that universal providence, particular by particular" (118.22–27). Here one might notice that Lipsius accepts the Stoic doctrine of God as the mind or soul of the world and, as such, everywhere interpenetrating its material constitution (as our souls do our bodies), and that he thought that these ideas were not inconsistent with the best of the Christian theological tradition.[21] His distinction between providence as *in* God and fate as (instead) *in* changeable things does not amount, therefore, to asserting the sort of modern popular view that makes God and his providence some metaphysically, if not physically, distant entity affecting the world from afar through his all-seeing distance vision, and so on. For Lipsius, as for the ancient Stoics, God is present everywhere, interpenetrating everything. It is merely that, as the providential mind dispersed through the world, God thinks the one grand thought that from eternity decrees the whole of what happens, while fate, the product of that thought, is dispersed through the materials of the world in the form of the various *causes* at work in it.[22] So far, then, in his account of God and fate, Lipsius's Christian Stoicism is an entirely faithful presentation of ancient Stoic theory.

It is in relation to the range of these causes, subordinate to or expressive of fate, that Lipsius registers his departures from ancient Stoic doctrine, or at any rate what he takes to be such. According to the Stoics, as he correctly reports, fate as a whole is "an order of *natural* causes from all eternity" (121.16; my emphasis).[23] For the Stoics, natural causes would, of course, include human beings, acting through their inherent natural powers of deliberation, choice and decision – in addition to whatever causes might be functioning in the automatic workings of inanimate and animate nature. But sixteenth-century common sense, brought up on Christian doctrine, would hold it obvious that even if everything has been foreordained by God, some of what he foreordains will come about not by either sort of natural causes at all, but by divine miraculous intervention in the natural and human orders. So among the causes through which, taken together, fate works, we must admit not only these two sorts of natural ones, but also ones that come about miraculously in contravention of the natural order and/or cause miracles. Secondly, when the

Stoics say that the fated order exists throughout eternity, that might be taken to mean (as Christian common sense would deny) that natural causation was at work throughout not just all time but eternity too. For Christians, God created the world at a certain point in his own "history," and "before" that there existed no such order of natural causes at work. So that qualification must be taken into account too, in adapting the Stoic theory of fate for sixteenth-century Christians. Thirdly, as Lipsius understood them, the Stoics deny that any of the causes that there are are "contingent" causes – causes of things that happen purely by chance and contingently. Lipsius does not explain or illustrate what he means by a contingent happening, nor does he say what makes him think the Stoics denied all contingency. He certainly does not mean to affirm that there are *real* chance or contingent events, ones that have no causes that in fact necessitate their occurrence, ones that just happen "out of the blue," causelessly: his acceptance of universal fate prohibits anything like that. He must mean by contingent events ones that, in being necessitated by their causes, are necessitated in such a way as to make it correct to denominate them as contingencies. If so, it seems clear that in fact the ancient Stoics had no difficulty in accommodating such events (e.g., a fair coin's randomly falling heads up when flipped). On Stoic theory, these things do have causes that just as much necessitate them as they necessitate further outcomes; it's just that we cannot remotely begin to find out in advance when the situation is one in which inevitably a (true) coin, when flipped, does come up heads rather than inevitably coming up tails. Chance and contingency for the Stoics are features of causes entirely in relation to our own ignorance. So this seems a case where Lipsius has misunderstood Stoic theory: he is wrong to say simply that the Stoics denied the existence of contingencies, chance events.

However that may be, on Lipsius's view, fate renders all events necessary, in the sole sense that they have as their original or first cause God's providential decree. It is this decree that ultimately brings them about, and it does so ineluctably in each and every case. However, fate or the embodiment of this decree is found dispersed in a variety of distinct types of "secondary" causes that Lipsius distinguishes, through which it works: "in causes (secondary ones, I mean) that are necessary, it works necessarily; in natural causes, naturally; in voluntary causes, voluntarily; in contingent, contingently" (119.24–26). At this secondary level, fate does not always work by using force, or by in that sense necessitating what it causes. For example, when a tree grows up and puts out its leaves, the tree is not violently assaulted by fate or by anything else in such a process; rather, it acts from itself, from its own inherent nature. It is fated to this result, if in fact it *does* result, through its own nature as the principal cause of what it does. Likewise (but, given the specific type of cause in question, very differently), a person voluntarily acts on certain reasons: he has not been forced by fate from outside himself to do what he does, for example by its moving his limbs against his will. Nor does fate act as a force from inside either, moving his limbs against his will. *He* is the principal cause of his decision and his action; he acts on the reasons that seem to *him* at the time to justify it. That is why the action counts as voluntary – not contingent, not natural (in the narrow sense of the tree's behavior in growing and putting out leaves) and not necessary either. Only when the specific secondary cause at work in a particular case is a violently necessitating cause (for example, when the brute force of the wind picks something up and moves it off somewhere) should we speak of fate as necessitating anything, through one of its secondary causes, in the sense of violently forcing something off in some way against its will or against what it is natural to it to do on its own. Furthermore, when something is fated through one or another of these different sorts of secondary cause, it is not just fated to *happen,* but to happen at just that place, just that time, and through just the precise types of causes and the specific circumstances through which it did or does come about.[24]

Now Lipsius's account of how voluntary action is compatible with the universal operation of fate is eminently Chrysippean, even in many of its details. As we have seen, he announces his conviction in chapter 18 that Chrysippus had cleared the Stoic school of the charge of "depriving man of free liberty," and in fact Lipsius's own account of the compatibility of fate with human freedom shows how Chrysippus did indeed clear the Stoic school of this charge. However, in accordance with his scheme in chapters 19ff. of setting aside the ancient dissensions and not disputing the charges of impiety against the Stoics, he treats this as another departure in his own view from that of the ancients. The ancient Stoics, he now avers, denied our free will, because they made the operations of fate, as they affect our actions, ones accompanied with "violence" (121.23ff.). Likewise, he blankly reaffirms the view that he had already cast doubt on in chapter 18, namely, that the Stoics made Zeus himself subject to some antecedent overriding fate. He counts that as a fourth way in which his "true" account of fate departs from that of the ancient Stoics (121.9ff.). In truth, however, it is only (at most) in the first two points that I mentioned earlier that his understanding does depart from that of the ancients: in its recognition of miracles as among the fated events and causes, and (perhaps) in its recognition of some fated events as contingencies or chances. Lipsius's own "true" view of fate, both in recognizing human freedom and in denying God's own subjection to fate, is in fact simply presenting the ancient Stoic understanding of fate, without significant change of any kind.

Earlier I outlined the four heads under which Langius organizes his discourse from *On Constancy* I.13 on. It is primarily in the discussion of fate (I.18–22, just examined) that Lipsius's attempts to adjust ancient Stoic doctrine to his sixteenth-century common sense can be seen and appreciated. The remaining sections of the discussion (in fact, the whole of Book II), devoted to showing that there is profit for everyone in the "public evils" of his time through chastisement or because they offer opportunities to exercise good moral qualities, and that in fact the current conditions are really not all that unusual or all that awful anyhow, rely much less upon special features of early modern Christian common sense than the discussions in book I that I have focused upon do. So I will not say anything further about *On Constancy*.

The *Manuductio ad Stoicam Philosophiam* (in three books) and *Physiologia Stoicorum* (in two) are, like *On Constancy*, written as dialogues – between Lipsius himself and an "auditor." However, in their case the speakers are not individualized and the "dialogues" read rather like elaborate catechisms rather than like a true discussion of the sort we do find in *On Constancy*. The Lipsius-speaker expounds to the auditor the relevant Stoic doctrines, with very extensive citations from ancient Latin amid Greek authors, and explications and discussions of his own aimed at bringing out the significance, and relevance to late sixteenth-century thought, of what one finds there. The title of *Manuductio* is obviously modeled on Epictetus's Greek *Enchiridion*. However, in Greek an *enchiridion* is a handbook, something small enough for you to hold in your hand and guide yourself with – a *vademecum* – whereas in Latin a *manuductio* is something that takes *you* by the hand and guides you. The main interest, amid the main achievement, of these works is that they provide an amazingly rich and full report of the ancient sources for Stoic philosophy, almost always acute and accurate – much more extensive than, as I have said, those we find in *On Constancy*. In the twenty years between *On Constancy* and the later works, Lipsius obviously did a prodigious amount of reading and note-taking in a pioneering and path-breaking attempt, as a scholar, to make available to his contemporaries the riches of this buried heritage. To a considerable extent that scholarly ambition, by itself, motivated the publication of these works, and Lipsius deserves our admiration and gratitude for his achievement in them. For two centuries and more, they were the main source one could go to to learn about and examine considerable parts of the ancient testimony on Stoic philosophy – much like more recent handbooks, such as those of Zeller or Long and Sedley. However, this labor was also carried out in the interest of Lipsius's hope of persuading his contemporaries to adopt for themselves the ancient philosophy of Seneca and the other heroes of the ancient Stoic tradition – the hope that educated people of his time could come actually to *live* the life of reason as the Stoics defined it, instead of living by false opinions about human values derived from a crude interest in the lowest-common-denominator pleasures, or by factionalizing religious commitments. He obviously hoped that if educated people could come to know, as he had come to know through his own scholarly labors, the rich and inspiring detail of the ancient Stoic theory, they might learn to adopt that philosophy (suitably revised so as to meet the needs of sixteenth-century common sense) as their own guide to life.

This interpretation of the underlying purpose or hope of Lipsius's Stoic writings – both *On Constancy* and the treatises of 1604 – might provide new light on some of the details of Lipsius's life with which I began this essay, and on his own character and way of life. Lipsius has been severely criticized for his alleged changes of religion – from his ancestral Catholicism, to Lutheranism in Jena in 1572, to Catholicism in Leuven in the later 1570s, to Calvinism in Leiden between 1579 and the early 1590s, and finally back to Catholicism as professor in Leuven from 1592 until his death. On the assumption that, really, he was some sort of Catholic throughout, he has been thought either weak and opportunistic, or simply more concerned for his comfort and peace than for his principles. But, judging from his Stoic writings, what he really thought, more or less all along, was that philosophical truth provided the only acceptable ground on which to live one's life. For him, to the extent that religion was not simply identical with sober and thoughtful devotion to the philosophical truth about God and his relation to the world and to human life, religion was simply a menace: religion as faith, cult, traditional practice, ritual worship, as some exclusively acceptable way of relating oneself to the philosophical truth about God and human life through some specific forms of faith and cult – all that simply led to civil strife, unrest, oppression, war. In that case, we should perhaps see him as actually having lived throughout according to his principles – the same ones all along. Of course, and in perfect accord with those principles, he sought good conditions in which to continue his scholarly work and his teaching career – first in a Lutheran academic context, then in a Catholic one, then in a Calvinist one and finally again in a Catholic one. It would be a gross misunderstanding to suppose him a man concerned for his own comfort and convenience and willing cynically to adopt or drop religious affiliations as convenience dictated. And it would certainly be a mistake to suppose that he was all along a committed Catholic who, however, for convenience and the advancement of his career, was willing to practice one or another Protestant faith.

In fact, a frequently cited letter of Conrad Schusselburg, a Lutheran colleague of Lipsius's at Jena, supports just this interpretation.[25] Schusselburg reports visiting Lipsius at his house in Leiden in 1582 (he takes care to name another person as present at the conversation, so as to reinforce the veracity of his report). Questioning Lipsius about his "apostasy" from Lutheranism at Jena to Calvinism at Leiden, and suggesting (as a committed Lutheran necessarily would) that that amounted to denying and deserting Christ himself, he got the following response: "I have not denied Christ, nor deserted him, even though here I don't profess the Lutheran doctrine, and consort with Calvinists. For every religion and no religion are to me one and the same. With me, the Lutheran and the Calvinists' doctrines walk side by side." And when Schusselburg suggested that if he continued in that way to approve equally of each of *these* religious doctrines, the next thing you knew Lipsius would become a papist again, as he had started out, Lipsius replied: "That's all the same to me." Of course, as we know, this is precisely what did occur.[26]

It is well known that in his *Six Books of Politics* (1589), written while he was a professor in Calvinist Leiden, Lipsius defended the principle that the sovereign's religion should prevail in the public life of any country; apparently he saw no other hope for peace and tranquillity in a world splintered by religious factionalism. This was, of course, not a very politic position to adopt in the United Provinces at a time when the Spanish king still claimed sovereignty there: in that context it inevitably sounded pro-Catholic and anti-Protestant.[27] The resulting controversy led to Lipsius's withdrawal back to Leuven and his final return to Catholic allegiance. In retrospect, it might seem odd that, with a commitment to a live-and-let-live tolerance in his own life and with the hope embodied in his Stoic works for the spread of this tolerance through philosophical education, Lipsius did not see that the experience of the Low Countries, and particularly the United Provinces, was leading toward a final accommodation between the various Protestant and the Catholic religions, on the basis of principles of political and social toleration accepted by committed

religionists. However, with his personal belief in philosophy itself as the
only salvation, and his sense that a true religious commitment simply
forestalled any possibility of accepting on equal terms persons of other
communions, it is perhaps not so surprising that he did not see his own
philosophical cause as linked to that of the Calvinist leaders at Leiden
who were groping their way toward this outcome.

J. B. Schneewind links the revival of Stoicism through the work of
Lipsius, and of Du Vair in France, with the ethical theory of Descartes
and Leibniz, under the heading of "origins of modern perfectionism" –
perfectionism being the chief seventeenth-century alternative to the ethical and political philosophy of the seventeenth-century natural lawyers.[28]
This is surely correct. Stoicism is without doubt what we nowadays call a
perfectionist ethical doctrine, and there seems no doubt that Descartes's
and Leibniz's work in these areas did owe a lot to the revival and spread
of Stoic ideas largely through Lipsius's (and Du Vair's) work. However,
we miss something important if we consider Lipsius's neo- or Christian
Stoicism simply in relation to these rather distant later influences. Lipsius
himself was not concerned at all with problems of ethical theory, understood in these later terms. He was returning to an ancient tradition in
which philosophy was not to be regarded primarily as a theoretical inquiry at all, but rather as a practical one, as spelling out a way of life. It
was the ancient Stoic – philosophical, as against religious – way of life,
so exemplarily led, he thought, by his hero Seneca, that he wanted to
revive.

Notes

1. I draw these biographical data from Jason Lewis Saunders, *Justus Lipsius:
The Philosophy of Renaissance Stoicism* (Liberal Arts Press, 1955), chap. I; and
Jacqueline Lagrée, *Juste Lipse et la restauration du Stoïcisme* (Vrin, 1994), pp. 17–
20. The publication year of the *Variae Lectiones* is given as 1569 by Saunders,
1567 by Lagrée; a check of the Harvard University Library catalog shows a
record for a book of this title published in 1569 by Plantin at Antwerp.
2. Seneca, *Moral Essays* (Loeb Classical Library), 3 vols., tr. John W. Basore
(Harvard University Press, 1928–35); and Seneca, *Ad Lucilium Epistulae
Morales* (Loeb Classical Library), 3 vols., tr. Richard M. Gummere (Harvard
University Press, 1917–1925).
3. Justus Lipsius, *Opera Omnia* (Wesel, 1675). I cite the *Manuductio* and *Physiologia* by book and chapter of the original publication in Latin. It seems that
neither work has ever been translated as a whole into a modern language.
Lagrée translates excerpts from both works, and her exposition of them provides the easiest access for a contemporary reader to their contents.

4. See the passage of the Introduction to the Reader in Lipsius's Seneca edition quoted by Lagrée, *Juste Lipse*, p. 199 n6.
5. Diogenes Laertius, *Lives of Eminent Philosophers* (Loeb Classical Library), 2 vols., tr. R. D. Hicks (Harvard University Press, 1925); Plutarch, *On Stoic Self-Contradictions* and *Against the Stoics on Common Conceptions* (Loeb Classical Library), ed. and tr. Harold Cherniss (Harvard University Press, 1976); Stobaeus, *Eclogae*, in *Ioannis Stobaei anthologium*, ed. C. Wachsmuth and O. Hense (Berlin: Weidmann, 1884–1912); Sextus Empiricus, *Works* (Loeb Classical Library), 4 vols., tr. R. B. Bury (Harvard University Press, 1933–1949).
6. Once, in discussing passages of Cicero, Stobaeus and Sextus Empiricus that he finds confusing and contradictory, he mentions that he has only the Latin translation of Sextus to consult, so that perhaps the contradiction could be removed by reading a different Greek text at the relevant place. See *Manuductio* 11.23 (vol. IV, 740 of the Wesel *Opera Omnia*). (In fact, Lipsius has misunderstood Sextus.)
7. See J. B. Schneewind, *The Invention of Autonomy* (Cambridge University Press, 1998), pp. 170–1. Citing Anthony Levi, *French Moralists: The Theory of the Passions 1585–1659* (Oxford University Press, 1964), p. 67, Schneewind reports that Lipsius's Latin text went through more than 80 editions and was translated into several vernaculars. There were at least seven editions of the Latin work in Lipsius's own lifetime (as a search of RLIN reveals). Besides that of Stradling in 1594, there were several other translations into English published in the seventeenth century. There were Dutch, French and German translations before 1600, too, as well as English ones. I note that a Catalan translation of the work appeared in 1616!

   For ease of reference, I cite *On Constancy* by the page numbers (and sometimes the lines) of the widely available 1939 edition by R. Kirk of the 1594 English translation by John Stradling: *Two Bookes of Constancie written in Latine by Iustus Lipsius*, Englished by Sir John Stradling (1594), ed. with intro. by Rudolf Kirk (Rutgers University Press, 1939). I often alter Stradling's translation slightly, usually simply to make it conform to modern English spelling and usage.
8. Schneewind, *The Invention of Autonomy*, pp. 170–1, quotes these words, but his context might lead a reader to think that Lipsius was comparing himself only or primarily with contemporaries or modern predecessors. Lipsius's comparison is with the ancients.
9. It is noteworthy that even in the *Manuductio* Lipsius devotes no separate discussion to the Stoic theory of the emotions as based in judgments of a person's reason, and does not attempt to distinguish the Stoics' view on this point from that of Plato and Aristotle. On the Stoic theory of emotions, see A. A. Long and D. N. Sedley, *The Hellenistic Philosophers* (Cambridge University Press, 1987), 2 vols., chapter 65.
10. However, later on, in chapter 7, Langius does say explicitly that he does not wish to disallow "fervent affection" for one's country, but only insists, in apparent accordance with the Aristotelian view, not the ancient Stoic one, that this affection must be "tempered with moderation"; otherwise, it is a vice,

a "deposing of the mind from its right seat" (86.29–34). See also chapter 11, 95.15-16, to the same effect: affection for our country must be "first bridled and restrained to a mean," and then it will conform with right reason and deserve the good name of love of country.

11. It is conceivable, of course, that Lipsius did not pay sufficient attention to his sources (such as Seneca's *On Anger*), which clearly mark off the Stoic moral psychology from the Aristotelian one, even to be clearly aware himself of the differences. In his note To the Reader, Lipsius complains at some length about those who, calling themselves philosophers, "dote upon thorny subtleties" and do nothing but engage in subtle disputations instead of making philosophy what it truly is, the "most serious instrument of life" (206). And in *On Constancy*, book I, chapter 18 (116.9–10), he complains that Chrysippus himself corrupted the Stoic school by turning it toward "crabbed subtleties," in its investigations. (One should, however, recall that the Stoic doctrine of the passions is due already to Zeno; Chrysippus, with his "crabbed subtleties," is simply carrying on the project by explaining in careful terms the Zenonian doctrine.) On the classical Stoic theory of the passions, see Long and Sedley, *The Hellenistic Philosophers*, chapter 65, and Michael Frede, "The Affections of the Soul," in *The Norms of Nature*, ed. M. Schofield and G. Striker (Cambridge University Press, 1986), pp. 93–110. Lipsius is not a philosopher's philosopher, so he may not have seen the value or point of careful distinctions in developing what he regarded as the sole thing of value, the end result of a philosophical theory for the improvement of human life.

12. I do not recognize these definitions, and do not know Lipsius's source for them (if he had one).

13. Plato, *Complete Works*, ed. John M. Cooper and D. S. Hutchinson (Hackett, 1997).

14. This would make the implied psychological view closer to that of the ancient Stoics, though, of course, the anti-Stoic supposition of a second "part" of the soul besides reason would remain.

In *Manuductio* II, 11, Lipsius pays brief (and accurate) attention to the Stoic doctrine of *phantasiae*, or appearances or impressions of the senses as the source of beliefs, but not equivalent to them. I am not sure, however, that even then he understood the doctrine or its significance correctly. He does not mention "assent" as a separate mental act needed before a *phantasia*, having been received by the mind, then gives rise to a belief.

15. For this division see Diogenes Laertius, *Lives of Eminent Philosophers*, 7.110 sub fin; see also Long and Sedley, *The Hellenistic Philosophers*, vol. I, pp. 410–12. Lipsius does not set out to discuss this theory in either of his two late Stoic works.

16. In *Physical Theory of the Stoics* 1.6–7, Lipsius goes to considerable trouble, drawing on a very extensive survey of ancient sources, to show that this doctrine is not alien to the Christian tradition's understanding of God.

17. See the passages collected in Long and Sedley, *The Hellenistic Philosophers*, chapter 55.

18. Seneca, *Moral Essays*, vol. I.

19. In *Physical Theory of the Stoics* 1.12, Lipsius returns to this passage of Seneca and the difficulties it might be thought to raise. He quotes much more extensively and more effectively from the ancient sources, including especially the Greek ones, and that enables him to give a decisive interpretation: Seneca's statement in *On Providence* 5.8 means that God does not and, given the perfection of his understanding, cannot change his law (i.e., his own mind), as that is expressed in the original decree. It has no implication for God's own subjection to his own or some other necessity, once imposed.

20. He does much better in his discussion of Stoics on fate in *Physical Theory of the Stoics*, 1.10ff.

21. See *Physical Theory* 1.7.

22. Lipsius correctly denies that the Stoics are pantheists, if that means that everything there is is god: matter (most notably, matter other than the divine spirit or *pneuma* that God or reason is immediately spread through and uses as an instrument for affecting the rest of matter) is not God. See *Physical Theory* 1.8.

23. In *Physical Theory* I.12, Lipsius cites in this connection a passage from Chrysippus's *On Providence* that is preserved only in the Latin author Aulus Gellius, *Attic Nights* (Loeb Classical Library), 3 vols., tr. John C. Rolfe (Harvard University Press, 1927), 7.2.3; it is printed in as 2.1000 in Johannes von Arnim, *Stoicorum Veterum Fragmenta*, 4 vols. (Teubner, 1903–24). Aulus Gellius quotes it in Greek: "fate is a natural ordering from eternity of all things: the ones follow on and are succeeded by the others and the connection is inviolable." Lipsius also cites a number of related passages from Stobaeus.

24. In discussing "order, time and place" at the end of chapter 19, Lipsius clearly relies implicitly on the Stoic conception of "co-fated" events (he provides examples of his own from Roman history), such as Tarquin's being fated to lose his kingdom but first co-fated to commit the adultery that led to that outcome. Lipsius's source is presumably Cicero's *On Fate* (with *De Oratore* III, *Paradoxa Stoicorum*, and *De Partitione Oratoria*) (Loeb Classical Library), tr. H. Rackham (Harvard University Press, 1942), 30–1.

25. To whom was Schusselburg writing? At what precise date? I cannot tell from the excerpted citation in my source, Saunders, *Justus Lipsius*, p. 19 n4. It does seem that Schusselburg was writing during Lipsius's lifetime or soon after his death, as an apologist of Lipsius against charges of infidelity and the like.

26. Schusselburg's attribution to himself in 1582 of this "prophecy" suggests that he was writing after 1592, when Lipsius did return to the Catholic Church in accepting the professorship at the University of Leuven.

27. For the history of the Low Countries' conflicts with Spain, see Jonathan Israel, *Conflicts of Empires: Spain, the Low Countries and the Struggle for World Supremacy, 1585–1713* (Hambledon Press, 1997); and Israel, *The Dutch Republic: Its Rise, Greatness and Fall, 1477–1806* (Clarendon Press, 1995).

28. See Schneewind, *The Invention of Autonomy*, chapters 9 and 12.

2

Affective Perfectionism

Community with God without Common Measure

Jennifer A. Herdt

1. Voluntarism and Antivoluntarism – Radical Alternatives?

One of the central themes woven through J. B. Schneewind's *The Invention of Autonomy* is that of community with God.[1] Schneewind draws on the notion of community with God in order vividly to capture what was at stake between voluntarists and antivoluntarists in the seventeenth and eighteenth centuries; voluntarists denied that God and human beings are members of the same moral community, while antivoluntarists insisted that God and humans must share membership in this community. In effect, voluntarists held that God, to be God, must be sovereign and free, while antivoluntarists retorted that God must for the same reason instead be loving and just. It was antivoluntarism that won, historically speaking, the day, since most people found an arbitrary tyrant as God unacceptable. But antivoluntarism had difficulty retaining a substantial role for God within human morality, and, ironically, the dedicated efforts of antivoluntarists to defend God's moral character gave rise to forms of moral philosophy that marginalized or eliminated God's role altogether: intuitionism, utilitarianism and Kantianism.

The point of departure for this essay is a nagging suspicion that the range of options represented within modern moral thought was in fact rather limited. I wish to raise the possibility of a third alternative alongside affirming or denying moral community with God, to ask if the affirmation and the denial of moral community with God were perhaps not radical alternatives to one another, but rather had in common a certain framework for thinking of God's transcendence that in fact undermined that transcendence. In this light, it would hardly be surprising that they were

30

unable stably to maintain a conception of God's central importance for human morality. A radical alternative would have suggested that human beings can do justice to God's transcendence only by at once affirming and denying moral community with God, that is (to phrase the alternative less paradoxically), by understanding God's sovereignty and God's love in a way that united rather than divided them.

The scope of this essay remains quite modest in that it does not claim to present anything more than a partial example – in Cambridge Platonism – of such an alternative within modern moral thought.[2] Such a partial exception to the rule implies only that an alternative was within the realm of possibility, without changing the historical judgment that it was not adequately represented within modern moral thought. Applying to debates over voluntarism in modern moral thought the concept of "noncontrastive transcendence" articulated by Kathryn Tanner, the essay sketches the barest outlines of what such an alternative would look like.[3] Its aim is simply to propose that the conflict between voluntarist and antivoluntarist thought did not reveal tensions internal and ultimately fatal to Christian moral thought per se, but tensions fatal to a specific framework for Christian thought, one that failed to conceive of transcendence in a sufficiently radical way. I begin with a fuller account of Schneewind's rendition of the opposition between voluntarism and antivoluntarism.

Voluntarists insisted on the inscrutable freedom of God; God's will is the source of the moral law, but God is not subject to the moral law, since God has no superior who can oblige him. Voluntarists believed that their position was the only way to keep God centrally important to morality. Pufendorf, along with later natural lawyers, embraced voluntarism on just these grounds; he worried, as Schneewind discusses, that the Grotian account of natural law, by claiming that the moral law would in a certain sense be binding even if God did not exist, threatened to render God unimportant to human moral obligation. Pufendorf's insistence that God is not bound by the moral law and that we are bound only through the sanctions imposed by God arose out of a concern to preserve God's sovereignty and moral relevance. At the same time, Pufendorf wished to assert that God's sovereignty is a form of authority rather than merely power over us. It was difficult, though, to see how authority, understood as the exercise of power within just limits, could be meaningful prior to the determination, through God's will, of what counts as just.[4] The God of the natural lawyers thus appeared to many as an arbitrary tyrant, "a God," as Thomas Burnet accused Locke of presenting, "without moral attributes."[5]

Many modern moral philosophers, notably perfectionists and rationalists, concluded that unless human beings and God can be seen to be members of the same moral community, unless we and God share the same morality, God will be nothing more than an arbitrary tyrant, and we will be unable to love God. This impulse to affirm moral community with God carried through all the way to Kant, for whom it implied that we must have equality with God. Community with God means for Kant not merely that we are able to perceive independent and eternal moral truths that bind God and ourselves alike, but that our will legislates a law that is also a law for God.[6] It is the capacity to legislate the law that binds us, which makes us autonomous like God. As Schneewind notes, Kant explicitly aligns human and divine moral agency; when we seek a harmonious unity of ends, we think of ourselves as "analogous to divinity."[7] But once we have become equal to God as moral legislators, God becomes irrelevant to our own moral agency. God is necessary neither as legislator of moral law nor as the source of motivation to obey the moral law. God enters in as a postulate of practical reason, the sole role of which is to preclude the pointlessness of morality.[8]

Reflecting on Kant's affirmation of shared human–divine membership in the moral community, Gordon E. Michalson, Jr., writes that "continuity and discontinuity exist side by side in Kant's idea that God and humanity are members of the same moral community." On the one hand, this is a "seemingly innocent, even pious, proposal, evoking the comforting biblical imagery of the kingdom." But on the other hand, the proposal is subversive: "Kant's actual way of rendering the moral community underscores the immanent source of holiness itself. Heaven not only comes to earth, it is progressively displaced by it."[9] Until Kant, it was possible to see the affirmation of community with God as a guarantee of the justice of God's reign, but in Kant we see that community with God denies God's reign altogether; God is no longer the moral sovereign and in that sense no longer calls for special attention. "Prerogatives" and "characteristics" traditionally attributed to God are transposed by Kant onto "the immanent domain of rational activity." This feature of Kant's thought, which Michalson terms his "principle of immanence," while ostensibly retaining God's transcendence (God lies beyond the reach of speculative reason), in fact makes room for human reason to take on the persona of divinity, and in this sense, the "source of holiness" is immanent.[10]

The problem confronting the antivoluntarists was that if moral principles are eternal and immutable, binding quite independently of God, if we are capable on our own, apart from grace, of understanding and pursuing the greatest possible happiness, or the demands of order, or the eternal fitnesses of things, God begins to appear superfluous to the project of morality. Schneewind suggests that antivoluntarists sought to retain God's significance for morality by insisting that God guarantees moral harmony and order – harmony between the good of the individual and the common good, order that sees that virtue is rewarded and vice punished. But insofar as human beings can and do take it upon themselves to organize society in ways that create such harmony, God may be displaced from this role as well. Just such a move was made by thinkers from Helvetius to La Mettrie to Bentham. And although the postulates of practical reason suggest that Kant agreed with the antivoluntarists that God is necessary as the preserver of moral order, his insistence that the postulates play no role in moral knowledge or motivation reveals his close proximity to those who saw the creation of moral order as a purely human project. As the final chapter of *The Invention of Autonomy* concludes, "for the Leibnizians God sees to it that the world is necessarily the best world there can be. Kant leaves with us the responsibility for perfecting the world as well as ourselves."[11]

In exploring the impasse between voluntarists and antivoluntarists, Schneewind uncovers for us what seems to be a tension dogging Christian moral thought. The voluntarists preserved God's freedom and power, while the antivoluntarists preserved God's lovability. God could be kept relevant to human moral knowledge and motivation only by keeping God out of the human moral community; once it is affirmed that we and God are equal members of the moral community, we need no longer look to God for our understanding of and ability to adhere to morality. In a sense, both voluntarism and antivoluntarism undermine God's worthiness to be worshipped, but from opposite directions. Voluntarism reveals that God is unworthy of worship because God cannot intelligibly be said to be good, while antivoluntarism reveals that God is unworthy of worship because God is not sovereign.

Schneewind's account of voluntarism's central role in the secularization of modern moral thought is, I think, compelling. Interestingly, Schneewind wrote in a 1984 essay that the problem of voluntarism or intellectualism in religious morality, "of significant concern to theologians, is of considerably less moment to morality as such" and proposed the metaphor of the "Divine Corporation" as a more complex and holistic account of morality in terms of a "just cooperative enterprise."[12] In his 1996 Presidential Address to the American Philosophical Association, however, the problem of voluntarism held center stage, as Schneewind claimed that "the ethical theories most distinctive of modernity – utilitarianism, intuitionism, and Kantianism – were all initially proposed as ways of understanding morality that would defeat voluntarism."[13] It would seem that as Schneewind worked on the project that came to fruition in *The Invention of Autonomy*, he realized that controversies over voluntarism (to which intellectualism was clearly not the sole response) could in fact be seen as underlying the complex whole of modern moral philosophy sketched in "The Divine Corporation." Different as the three distinctively modern theories of morality seem to be, all can be traced back to attempts to oppose voluntarism. Moreover, all three tend to render God irrelevant to morality.

In effect, Schneewind offers an internal explanation for the secularization of moral thought. Just as he argues that virtue ethics took a back seat in modern moral thought not because it was neglected but because its weaknesses were revealed, he likewise suggests that God became marginal to human morality not in the first place because antireligious thinkers sought to displace God's role in morality, but because sincerely religious thinkers were unable to show in detail how to make sense of God's role within morality in a way that was not morally offensive or simply gratuitous. That is, tensions internal to Christian moral thought, made pressing given a social context in which authorities of all kinds were being questioned, undermined it.

2. Varieties of Divine Transcendence

While voluntarism and antivoluntarism seem starkly opposed, with the former denying community with God and the latter affirming it, from another perspective it appears that the antivoluntarist stance did not offer a sufficiently radical alternative to voluntarism. In order to see this, we must take a closer look at the notion of community with God. Schneewind suggests that what it means for God to share our morality, for us to share moral community with God, was fleshed out in different ways by different thinkers. For Richard Cumberland, sometimes considered the first utilitarian, it meant that God and we are both bound by the same eternal and necessary moral law that requires us to aim at the same end, that of the greatest possible happiness.[14] For the perfectionist Herbert of Cherbury, it meant that we and God think of morality in the same terms, because we have access through our minds to the divine mind and thus can share, through perfecting ourselves, in the divine activity of bringing about the greatest good.[15] Malebranche believed that both we and

God are bound to follow the demands of order; Samuel Clarke insisted that we can, like God, understand and conform to the "eternal fitnesses" of things.[16] More generally, eighteenth-century rationalists insisted both that our motivation to be moral is the same as God's and that our way of knowing morality is the same as God's. Schneewind suggests that antivoluntarist thought tended to move in the direction of insisting that we and God must share a common set of moral *principles* and that this is possible only if moral principles are necessary truths: "as the work of Cumberland, Leibniz, Clarke, and Price makes clear, the only principles that seemed capable of satisfying this requirement are so abstract that they are, in effect, principles that spell out the essential conditions of practical reasoning as such."[17] The logic of the argument pressed in the direction of purely formal principles. Nothing empirical, nothing arising from the contingent particularities of human nature, can serve as moral principles, since these will not be binding on God. This paved the way for Kant, who argued that the nature of practical reasoning is such that it prescribes to itself the moral law – only this will provide a moral law binding on all rational beings. Moral truth is not independent of us, but rather something we make for ourselves.[18]

The concept of community with God appears fairly straightforward to apply to these seventeenth- and eighteenth-century thinkers. If, however, we consider closely Schneewind's discussion of Luther and Calvin, where the theme of community with God is first discussed, we can discern some ambiguity in its application. At first it seems absolutely clear that Luther and Calvin, with their voluntarist emphasis on the omnipotence of God, deny that God and human beings belong to the same moral community; of Luther, Schneewind writes that "God is outside and infinitely distant from any human community formed by morality."[19] God is under no law and needs no law, while we require a law to control our sinful passions. Moreover, given Luther and Calvin's doctrine of grace, morality concerns only life on earth and has no further bearing on the soul after death. God can "touch our lives by his mysterious grace, for which we may hope. But because we cannot by ourselves do anything to bring him to give us grace, he is in an important sense above the human community and not part of it."[20]

Yet when Schneewind compares Luther and Calvin with Hobbes, he notes that "Luther and Calvin do not intend voluntarism to take God out of the human community. They use it to ensure that his inscrutable ways will always be in our thoughts."[21] Hobbes shares their voluntarism, but for him it serves a different purpose, that of showing that the "content and maintenance of morality are our business. God gives our theorems their formal status as law, but we cannot think that he does anything more than that. He leaves us to our own devices."[22] While Hobbes unambiguously denies a common divine–human moral community, Schneewind's treatment of Luther and Calvin reveals them to be of two minds on this question. God is for Luther and Calvin in some sense inscrutable, but because they accept Scripture and Jesus Christ as revealing God's nature, they are nevertheless able to affirm the goodness and lovability of God. God is on the one hand utterly transcendent, while on the other hand intimately close to human beings. The modern natural lawyers, in contrast, embraced an empiricist methodology and therefore set aside Scripture as a source of knowledge of God's character. God's moral authority was therefore less easily justified than for earlier voluntarists.

What appears in Luther and Calvin as a two-mindedness or uncertainty may, with the help of terminology devised by Kathryn Tanner, be understood, rather, as an expression of radical divine transcendence. Tanner proposes a distinction between "noncontrastive" and "contrastive" accounts of divine transcendence. To hold a noncontrastive account is to maintain that God is "transcendent beyond opposition with the non-divine," that is, that the distinction between God and the world cannot be adequately characterized in terms used to make distinctions *within* the world, and thus that transcendence cannot be articulated solely in terms of separation or noninvolvement.[23] David Burrell gets at something similar when he writes that "what is needed, then, to articulate the distinction between God and the world in such a way as to respect the reality appropriate to each, is a distinction which makes its appearance, as it were, within the world as we know it, yet does not express a division within that world" – not a simple matter.[24] A God regarded as creator, for example, cannot be "neatly other," but nor can the distinction between creator and creation be a distinction internal to creation.

Christian faith has traditionally maintained both that God transcends the world (a God who creates the world is clearly not *part* of that world) and that God is intimately and directly involved with the world God creates and sustains.[25] Because God's transcendence is not contrasted with, it does not imply a barrier to, immanence and vice versa. A noncontrastive understanding of transcendence is exemplified by applying the same terms to God and human beings analogically rather than univocally, or by asserting God to be identical with what is simply predicated of human beings; that is, God is righteousness while human beings are righteous. Through these and other "rules" for theological discourse, it avoids both direct contrast and direct identity between God and created reality. On the other hand, explains Tanner:

> Divinity characterized in terms of a direct contrast with certain sorts of being or with the world of non-divine being as a whole is brought down to the level of the world and the beings within it in virtue of that very opposition: God becomes one being among others within a single order. Such talk suggests that God exists alongside the non-divine, that God is limited by what is opposed to it, that God is as finite as the non-divine beings with which it is directly contrasted.[26]

Contrastive transcendence actually undermines God's transcendence.

William Placher, in *The Domestication of Transcendence*, seeks to trace a historical shift toward contrastive understandings of transcendence. He argues that Luther and Calvin preserved a noncontrastive account of divine transcendence, while later thinkers embraced a contrastive account:

> Increasingly, Christian writers in the seventeenth century, since they did not want to think of God as utterly beyond their comprehension, thought of God's otherness in terms of distance and remoteness from the world. Such a "contrastive" account of transcendence . . . makes divine transcendence and involvement in the world into a zero-sum game: the more involved or immanent, the less transcendent, and vice versa.[27]

One indication of Luther and Calvin's preservation of noncontrastive transcendence is, Placher suggests, their insistence that God is always fully engaged with the world, rather than remaining generally absent but intervening from time to time. Providence is all-pervasive; though God does work at times through secondary causes, these causes do not in any sense displace Providence.[28]

Within a contrastive understanding of transcendence, one would expect the emphatic denial that human beings share moral community with God. If human beings are constrained by moral principles, God is free of such constraint. If morality is for human beings, it is not for God. A natural reaction against this would be to assert that God is indeed a member of the human moral community, that God is bound by the same moral principles that bind us, and in the same way. This is an assertion that, as we see in the course of modern moral philosophy, renders God increasingly immanent and thus redundant. But this reaction is not a true alternative. A contrastive account of God's transcendence and an assertion of God's immanence are, rather, two sides of the same coin; contrastive accounts have the ironic result of bringing God down to the same level as that with which God is contrasted, of using language in a univocal way even in contrasting God with created beings, of limiting God and rendering

God finite, while an account of God as immanent, on the other hand, *begins* at this point with God as limited and finite, contained within the world. In a sense, then, denials of transcendence and assertions of contrastive transcendence both remain within the same framework, one that assumes that God can be directly and adequately characterized in terms of human concepts.

A true alternative to the denial that God shares moral community with humanity is offered only by a noncontrastive understanding of transcendence, which renders it problematic either simply to deny or simply to affirm that God and human beings share moral community – God's transcendence is "beyond relations of identity or simple contrast."[29] On such an account, God is surely not just another being in the human moral community, but God is also not a being outside of our moral community. One would want to say something more like "God is moral community itself" to point to the inadequacy of the distinction between "inside" and "outside" for talking of God. It is thus only within the framework of a contrastive understanding of transcendence (and its intimate flip side, an immanentist understanding) that it is possible neatly to group thinkers according to whether or not they regard God and human beings as part of the same moral community.

Placher, as I have noted, locates the shift from noncontrastive to contrastive understandings of transcendence in the late sixteenth and seventeenth centuries, pointing to such thinkers as Cajetan and Suarez, Turretin, Descartes and Leibniz. Tanner, in contrast, emphasizes contrastive aspects of late medieval nominalism, particularly in Gabriel Biel. She argues that Biel represents a late medieval trend in which absolute freedom is claimed for human beings, and human powers are seen as exercised quite independently of God. Biel reinterprets the distinction between God's absolute and ordained powers in such a way that they are separate domains rather than different aspects of God's agency. As Tanner notes, "a dome is thereby formed, around a self-enclosed created order of causes that proceed *ex puris naturalibus.*"[30] Within this sphere of pure nature, human beings are understood as free in a new way, unsupported by God in their exercise of agency. According to Biel, human beings are capable, quite apart from grace, of arriving at absolute love of God, love of God for God's own sake; *facere quod in se est* refers explicitly to what one can do without the assistance of grace.[31]

Biel assumes that unless such a realm of pure nature exists, human and divine freedom would necessarily conflict. "Such a conflict results," notes Tanner, "only if divine and created agencies are included within a single linear order of predication."[32] This collapse into a single dimension is just what a noncontrastive account avoids; within the horizontal dimension of the created order, human beings can be affirmed to be free, to be "master . . . of that which conditions choice on the created level" without claiming that human beings are free from God, unsupported in the vertical dimension by "the divine agent who creatively founds the whole of created beings and their effects and their modes of relation."[33] Created being is always understood to be constituted by, and nothing apart from, God, so "one must say created being becomes what it is and this all the more fully, not by way of separation or neutrality from God, but within the intimacy of a relationship to divinity as its total ground."[34] Human freedom does not require independence from the vertical dimension, and indeed such independence is seen as utterly impossible.

Tanner's suggestion that Biel's worries about conflict between divine and human freedom relate to a loss of the distinction between horizontal and vertical dimensions is a helpful one. I would suggest that it is also important to see how such concerns among late medieval nominalists arise out of their particular understanding of freedom, an understanding that sets the stage for a clash between God's freedom and that of human beings. Ockham and his followers conceived of freedom as the will's indifference, its capacity to choose either this or that; Scotus paved the way with his interpretation of contingency in terms of created entities potentially having been otherwise than they are, an interpretation leading him to the assertion that "the divine will is related to any other object only contingently, so that as will it has the capacity to will either this or its opposite."[35] Ockham went so far as to propose that God can command even that we hate him, although he noted that a practical contradiction would ensue between loving God above all by obeying this command and hating God in obeying it.[36] This implies that God's freedom is no longer seen as action in accord with the divine nature, action that draws all things into participation in divine goodness; nor can human freedom be understood as acting in accordance with our own nature as beings oriented toward participation in goodness itself, that is, in God. Will is no longer understood, as in earlier Franciscan thought, in terms of love of the good, but rather in terms of radical, arbitrary choice; God's will is what lends goodness to things.

Beginning in the 1950s, a number of scholars of late medieval thought mounted an attack against this received understanding of Scotus, Ockham and Biel, arguing that "the priority of God's will is not stressed as much as the simplicity of God's being and the resulting unity of his intellect and essence."[37] If these scholars are correct, we are closer to understanding why divine transcendence continued for the most part to be articulated in noncontrastive terms into the early modern period; as long as will and intellect are one, God's will does not appear arbitrary. Nevertheless, even if insistence on the unity of God's will and intellect prevented the radical implications of liberty of indifference from being fully felt, we do see in Ockham's thought how the exercise of God's freedom begins to appear as an arbitrary limitation on human freedom. God, as omnipotent, can impose his will on us and can obligate us through the expression of his will. Given this understanding of divine and human freedom, the two are seen as competing head on with one another, with God, of course, winning. Servais Pinckaers, observing that man, like God, enjoyed for Ockham complete freedom of will, notes that "yet, as a creature, he was subject to the divine power and his freedom came into direct confrontation with the will of God, which acted upon his freedom and limited it by the divine power of obligation."[38] While human beings are theoretically free to choose anything, in fact we are constrained to choose according to God's will. Morality is centrally about obligation, and obligation is about the way in which God's will trumps our will.

It is not just human freedom that is constrained, on such an account. An even more remarkable result of conceiving of freedom in this radical way is that late medieval voluntarists ended up limiting *both* human and divine freedom. In Biel's thought, human beings have a capacity, exercised independently of God within the realm of "pure nature," to do good works, which then creates an obligation on God's part (according to God's ordained power, of course, not God's absolute power) to give these persons salvation. Human beings are obligated to do God's will, but God is obligated to save them when they do.[39] This is what one would expect in a contrastive account of transcendence. God and human beings are free in a univocal sense, so the scope of the free action of each must be clearly marked out. God is hence on the same plane as God's creatures, and God's transcendence has effectively been undermined.

Placher notes in passing the roles played by Duns Scotus, Gabriel Biel and William of Ockham in the "domestication of transcendence."[40] He fails, though, to acknowledge the ways in which Luther and Calvin were indebted to late medieval accounts of radical freedom. Placher tries to play down Luther's denial of free choice, but it is not accidental that, as Placher is at one point forced to admit, "Luther made it sound as if God's ultimate control of events implies the denial of human freedom on any level."[41] Rather than understanding God as goodness itself, Luther and Calvin regarded the good as defined by God's will. The freedom of spontaneously expressing one's nature – even if that nature is perfection itself – they saw as a form of enslavement; only liberty of indifference can therefore preserve God's omnipotence. Luther and Calvin solved the problem of competition between human and divine freedom in a different way than Biel, but retained the same understanding of freedom. They were concerned to free God from any constraint or obligation within the economy of grace. Thus, while human beings can be said to do some things voluntarily or willingly, we do not possess liberty of indifference; only God does. God is the agent of any good that we do, and receives the credit.

Despite those elements of their thought that preserved a noncontrastive account of transcendence, and thus make it difficult to determine whether they affirm or deny community with God, Luther and Calvin did thus offer a contrastive account of freedom as a zero-sum game: liberty of indifference is the only true freedom, but in order to secure God's sovereign liberty, human liberty must be denied. By going back to the late medieval developers of this concept of freedom and seeing how they themselves fall into a contrastive account of freedom, we come to expect contrastive transcendence to lurk wherever freedom is understood as radical liberty of indifference.

Turning now to modern moral thought from the seventeenth century on, we might expect that modern voluntarists, like their late medieval and early modern predecessors, would fall into contrastive accounts of transcendence, while antivoluntarists would preserve noncontrastive accounts. As has been discussed, though, modern antivoluntarism, rather than offering a true alternative to voluntarism and its contrastive understanding of divine transcendence, offered only an apparent alternative, one that progressively *immanentized* God and thus rendered talk of God redundant to moral discourse. One significant sign of this is the readiness of modern antivoluntarists straightforwardly to affirm shared divine–human membership in a single moral community. In the next section I will argue, however, that for at least some of the seventeenth-century antivoluntarists, specifically the perfectionist Cambridge Platonists (Benjamin Whichcote, John Smith, Ralph Cudworth and Henry More), one may not so straightforwardly say that God is a member of our moral community, bound as human beings are by shared moral principles, acting through the same mode of agency. One can, though, affirm community with God in another sense, as I shall endeavor to explain by delving in turn into the Cambridge Platonists' understandings of friendship with God, of freedom and of grace. The way in which these thinkers simultaneously affirm and deny community with God points to the fact that they are drawing from a noncontrastive understanding of divine transcendence. Moreover, unlike Luther and Calvin, they do not understand freedom in terms of liberty of indifference and do not understand morality in terms of an expression of God's will that constrains (or competes with) human liberty. The Cambridge Platonists serve as the exception that proves the rule of antivoluntarism's failure to offer a true alternative to voluntarism. They prove the rule even more so in that they are themselves only a *partial* exception, as they do show evidence of a shift toward a contrastive understanding of divine transcendence, though in different ways than Luther and Calvin. This is what makes it possible for someone like Frederick Beiser to see the Cambridge Platonists as marking the decisive beginning of the Enlightenment, even as someone like Ernst Cassirer saw them as largely conservative.[42] Even those modern moral thinkers who sought to counter not simply voluntarism, but also the contrastive account of transcendence shared by most voluntarists and antivoluntarists, did not fully free themselves from a framework that set God and humanity in competition with one another.

3. The Cambridge Platonists: Non-contrastive Antivoluntarism?

Community with God: Friendship and Participation
The Cambridge Platonists used a variety of terms to talk about what we might consider community with God – "reconciliation," "union," "agreement," or "converse with God," "participation in (or partaking of) God," "enjoyment of God" and "sympathy or friendship with God."[43] John Smith wrote of the divine virtue "which ariseth out of an happy Union of Souls with God" *(Discourses,* 20) and claimed that the essence of true religion is "to unite the soul in the nearest intimacy and conjunction with God" *(Discourses,* 390–1). Benjamin Whichcote preached that "we then relish the truest Pleasure and Satisfaction, when we find our selves reconciled to God, by Participation of his Nature" (Patrides, 72). In his sermon preached before the House of Commons, Ralph Cudworth urged his audience to recognize that "happiness is nothing, but the releasing and unfettering of our souls, from all these narrow, scant, and particular good things; and the espousing of them to the Highest and most Universall Good, which is not this or that particular good, but goodnesse it self" – God (Patrides, 112). The Cambridge Platonists did insist that morality is eternal and immutable and is not a creation of God's will, but this claim

must, I believe, be interpreted in light of the affirmation that human beings achieve goodness through participation in and friendship with God.

In his treatise on *The Excellency and Nobleness of True Religion in Its Nature and Essence*, John Smith writes that "a Good man, one that is informed by True Religion, lives above himself, and is raised to an intimate converse with the Divinity. He moves in a larger Sphere then his own Being, and cannot be content to enjoy himself, except he may enjoy God too, and himself in God" (*Discourses*, 389). This suggests that friendship between God and human beings creates a new good common to both, something new to love that is neither oneself nor Godself. The good man enjoys neither himself alone nor God alone, but rather himself and "God too"; that is, he enjoys himself "in God," he enjoys his relatedness to God and God's relatedness to him. While Smith stresses the nobility of the good man, who "lives in converse with his own Reason" and "lives at the height of his own Being" (*Discourses*, 387), at the same time he insists that the good man is characterized by self-denial and resignation to God. The good man is not independent of God, does not rest in his "own" reason or being. Rather, Smith insists:

> The Soul loves it self in God, and lives in the possession not so much of its own Being as of the Divinity; desiring only to be great in God, to glory in his Light, and spread it self in his Fulness; to be fill'd alwaies by him, and to empty it self again into him; to receive all from him, and to expend all for him; and so to live not as its own, but as God's. (*Discourses*, 389).

Smith here stresses the back-and-forth nature of friendship with God – being filled and emptying, receiving and expending. It is this ongoing process of relation with God in which the soul glories. Living in this relationship with God is the only sense in which a human person may "possess" the Divinity.

Given that God is the source and ground of all that is, including the human capacity for friendship with God and participation in God's goodness, human beings are never independent of God. The mistake of the wicked, suggests Smith, is to *imagine* themselves self-sufficient; "they will be something in themselves, they wrap up themselves in their own Being, move up and down in a Sphere of Self-love, live a professed Independency upon God, and maintain a Meum & Tuum between God and themselves" (*Discourses*, 390; see also Whichcote, Patrides, 57). Talk of friendship with God preserves a distinction between God and human beings even in intimate relation – friendship does not imply a loss of either party's distinct identity. At the same time, the Cambridge Platonists guard against interpreting friendship with God wholly in terms of human friendship by noting the utter dependency of human beings on God as their creative source.

The language of "participation" in God is another reminder that friendship with God is unique, that human beings are not in an ontological sense independent of God. Other perfectionists (such as Herbert of Cherbury) used the language of participation primarily to account for human access to moral principles in the divine mind. But for the Cambridge Platonists, participation in God's mind is first and foremost a participation in the love of God, not in abstract rules of practical reasoning.[44] They are what we might call "affective" perfectionists, in contrast to "rationalist" perfectionists like Herbert of Cherbury and Descartes. It is not that rules exist that both we and God are constrained to obey; morality is eternal and immutable because it is an expression of God's nature, not because it constrains God's will.[45] God just is God's goodness, and we flourish only insofar as we participate more and more fully in that goodness; as Cudworth says, "those expressions of goodnesse and tender affection here amongst creatures, be but drops of that full Ocean that is in God" (Patrides, 106).

If community with God is understood in terms of participation in God, then it is meaningless to speak of equality with God. That which is capable of participating (and thus also of failing to participate) in goodness is clearly not equal with "Goodness Itself." At the same time, this inequality is not domination. The power of God is seen not primarily in laws that the divine will obliges human beings to obey. Rather, this power is the power of being that grounds the existence of all that is and the goodness of all existence. Cudworth writes that "Gods *Power* displaied in the World, is nothing but his *Goodnesse* strongly reaching all things, from heighth to depth, from the highest Heaven, to the lowest Hell: and irresistibly imparting it self to every thing, according to those severall degrees in which it is capable of it" (Patrides, 107). God, as Being itself and Goodness itself, thus transcends human being and goodness, but is hardly alien to them.

The language of participation in the divine can thus point simultaneously to intimate human–divine relationship and radical divine transcendence. Some ways of talking of participation in the divine, however, can go along with an understanding of divinity as immanent *rather* than transcendent. If divinity is something that human beings can possess insofar as they acquire certain characteristics – perfection, rationality, stability, unity, and so on – then it is just another *kind* of being alongside others within the cosmos. Within such a framework, which was, as Tanner notes, common in ancient Greek philosophy, "divinity is a predicate determined by commonality and susceptible of difference: it is the sort of thing which can be said to be shared generically with specifying differences of degree."[46] Divinity understood in this way can at most order a preexisting cosmos, not be its creative source and sustenance.

The Cambridge Platonists do indeed speak at times as though divinity is something that human beings can possess, something that can be univocally predicated of God and human beings.[47] Smith, for instance, writes that "God is the First Truth and Primitive Goodness: True Religion is a vigorous Efflux and Emanation of Both upon the Spirits of men, and therefore is called a participation of the divine Nature" (*Discourses*, 380). It sounds here as though the divine nature is something capable of being shared between God and ourselves. Insofar as we ourselves possess truth and goodness, we *have* the divine nature. And More, in his *Enchiridion Ethicum,* considers "Right Reason" a "Divine thing," "equally referable to Gods and Men."[48] It is not accidental, I think, that this work was intended as moral philosophy rather than theology. More borrows heavily from pagan authors, and in the passage just quoted, for instance, has been citing from Cicero. Sterling Lamprecht writes that "the seeming secularization of the foundation of theological doctrine" in the thought of the Cambridge Platonists "was offset by the constant reiteration of the semi-divine nature of the voice of reason."[49] While Lamprecht seems to regard this as testimony to the deep religiosity of the Cambridge Platonists (and I do not doubt this), it was, ironically, just this notion of the "semi-divine" that undermined the transcendence of God and made secularization possible.[50]

In More's *Enchiridion Ethicum,* univocal references to "divinity" are paired with a strong consequentialist impulse, a tendency to think of moral laws as laws that prescribe means to the end of maximizing human happiness.[51] He says of right reason that it "generously dictates, like to a common Parent, such laws as tend, in their own Nature, to the Happiness of all Mankind" (*Enchiridion*, 15). With participation understood not in terms of relationship with one's creator, but rather as acquiring a "divine thing," the end to be achieved through participation is easily separable from the means by which it is achieved. Given a relational end such as friendship, the "means" to the end serve to constitute that end, that is (in terms of human friendship), spending time with one's friend, sharing joys and sorrows with one's friend, doing what pleases one's friend. More's univocal account of participation encourages him to set forth a consequentialist formulation of the final end or good to be aimed at. Participation in God is seen not as an end in itself, but rather as a means to human happiness, and we can begin to calculate such happiness in a quantitative way: "if it be good for one man to have wherewithal to be happy, it evidently follows, 'tis twice as good for two men to be happy, thrice for three, a thousand times for a thousand; and so of the rest" (*Enchiridion*, 26). Moreover, human happiness is something human beings can aim at achieving on their own, whereas friendship with God, though not something God brings about without human co-operation, is also clearly not an end that human beings can achieve on their own; friendship requires mutuality. Schneewind notes a general tendency within perfectionist thought to move toward consequentialism; God understood as a loving being rather than an arbitrary lawgiver could quite plausibly be regarded as aiming at maximizing human happiness, something human beings could themselves aim at apart from God.[52] My suggestion is that consequentialist perfectionism was made possible by understanding divinity in an immanent, univocal sense; human beings who participated in and thereby possessed divinity could think of the point of morality as the achievement of certain human ends, fully immanent to created reality.

Still, this kind of univocal participation language is frequently corrected in the less determinedly "philosophical" writings of the Cambridge Platonists by its explication in terms of the notion of "Christ within." Smith, speaking of the "Divine Knowledge," life and virtue of "the true Metaphysical and Contemplative man," cautions that "by the Platonists leave such a Life and Knowledge as this is, peculiarly belongs to the true and sober Christian who lives in Him who is Life itself, and is enlightened by Him who is the Truth it self, and is made partaker of the Divine Unction" (*Discourses*, 20–1). Cudworth writes in a similar vein: "this Divine life begun and kindled in any heart, wheresoever it be, is something of God in flesh; and, in a sober and qualified sence, Divinity incarnate" (Patrides, 105). This language of Christ within functions not so much to exclude non-Christians from consideration, since the Cambridge Platonists were quite willing to presume that non-Christians (not least Plato) might have Christ within without explicit knowledge of Christ. Rather, this language serves as a reminder that divinity is not, after all, a predicate we can possess, though we can enter into the most intimate relation with God. The languages of friendship with God and of participation in God as the source of all being work in concert to preserve the noncontrastive insistence that divine immanence and transcendence are complementary rather than in tension with one another.

Freedom

Smith argued that to embrace friendship and converse with God is to accept one's dependence on God. At the same time, this relationship with God cannot be forced; as the metaphor of friendship makes clear, it must be freely welcomed by all those who participate in it. On this account, it is thus proper to say that friendship with God is not something that God can achieve *without* human beings, even though a noncontrastive account of transcendence must also speak of nondivine being "as always and in every respect *constituted* by, and therefore *nothing apart from,* an immediate relation with the founding agency of God."[53] Therefore, God can achieve friendship with human beings only *through* human embrace of that friendship.

Among the Cambridge Platonists, it is Cudworth who dedicates the most time and effort to giving an account of human freedom or "self-power," and my discussion will focus on him.[54] His aim is to give an account that makes it clear that only God possesses perfect freedom, and that only friendship with God allows human beings to participate in this freedom, but at the same time to show that human beings have it in their power to turn to or away from God and thus from true freedom.[55] Cudworth is very clear that liberty of indifference cannot be identified either with God's freedom or with human freewill or self-power. "Indifferency," he writes, "is to will merely because we will and without any other reason," and if this is freedom, then freedom is madness.[56] His rejection of liberty of indifference made it possible for him to affirm human freedom in the context of divine sovereignty. Nevertheless, it is also apparent that Cudworth was not confident of the adequacy of his account. He wrote several treatises on freewill, none of which were published during his lifetime and most of which remained in draft stage. In part, this simply reflects the quirks of Cudworth's personality. It may also, though, point to Cudworth's failure fully to break free from a contrastive voluntarist framework.

The usual tendency among antivoluntarists was to regard the structure of divine and human agency as parallel. Clarke, for instance, held that God obliges himself to act in accordance with the eternal fitnesses or relations of things to one another, and that human beings can and should do so as well: "by this understanding or knowledge of the nature and necessary relations of things, the actions likewise of all intelligent beings are constantly directed . . . unless their will be corrupted by particular interest or affection, or swayed by some unreasonable and prevailing lust." Since God's will cannot be either corrupted or swayed in this way, "he must act always according to the strictest rules of infinite goodness, justice, and truth, and all other moral perfections."[57] Both God and we possess absolute freedom of will, freedom to determine ourselves according to these fitnesses.[58] Cudworth's account of freewill departs from this usual antivoluntarist model, and is thus an indication of the extent to which the Cambridge Platonists do maintain a noncontrastive account of divine transcendence; they affirm that both God and human beings are free, but insist that freedom takes significantly different forms in each. God is free, a "self-determining Agent," in that God unfailingly acts according to the perfect divine nature; God's actions are "not imposed upon him by anything from without" (BL 4980, 117). For two reasons, then, we cannot say that we share moral community with God in the sense that both we and God are bound by the same moral principles. First, moral principles are not external to or distinct from God's own nature. Cudworth claims that the argument that eternal and immutable morality proves the existence of something independent of God that constrains God's agency "will prove a mere mormo, bugbear, and nothing so terrible and formidable," for "there is no other genuine consequence deducible from this assertion, that the essences and verities of things are independent upon the will of God, but that there is an eternal and immutable wisdom in the mind of God" (TEM, 26). Second, to say that moral principles are *binding* on God implies a commitment to a false understanding of freedom as liberty of indifference, freedom to choose against God's own goodness, a freedom that would in fact be madness, action for no reason.

Cudworth contrasts the unity of God's nature with the complexity, diversity and inner conflict that characterize human nature. Human beings require a ruling power within the soul to bring unity into the diversity of their various drives and desires; God does not. "[A] perfect being can be neither more nor less in intention . . . it can have no such thing as self-recollection, vigilant circumspection or diligence in execution, but it is immutable or unchangeable goodness, and wisdom undefectible" (Freewill, 186). The soul's ruling power or *hegemonicon* is the locus of freewill. (I follow Cudworth in writing "freewill" as a single word in order to mark his insistence that there is no "blind faculty of will, which does nothing else but will" indifferently to good and evil [Freewill, 177].) Within the soul are many powers or principles, all of which Cudworth terms "natural and necessary": unconscious plastic life, passions, imagination, conscience, intellect (Freewill, 175). The ruling power of the soul is none of these but is rather the reflexive activity of the soul, "the soul as comprehending itself, all its concerns and interests, its abilities and

capacities, and holding itself, as it were in its own hand, as it were redoubled upon itself" (Freewill, 178). The soul as "redoubled" is what we
might call the self; it is "that which is properly we ourselves (we rather having those other things of necessary nature than being them)" (Freewill,
178). What Cudworth seems to have in mind here is that human beings
can reflexively endorse certain of their powers and desires; we can make
them our own, take responsibility for them, by identifying with them – or
render them not our own by refusing such identification.[59] In so doing,
human beings exercise freewill.[60]

God clearly has no need for freewill in this sense; God is always already
fully self-identified, wholly God-self. Divine and human agencies thus di-
verge. Unlike God, "we ourselves are not perfectly ourselves, but broken
with a kind of duplicity like a ray of light refracted" (BL 4980, 281). There
is "a kind of duplicity in the human soul: one, that which is ruled, another,
that which ruleth" (Freewill, 184). We need this inner rule, inner hierarchy, because we are "imperfectly ourselves" (BL 4980, 281). This talk
of the dividedness of the human soul has led some scholars to think that
the Cambridge Platonists regarded freewill as an imperfection; Walker
writes, "they regarded it as an imperfection, since its essence is a liability
to sin."[61] But Cudworth clearly insists that human freewill is a relative
good, a perfection for human beings, though not for God (BL 4980,
117; BL 4980, 298 calls freewill a "lower perfection"). The exercise of
freewill allows human beings to become more perfectly themselves and,
at the same time, to be more closely reconciled with God (Freewill, 185).
Only through participation in God's goodness is freedom as such attained, freedom that reflects the unity of the agent and the ease of acting
according to that unified nature. At the same time, it is only through the
exercise of the *human* mode of agency, freewill, that such community can
be achieved. We are not indifferent to the good, but we must freely embrace, identify with, the love of good that we find within ourselves, and
in so doing we are then drawn to God – not imposed on by God. Even as
human beings come closer to God and thus to true freedom, their freedom is never simply theirs but always due to their relation to God; at the
same time a necessary condition of this relation is the constant exercise
of their own agency, their own freewill, in clinging to God.[62]

On Cudworth's account, freewill is not a God-like power, not something that, as in some Renaissance Neoplatonism, encourages self-
glorification.[63] It reflects, rather, our dividedness, our lack of unity. Because of this clear distinction between divine and human modes of agency,
human freewill and divine freedom do not compete with one another;

human freewill has its own mode of action, but at the same time, freewill finds its fulfillment in participation in God. Human freewill does not displace divine sovereignty; divine goodness attracts but does not force or constrain us. This supports a noncontrastive understanding of God's transcendence; God's freedom and agency cannot be identified with human freewill and agency, but neither can they be simply opposed to one another.

Thus far I have offered a noncontrastive interpretation of Cudworth's account of freedom and freewill. One might think, though, that Cudworth's account actually immanentizes God. If human beings may somehow "become divine" and lose their own distinctive identity in God, God at the same time loses radical transcendence and becomes a feature immanent to the world. This possibility lurks in Cudworth's discussion of freedom as the completion of human freewill. Is freewill then abolished once true freedom is attained? As Schneewind poses the question (with regard to Smith's reflections on freedom), are the "blessed few" who achieve this freedom "so fully tied to the divine order of goodness that they have no real agency of their own?"[64] Cudworth is, I think, resistant to this immanentizing view; he writes that it is more honorable for God to have "lively Attendants" that can "serve him, love him, and praise him heartily from an inward unforced and unconstrained principle of their own" (BL 4979, 108; BL 4980, 300). He also notes that God cannot act in some external way to transform us from wicked into good persons without thereby destroying our personhood (BL 4980, 298). In fact, in his insistence that human beings must be something "on their own," he departs from a noncontrastive account of divine transcendence in the *opposite* direction – toward a contrastive rather than an immanent account.

While Cudworth is clear that true freedom is not the arbitrary willing associated with liberty of indifference, and thus rejects outright the most obvious feature of a contrastive voluntarist framework, he nevertheless finds it difficult to affirm both human freedom and divine sovereignty. This had to do with the fact that he associates God's sovereignty through the determination of all things with the position of the voluntarists and reacts against it. If God determines all things, he writes, "this is to swallow up all things into God, by making him the sole actor in the universe, all things else being merely passive to him, and determined in their actions by him" (Freewill, 205). This indicates that Cudworth does see human and divine freedom (despite his distinction between human "free will" and divine "freedom") as at least potentially in competition with one another, divine freedom threatening to overwhelm human free choice. When he thinks in this way, he is clearly regarding God as a being within the world, rather than as Being-itself that grounds the world. He is thinking of God as acting on the same horizontal plane as human beings. Tanner locates a similar feature in Molinist assumptions that "the freedom of human beings must be a freedom from God."[65] It is thus not surprising to find points in Cudworth's discussion where he seems drawn to something akin to Molinism.

Luis de Molina and his followers in the second half of the sixteenth century developed an account of human freedom as freedom from divine determination. They sought at the same time to maintain divine sovereignty by introducing the concept of *scientia media* or middle knowledge. God foresees by middle knowledge how each human being would freely choose to act in a given set of circumstances, and chooses to create a world providing the set of circumstances in which persons will freely choose the outcome that God wishes to bring about.[66] While Cudworth, to the best of my knowledge, never makes reference to Molina, he does employ a theatrical metaphor that hints at a Molinist position.

Cudworth asks us to imagine a drama in which the players are not simply actors, but "partiall Poets themselves," that is, partial authors of the play. The various parts are not all written out ahead of time; "the Poet is supposed to leave void Spaces for the Actors to speak between something of themselves but by a divine Sagacity foreknowing what every man would interpose of his own." The world is such a drama and God is the Poet; God's foreknowledge of the free actions of the actors allows him to act in ways that will make up "good sense of the whole" (BL 4980, 206). This metaphor implies that human freedom requires "void spaces" left empty by God. On a noncontrastive account, one would instead affirm that "God must be directly productive of everything that is in every aspect of its existence," but that this "production" is not an example of and thus does not compete with the way in which human beings can produce their own actions.[67] A noncontrastive use of the drama metaphor would emphasize that both Poet and actors are free, but that they act on different planes; the Poet writes the entire play, leaving no blanks, but never appears on stage; each actor's performance is his or her own, and freedom on the actor's plane appears in the interpretation of the given parts. Although Cudworth is arguing against voluntarism, he remains within the contrastive framework typical of voluntarism insofar as he regards divine freedom as even *potentially* threatening to constrain and limit human freedom.

Grace and (Plastic) Nature

The Cambridge Platonists' understanding of grace betrays a similar am-
bivalence between a noncontrastive and a contrastive account. As the
discussion of freedom and that of grace are so closely linked, I will give
only a brief treatment of the latter. On the one hand, the Cambridge
Platonists denied the existence of a self-enclosed realm of "pure nature,"
in the sense that they consistently held that human beings are fulfilled
by participation in God, and that there is no purely natural end to which
this supernatural end is added on.[68] C. A. Patrides sees this as lying at the
heart of Cambridge Platonist thought: "all that the Cambridge Platonists
ever uttered reverts in the end to Whichcote's refusal to oppose the spiritual to the rational, the supernatural to the natural, Grace to Nature."[69]
The Cambridge Platonists could have agreed with Rahner when he says
that "man can experiment with himself only in the region of God's supernatural loving will, he can never find the nature he wants in a 'chem-
ically pure' state, separated from its supernatural existential."[70] Since
the creator is intimately related to creation, "pure nature" can only be a
secondary abstraction that attempts analytically to separate out that relation. Cudworth, for instance, writes that human nature *as God first made it*
"was to be conjoyned with the Divinity" (BL 4981, 94). God's "preventing
and exciting" grace is given prior to any exercise of freewill on our part
(BL 4981, 92); grace is therefore all-pervasive. We cannot claim, moreover, that our own freewill makes us good; "when a man crawls from a
cave into the light, he has little reason to attribute to himself the healing
warmth of the sun" (BL 4981, 94).[71] Many of Cudworth's other comments
are consistent with a noncontrastive account, as when he writes that "the
aid and assistance of Divine grace [is] necessary both for the recovery of
lapsed souls and for their perseverance. The use of their own freewill is
necessarily required, for God, who made us without ourselves, will not
save us without ourselves" (Freewill, 208). This allows for the noncontrastive view that God in the vertical dimension brings about *all* things,
but that some things God brings about only through created causes such
as freely willed human action; it is God's grace that saves us, but only if
we freely cooperate with that grace.

In order to defend God against accusations of injustice, many modern moral thinkers began to develop accounts of the natural equality
of access to moral knowledge and motivation. On these accounts, grace
became superfluous. A view of nature as always pervaded by grace, of
an access to moral goodness that is supernatural but still available to all,
made it possible for the Cambridge Platonists to defend the significance

of grace (i.e., to defend God's sovereign yet intimate role in morality) while also defending the justice of God's reign. Schneewind argues that perfectionism has a tendency to be elitist, since only a few will be capable of perfecting themselves, while the rest must be motivated by threats and promises to conform externally to the requirements of morality.[72] Perfectionism thus failed to offer an account of natural moral equality. While Schneewind suggests that this elitism was particularly evident among the rationalist perfectionists, he locates it among the Cambridge Platonists as well.[73] In his discussion of Kant, however, he seems to recognize that affective perfectionism, since it does not rely on rare intellectual capacities, is not inherently elitist. In that context he remarks that while Kant rejected the elitism of Leibnizian perfectionism, he did not give up on self-perfection, but that for him, as for the Cambridge Platonists, self-perfection is "a matter of the heart rather than the head, of the will and the feelings rather than the intellect."[74] While almost any moral thinker can be read as elitist, since some account must be given of why not all human beings are in fact morally good, I would agree with this latter assessment from Schneewind; affective perfectionism does avoid elitism, at least in principle. At the same time, the Cambridge Platonists offered not so much an account of natural moral equality as of supernatural moral equality, an account that retained a place for grace and thus for God within morality.

Within a noncontrastive framework, concepts of causality that are employed within the world cannot in a simple way be ascribed to the creator of the world. Tanner notes that "if divinity is not characterized by contrast with any sort of being, it may be the immediate source of being of every sort."[75] God's creative agency must be described as "immediate and universally extensive"; God's "causality" is not another cause alongside others; it does not compete with the natural causes of things. At some points, though, Cudworth speaks as though we contribute *part* of what is needed for sanctification, while God contributes the other part; if we do what we can, God will always help us (BL 4980, 286). Tanner's comment on Molina is apt here; "human willing is not efficacious without divine agency working with it but human agency is solely responsible for its own action and therefore for that aspect of the created effect it works to bring about."[76] If what human beings do is regarded as something that God does *not* do, as in Molinism and at times in Cudworth's thought, a contrastive framework is at work.

Cudworth's difficulty in regarding God as the immediate source of all that is can be seen perhaps most vividly in his conception of "plastic nature." He worried that "it seems neither decorous in respect of God, nor congruous to Reason, that he should . . . do all things himself Immediately and Miraculously, Nature being quite Superseded and made to signifie nothing."[77] He suggested instead that plastic nature, an immaterial but unconscious power, serves as an intermediary between God and the world, acting as efficient cause of God's providential plans. While Cudworth was eager to embrace what he called the "atomick philosophy," as long as it is regarded solely as an account of material reality, rather than of reality as such, it encouraged him to think of God in terms of another *kind* of substance, incorporeal rather than corporeal (TIS, 10, 22). Moreover, he was unable to understand God's creative agency as immediate, because he tended to conceive of God's agency in terms of efficient causes, and was troubled by the thought that if God is the efficient cause of everything that takes place, then natural causes are simply an illusion and God is the sole agent in the universe. These worries indicate clearly that Cudworth is here assuming a contrastive account of divine transcendence; God cannot act directly in our world but only mediately. God is thus outside the human community, decorously cut off from the world.

4. Conclusion

The third part of this essay has sought to show the various ways in which the Cambridge Platonists seem both to affirm and to deny that human beings and God share a common morality, and to suggest that this hints at a noncontrastive understanding of transcendence. Significant elements of Cambridge Platonist thought preserve the position that God is not transcendent at the cost of losing all connection with the world, nor intimately bound up with the world at the cost of transcendence; rather, God's transcendence and immanence imply one another. Moral community with God is understood in terms of friendship with and participation in Goodness itself, rather than in terms of common obedience to external moral principles or a common mode of moral agency. At the same time, there are undeniable contrastive/immanentist elements within Cambridge Platonist thought. These indicate the extent to which their understanding of transcendence remained within a framework shared with the voluntarism they so fiercely rejected. The general tendency of modern antivoluntarist thought was to conceive of community with God in a way that required that God be seen as *similar* to human beings – just another member of the moral community, thinking in the same way, moved in the same way, bound in the same way. Within a noncontrastive framework for understanding transcendence, community with God would be a claim not of similarity or of equality, but a claim of relatedness. On such a view, God's "role" in morality cannot simply be displaced by human activity, since apart from God, the end of human action cannot even be defined, let alone achieved.

What explains the noncontrastive elements within Cambridge Platonist thought, in the midst of a context dominated by contrastive thinking and its intimate opposite, immanentist thinking? I do not have an exhaustive account to offer, but such an account would, I think, need to point to the way their perfectionism focuses on love rather than the speculative intellect, what I earlier termed their "affective" perfectionism.[78] David Burrell argues that the only way of relating to another intrinsically without requiring a common measure or reciprocity is the intentional one of knowing and loving. So one can be related to another in sharing a common species, or in being actively engaged in a shared enterprise, or extrinsically in a limitless variety of respects, but the only way open for the One to relate to everything else existing in virtue of it is through knowing and loving.[79]

Contrary to what one might expect at first glance, conceiving of God's relation to the world in terms of love preserves, rather than undermines, God's radical distinction from the world. Most antivoluntarists conceived of community with God in terms of a "common species" or "shared enterprise." Hence, affirming community with God was affirming a "common measure" with God and undermining God's transcendence. By conceiving of community with God in terms of love, a relational but not a homogenizing concept, the Cambridge Platonists kept open the possibility of affirming both God's transcendence and God's relation to the world.

Notes

1. J. B. Schneewind, *The Invention of Autonomy* (Cambridge University Press, 1998).
2. In making this claim, I do not, of course, intend to exclude the possibility that elements of noncontrastive thought may be identified in other modern moral thinkers.
3. Kathryn Tanner, *God and Creation in Christian Theology* (Basil Blackwell, 1988), 45–6.
4. Schneewind, *Invention*, 135.
5. Schneewind, *Invention*, 149.
6. In his emphasis on the will's legislation of the moral law, Kant incorporated one of the key aspects of voluntarism, that good and evil are defined

by the moral law and not vice versa. Schneewind, *Invention*, 512. Kant's success in grafting this feature of voluntarism onto his antivoluntarist affirmation that the moral law must apply to all rational beings can be seen as further indication of the shared framework underlying voluntarism and antivoluntarism.

7. Schneewind, *Invention*, 512.
8. Schneewind, "Autonomy, Obligation, and Virtue: An Overview of Kant's Moral Philosophy," in *The Cambridge Companion to Kant*, ed. Paul Guyer (Cambridge University Press, 1992), 333.
9. Gordon E. Michalson, Jr., *Kant and the Problem of God* (Blackwell, 1999), 126.
10. Michalson, *Kant*, 20.
11. Schneewind, *Invention*, 530.
12. Schneewind, "The Divine Corporation and the History of Ethics," in *Philosophy in History: Essays on the Historiography of Philosophy*, ed. Richard Rorty, J. B. Schneewind and Quentin Skinner (Cambridge University Press, 1984), 176, 184.
13. Schneewind, "Voluntarism and the Foundations of Ethics," *Proceedings and Addresses of the American Philosophical Association* 70 (1996), 25.
14. Schneewind, *Invention*, 106.
15. Schneewind, *Invention*, 176.
16. Schneewind, *Invention*, 228, 323.
17. Schneewind, *Invention*, 510.
18. This "constructive antirealist" reading of Kant is not uncontested. John Hare argues that we are not for Kant authors of the moral law in a strong sense; we only "declare a correspondence of our wills with the law (which we do not create), and we are unlike God in being only members, not heads, of the kingdom of ends." "Kant on Recognizing Our Duties as God's Commands," *Faith and Philosophy* 17 (2000), 462. I cannot enter into this debate fully here, but while I agree with Hare that Kant strives to retain a special place for God in his moral thought, I am persuaded, with Gordon E. Michalson, Jr., that "at every important turn, beginning with his own moral argument for the existence of God, Kant's theistic commitment turns out upon inspection to be a subordination of divine transcendence to the undeniable prerogatives of autonomous rationality," *Kant and the Problem of God* (Basil Blackwell, 1999), ix–x.
19. Schneewind, *Invention*, 31.
20. Schneewind, *Invention*, 36.
21. Schneewind, *Invention*, 99.
22. Schneewind, *Invention*, 100.
23. Tanner, *God and Creation*, 82.
24. David Burrell, *Knowing the Unknowable God* (University of Notre Dame Press, 1986), 17.
25. Tanner, *God and Creation*, 38.
26. Tanner, *God and Creation*, 45–6.
27. William C. Placher, *The Domestication of Transcendence* (Westminster John Knox Press, 1996), 111.
28. Placher, *Domestication*, 117.

29. Tanner, *God and Creation*, 66.
30. Tanner, *God and Creation*, 134.
31. Heiko Oberman, *The Harvest of Medieval Theology: Gabriel Biel and Late-Medieval Nominalism* (Labyrinth Press, 1963), 133.
32. Tanner, *God and Creation*, 135.
33. Tanner, *God and Creation*, 90.
34. Tanner, *God and Creation*, 85.
35. John Duns Scotus, *Ordinatio* IV, dist. 46, translation from *Duns Scotus on the Will and Morality*, trans. and intr. Allan B. Wolter (Catholic University of America Press, 1986, 1997), 187. See also Burrell, *Knowing the Unknowable God*, 108.
36. Gordon Leff, *The Dissolution of the Medieval Outlook* (Harper & Row, 1976), 84.
37. Oberman, *Harvest*, 99 gives an overview of this discussion, though Oberman himself expresses some doubts about whether Ockham consistently maintains this unity of intellect and essence in God; on Scotus see Wolter, *Duns Scotus*, x–xi.
38. Servais Pinckaers, *The Sources of Christian Ethics*, trans. Mary Thomas Noble (Catholic University of America Press, 1985, 1995), 252.
39. Tanner, *God and Creation*, 136.
40. Placher, *Domestication*, 38–9, 75
41. Placher, *Domestication*, 124.
42. Frederick Beiser, *The Sovereignty of Reason* (Princeton University Press, 1996), 138; Ernst Cassirer, *The Platonic Renaissance in England*, trans. James P. Pettergrove (Gordian Press, 1970; orig. pub. 1932), 44, 71, 121–2.
43. Examples include "reconciliation" (Whichcote, Patrides, 46, 72); "union" (Smith, *Discourses*, 20); "agreement" (Cudworth, Patrides, 98); "converse" (Smith, *Discourses*, 16); "partake" (Cudworth, Patrides, 101–2); "participation" (Whichcote, Patrides, 72; Smith, *Discourses*, 380); "enjoyment of" (Smith, *Discourses*, 389); "friendship" (Cudworth, Patrides, 102); "sympathy" (Cudworth, Patrides, 112). Here and in subsequent references given parenthetically in the text, "Patrides" refers to *The Cambridge Platonists*, ed. C. A. Patrides (Harvard University Press, 1970), while "*Discourses*" refers to John Smith, *Select Discourses* (Garland, 1978).
44. Stephen Darwall perceptively notes that morality for Cudworth arises from a natural motivation rather than from intellectual forms in the mind, and that love is the volition essential to perfect mind. *The British Moralists and the Internal 'Ought'* (Cambridge University Press, 1995), 127–8. Many commentators overlook this, though Schneewind likewise notes that the Cambridge Platonists were set apart from other perfectionists by their focus on love. *Invention*, 194, 529.
45. Ralph Cudworth, *A Treatise Concerning Eternal and Immutable Morality, With A Treatise of Freewill*, ed. Sarah Hutton (Cambridge University Press, 1996), 26. In what follows, the former treatise will be cited parenthetically as "TEM," while the latter will be cited as "Freewill."
46. Tanner, *God and Creation*, 39.

47. This is John H. Muirhead's view of Cudworth's thought; he considers Cudworth's "view of the divine principle in the world" to be "not of an arbitrary Will acting on it from without, but of an immanent will to good, whether conceived as beauty, justice, or truth." *The Platonic Tradition in Anglo-Saxon Philosophy* (Humanities Press, 1931, 1965), 35. This clearly captures the way a contrastive account of transcendence tends to elicit, as though it were the only alternative, an immanentist account.

48. Henry More, *Enchiridion Ethicum*, English translation of 1690 (Facsimile Text Society, 1930), 114.

49. Sterling Lamprecht, "Innate Ideas in the Cambridge Platonists," in *Seventeenth-Century British Philosophers*, ed. Vere Chappell (Garland, 1992), 131.

50. I do not think that Passmore has it quite right when he argues that morality was ontologically dependent upon God for Calvinism but not for Cambridge Platonism; morality *was* for the Cambridge Platonists ontologically dependent on God as the good, but when God was understood in immanentist ways, it was indeed possible to redescribe "God" and thus morality in terms of aspects of "pure nature." J. A. Passmore, *Ralph Cudworth: An Interpretation* (Cambridge University Press, 1951), 87–8.

51. G. R. Cragg makes the apt comment that the Cambridge Platonists "conceived of reason as a divine light and of morality as the fruit of a divine life: by the beginning of the eighteenth century the one had become another name for common sense, and the other had been equated with utility." *From Puritanism to the Age of Reason: A Study of Changes in Religious Thought within the Church of England 1660–1700* (Cambridge University Press, 1966), 37.

52. Schneewind, *Invention*, 200, 205, 209–10, 470.

53. Tanner, *God and Creation*, 84.

54. Muirhead writes of Cudworth's account of freedom that "as an attempt to develop a rational theory of volition equally remote from ordinary determinism and libertarianism, it stands alone, so far as I know, in English philosophical literature, not only of his own but of the following century." *Platonic Tradition*, 69.

55. I offer a fuller account of this aspect of Cudworth's thought in "Cudworth, Autonomy and the Love of God: Transcending Enlightenment (and Anti-Enlightenment) Christian Ethics," *Annual of the Society of Christian Ethics* 19 (1999), 47–68.

56. British Library Additional Manuscript 4980, 118–19. Further references to Cudworth's manuscripts on freewill will be given parenthetically as BL, number of manuscript, page number(s), e.g., (BL4980, 118–19). I would like to thank Stephen Darwall for graciously sharing with me his transcripts of manuscripts 4978, 4982 and the first portion of 4980.

57. Samuel Clarke, *A Demonstration of the Being and Attributes of God and Other Writings*, ed. Ezio Vailati (Cambridge University Press, 1998), 84; see also 144.

58. Clarke, *Demonstration*, 89.

59. See Darwall, *British Moralists*, 135.
60. I leave to one side the question of whether Cudworth's account of freewill is not in fact a form of compatibilism; for my purposes, what is significant here is the distinction between human freewill and divine freedom.
61. D. P. Walker, *The Decline of Hell: Seventeenth-Century Discussions of Eternal Torment* (University of Chicago Press, 1964), 150.
62. In this sense, John H. Muirhead is right to insist that there could be for the Cambridge Platonists no conflict between freedom and determinism (*Platonic Tradition*, 30). As we will see in what follows, however, this is not the whole story.
63. See Charles Trinkhaus, "Marsilio Ficino and the Ideal of Human Autonomy," in *Ficino and Renaissance Neoplatonism*, ed. Konrad Eisenbichler and Olga Zorzi Pugliese (Dovehouse, 1986), 143.
64. Schneewind, *Invention*, 212.
65. Tanner, *God and Creation*, 145.
66. Gerard Smith, *Freedom in Molina* (Loyola University Press, 1968), 148–55. For a contemporary analytic reconstruction of Molinist thought, see Thomas P. Flint, *Divine Providence: The Molinist Account* (Cornell University Press, 1998).
67. Tanner, *God and Creation*, 47.
68. As Cassirer rightly notes, the Cambridge Platonists recognized no division between reason and faith, natural and intelligible being, rational and spiritual. *Platonic Renaissance*, 52. In holding to these unities, they "supernaturalized the natural" rather than "naturalizing the supernatural," to borrow a phrase from John Milbank, *Theology and Social Theory* (Blackwell, 1990), 30. John Tulloch argues that the Cambridge Platonists divinize the moral rather than humanizing the divine. *Rational Theology and Christian Philosophy in England in the 17th Century*, vol. II (Georg Olms Verlagsbuchhandlung, 1966; facsimile of 1874 ed.), 469.
69. Patrides, Introduction, 10.
70. Karl Rahner, *Theological Investigations*, vol. 1, trans. Cornelius Ernst (Helicon Press, 1961).
71. This implies that Beiser is somewhat off the mark when he claims that salvation is for the Cambridge Platonists a matter of law rather than grace. *Sovereignty of Reason*, 162.
72. Schneewind, *Invention*, 528–9.
73. Schneewind, *Invention*, 199, 202.
74. Schneewind, *Invention*, 529,
75. Tanner, *God and Creation*, 46.
76. Tanner, *God and Creation*, 145.
77. Cudworth, *The True Intellectual System of the Universe* (London, 1678; facsimile ed. Stuttgart-Bad Cannstatt: Friedrich Fromann Verlag, 1964), 178.
78. Also important to note is the deep influence of Plotinus on the later Cambridge Platonists. Plotinus's insistence that the "One" lies beyond being aims at a noncontrastive account of divine transcendence: "generative of all, The Unity is none of all"; the One or Unity "is not a being, for so

its unity would be vested in something else." Plotinus, *The Enneads*, trans. Stephen MacKenna (Faber and Faber, 1962), VI, 9, 3, p. 617; VI, 9, 5, p. 619. Plotinus's scheme of emanation, on the other hand, encourages an immanentizing view by placing the One at the head of a chain of being that simply proceeds from the One.

79. Burrell, *Knowing the Unknowable God*, 72.

3

Autonomy and the Invention of Theodicy

Mark Larrimore

J. B. Schneewind has taught us that the problem of evil played a part in Immanuel Kant's "invention of autonomy."[1] The effort to reconcile the apparent evil in creation with the perfect nature of God led Kant to develop a new conception of divine agency – "God prescribes a law for himself" – that eventually informed a new understanding of human agency: "autonomy."[2] Kant's concern was not the suffering of the innocent, the paradigm case of modern theodicy, but reconciling the insights of the "voluntarist" and "antivoluntarist" (or "intellectualist") conceptions of agency and goodness that Schneewind has shown frame the story of modern ethics. More generally, Schneewind shows that the problem of evil plays a prominent part in the history of modern ethics because it is the nemesis of religious antivoluntarism. A problem that "has confronted religious thinkers from at least the time of the Book of Job,"[3] it becomes virulent and then lethal to theism as the human capacity and obligation to make moral judgments grows. The invention of autonomy is one of the fruits of this collision.

Historians of "theodicy" tell a subtly different story. Odo Marquard is only the most prominent to have argued that theodicy, which moderns think a central part of the job description of religion, is itself a modern phenomenon.[4] Far from being a constant of human religious or existential experience, the philosophical problem of evil is a historical product. The problem of evil, too, had to be invented. We Schneewindians should not be surprised. Why should the history of responses to evils be any more uniform or monolithic than the history of reflection on good? We should rather suppose that the concerns of those writing and thinking about evils "are at least as likely to have changed as to have remained constant through history."[5] The histories of theodicy and autonomy are, moreover, not independent but simultaneous and indeed intimately related.

In this essay I shall assemble reminders for a "variable-aim view"[6] of the history of Western responses to evils, and in the process challenge some conventional views concerning this history. After some necessarily sketchy reflections on the prehistory of theodicy, I will look at the place of accounts of evil in the work of Gottfried Wilhelm Leibniz and Kant. Leibniz, coiner of the word "theodicy," is often thought to have inaugurated a "century of theodicy" that Kant's *Critiques* closed, but I will argue that the discourse of theodicy was something Leibniz was in fact trying to stop. Like premodern thinkers, Leibniz thought brooding over evil got you nowhere, and so tried (unsuccessfully) to wean people from it. Kant, too, thought the problem insoluble, but he also presented it as inescapable, something we could neither answer nor ignore. The philosophical challenge of theodicy did not so much generate autonomy as follow from it.

1. The Historicity of Theodicy

Like every philosophical problem, the problem of evil has a history. Like most current philosophical problems, its historicity is forgotten. Especially for those who understand religion in monotheistic terms, what Hume called "Epicurus's old questions" seem inescapable:

Is he [God] willing to prevent evil, but not able? then is he impotent?
Is he able, but not willing? then is he malevolent.
Is he both able and willing? whence then is evil?[7]

Certainly the cosmogonic myths of the world religions and the liturgical complexes in which they have their homes provide responses to evils. To see them as philosophical accounts in disguise would be to misunderstand them, however. The history of religious responses to evils is more practical than theoretical, and less concerned to dispel human incomprehension at evils than to find meaning in it. Even what Kant was to call the "most philosophical book of the Old Testament,"[8] the Book of Job, gives the platform to the philosophical arguments of the Wisdom tradition only to shout them down. Job never learns why he suffers and forswears the need to know. The Book of Job works as a narrative whole or, in liturgical uses, provides a template for innocent suffering. Philosophy's competence in these issues is rejected.

To understand how different the modern problematic is from pre-modern responses to evils, we need to understand how (to choose two examples) Aquinas could have argued:

Boethius introduces a certain philosopher who asks: "If God exists, whence comes evil?" But it could be argued to the contrary: "If evil exists, God exists."[9]

and how it could have been part of Luther's understanding of theology that

God so orders this corporeal world in its external affairs that if you respect and follow the judgment of human reason, you are bound to say either that there is no God or that God is unjust.[10]

It's not that these thinkers did not see the problem that theodicy addresses. They saw it in the light of different aims. By way of exploring how they could have seen past the "problem of evil," an inevitably incoherent and inescapably anachronistic endeavor, let me offer some perspectives on the very different contexts in which what seem to be precursors to theodicy occur.

I start with two distinctions from contemporary philosophy of religion that open the way to a variable-aim view of Western responses to evils. A first distinction is that between "theodicy" and "defense":

The aim of defense is to show that antitheistic arguments from evil are not successful on their own terms. The general aim of theodicy, by contrast, is to give positive, plausible reasons for the existence of evil in a theistic universe.[11]

A defense need be no more than hypothetical, a performance of reconcilability rather than a reconciliation. The point is not to get it right, but merely to link the allegedly incompatible assertions about divine attributes and the nature and extent of evils in some way. Defense aims to make us lose interest in the particular question. It seeks to deflect our interest from questions we have neither the capacity nor the need to answer, to make way for more edifying avenues of inquiry. In response to questions about evils, defense was the norm before the emergence of theodicy.

Defense by itself is not enough, of course. The challenge of evils could not be ignored, certainly not in times when evils of all kinds were a more regular feature of experience than we can even imagine. Here the distinction between what Marilyn McCord Adams and Robert Merrihew Adams call "atheistic" and "aporetic" understandings of the problem of evil is illuminating. Given the undeniable presence of evil in the world, the

atheistic understanding challenges us: how can one believe in an omnipotent and benevolent God? This is the *Fragestellung* (research project)
of most modern philosophers of religion, but it is fundamentally different from the approach of premodern thinkers. The philosophical difficulty of reconciling the divine attributes with evil, and indeed with each
other, was understood not as undermining the plausibility of theism but
"*aporetically*, as generating a puzzle," a "constructive challenge to probe
more deeply into the logical relations among these propositions, to offer more rigorous and subtle analyses of the divine perfections."[12] God
was a given. His infinity made a full understanding of his attributes impossible for finite minds. While defense parries, aporetic investigation is
spurred on to conceptual innovation, faith seeking understanding. (The
contrast is not Athens vs. Jerusalem. Epicurus didn't pose his questions
with atheistic intent, nor did Sextus Empiricus, who provides the oldest
extant version of the problem.[13])

Seeing that the atheistic isn't the only way to approach the issue is a
good first step. A good second step is to recognize what an odd thing
it is to lump all *mala* (evils) into one *malum* (evil). As Paul Ricoeur has
noted, "the whole enigma of evil may be said to lie in the fact that, at
least in the traditions of the West, we put under the same terms such
different phenomena as sin, suffering, and death." It was not Hebrews,
Greeks or Christians who "conceived the problem of evil in terms of one
all-encompassing problematic" but metaphysical dualists.[14] The Gnostic
Marcion employed a version of Epicurus's old questions because it served
his dualist purposes. He argued that evil shows that the creator of this
shabby world is not the one whom we should worship. Monotheism can
make no sense of evils, but Gnosticism can.[15]

The most important Western thinking on evils emerged in responses
to metaphysical dualists: Plotinus responding to the Gnostics, Augustine
to the Manichees. These efforts, generating or revealing dualisms of their
own, may seem to prove the dualists right. The fundamental response,
however, is to reject the question. One can't make sense of evil because
it is no more than the *privation* of good, of being. It can seem no more
than wordplay when Augustine reflects in his *Confessions:* "[W]hatever is,
is good, and evil, the origin of which I was trying to find, is not a substance,
because if it were a substance, it would be good."[16] But this is precisely
because speaking of evil in abstract, general terms is nonsense! Examples
reveal the explanatory power of the metaphysics of being as goodness.

[W]hat is the so-called evil but a privation of the good? In the bodies of animals
affliction with diseases and wounds is nothing other than the privation of health.

For, when a cure is worked, it does not mean that those evils which were present, that is, the diseases and the wounds, recede thence and are elsewhere; they simply are not. For a wound or a disease is not a substance, but a vice of the fleshly substance; the substance, surely something good, is flesh itself, its accidents being the aforementioned evils, that is, privations of that good which is called health. In like manner evils in the soul are privations of natural good. When they are cured, they are not transferred to another place; since they can have no place in the healthy soul, they can be nowhere.[17]

Seeing evil as disease-like makes the uselessness of generalizing clear. We would hardly be impressed by the impassioned call of Camus' Dr. Rieux – "there are sick people and they need curing" – if he did not know to distinguish one kind of illness from another.[18] Response to evils understood as privative is necessarily practical, even as the awareness it generates of the nature and relations of goods leads us to God, the source of being and goodness. It is this metaphysics that led Aquinas to assert that the very existence of evils proves there is a God: "there would be no evil if the order of good were taken away, since its privation is evil. But this order would not exist if there were no God."[19]

For thinkers in this tradition, the question *Si deus est, unde mala?* is poorly formed. It is only half of the question Boethius reported, and not the more important half: "If there be a God, from whence proceed so many evils? And if there be no God, from whence cometh any good?"[20] For Christian Neoplatonists, the key is to realize not just the duality of questions but also their *asymmetry*. Reflection on the privative character of evils exposes the wonder and fragility of substance. Pierre Bayle, whose renewal of the dualists' charge that monism can make no sense of the mixture of good and evil in the world makes him the most important reviver of Epicurus's old questions, thought that Christian philosophy was lost without the (revealed) knowledge of *creatio ex nihilo*. The idea "that Matter was *self-existent*" made ancient views like Epicurus's philosophically compelling in a way Manicheanism, Platonism and Christianity could never be.[21] The metaphysics of being as goodness and its understanding of evil as privation were casualties of the new science and philosophy.

The fragility of substance reminded premodern thinkers of their own fragility. Neoplatonic understandings of infinity undermined confidence in the finite human's grasp of the divine attributes, which can thus be known only in "equivocal," "negative" or at best "analogical" terms. The mystery of the Christian Trinity only sharpened the point. Epicurus's old questions can hardly get off the ground if human beings are unable with confidence to formulate even one of the constituent propositions! What strike us as theodicistic arguments crop up, but they are part of very different projects: penitence, meditation hoping to transcend the limitations of human categories, and, most fundamentally, mending and maintaining a relationship with God, the only thing certain. The problem of evil didn't really get going until human beings felt the world to be solid enough to want to make a home there[22] and confident enough of their own judgments to move beyond a humble and hopeful reticence about God.[23]

Sin only complicated things further. The Christians of most ages lived, moved and thought in a world (and in bodies) made intelligible by the battle between Christ and Satan, between flesh and spirit. For sinful humanity, it is not just foolish to seek the origin of evil; it is dangerous. Original sin has so clouded human minds and corrupted human wills that the very entertaining of the question of whether God's goodness or power is compromised by evils can be a sign of perdition. In an important sense, the response to the problem of evil for Christians was thus not philosophy but conversion.[24] Kenneth Surin has argued that for Augustine,

[W]ithout conversion, the very *process* of seeking an answer to the question 'whence is evil' will be undermined by the distorted thinking of a crippled intellect. For the perversion of the human will is complemented by a perversion of the memory and the intellect ('the eye of the mind'); and so evil, inevitably and paradoxically, comes to be yet more deeply entrenched in the unconverted person's attempts to find a solution to this "problem."[25]

The penitent sinner takes responsibility for human wretchedness. Far from complaining at adversity, she welcomes it as just chastisement. All are in need of correction, and God chastens those he loves. A well-known passage in Gregory the Great's *Moralia in Job* reveals an approach to suffering and happiness in this world dramatically different from that of post-Renaissance thinkers.

[B]ecause in the midst of divine judgments, the human mind is closed in by the great darkness of its uncertainty, holy men, when they see the prosperity of this world to be their lot, are apprehensive. For they fear that they are receiving the fruit of their labors now. They fear that divine justice discerns in them something hidden and, by showering them with external blessings, withholds from them the interior. . . . And so it is that holy men dread prosperity in this world more than adversity.[26]

If no earthly being deserves happiness or should desire it in this world, and if we are not and cannot hope to be impartial judges of the situation anyway, the temptation to theodicy is one to be resisted at all costs.[27]

In order for the atheistic approach to evils to displace the aporetic, evil had to be defined as a problem within philosophy's competence. As a philosophical discourse, theodicy requires a set of shared assumptions among critics and defenders of a doctrine of providence. Because we live with what Marilyn McCord Adams has called the "myth of shared values" – an unquestioning faith in a "value-neutral" understanding of good and evil shared by theists and atheists[28] – it is hard to grasp how unusual this situation is. Adams traces this "myth" to the presuppositions of ordinary language philosophy of the 1950s, but its roots surely go back considerably farther. William Placher has recently argued:

Only in the seventeenth century, when theologians and philosophers began to assume that they had clear concepts of what "sovereign," "power," and "good" meant as applied to God, that beliefs about God ought to fit together in a logically coherent system, and that talk of the Trinity was marginal to our understanding of God, did theodicy in its modern form emerge.[29]

At least as important was the development of a secular vocabulary for moral and political questions by the modern natural lawyers.

A final difference between premodern and modern responses to evils needs to be named. If a question is meaningful, different answers to it will lead to different forms of life. The problem of the compatibility of belief in a God omnipotent and just with the existence of evil in the world is something like the question "Should I leave my husband?" While in principle available wherever there are marriages, this question arises in a real way only where the marital bond can be dissolved (and by the wife) and where there is somewhere within society for a woman to go should she leave her husband. The modern discussion of the problem of evil presupposes not only that we are fit to judge the ways of God, but also that there is a life for us should we find God's ways unacceptable. As Lucien Febvre argued, relevantly different forms of life were not available to premodern Christians facing evils.[30] The problem of evil presupposes the autonomy of moral standards (or some kind of standard) for judging God – an unequivocal moral language that is used in the same way by God in judging human beings and vice versa – but also a view of the human and natural world divorceable from theology and a *social* space independent of the church.

The Hellenistic Precedent
It is probably no coincidence that the early modern period, in which changes in metaphysics, theology, law and social structure gave rise to

the demand for theodicy, also saw the retrieval of the arguments of the Hellenistic philosophies of Stoicism, Skepticism and Epicureanism. It is in the philosophies of the Hellenistic period that we find the philosophical antecedents of theodicy – if not theodicy itself. Theodicy-like discussion became possible when Epicureans criticized providence and Stoics came to its defense:

the world's nature is certainly not a divine gift to us: it is so deeply flawed. (Lucretius, *De rerum natura* 2.180–1)[31]

it was for the sake of gods and men that the world and everything in it was made (Cicero, *De natura deorum* 2.133)

What made the debates of Epicureans and Stoics a discussion, and providence a philosophical topic, was a shared paradigm: agreement on philosophical protocol and on the goal of human striving in *eudaimonia*. Stoics and Epicureans alike thought men capable of judging what was good or bad for human flourishing, and of discerning the underlying reasons for things.

The sources for our knowledge of Hellenistic philosophy are fragmentary and derivative. It is virtually impossible to know whether the Epicurean arguments marshaled later by Lucretius provoked the Chrysippean views indicted by Plutarch and developed by Seneca and Epictetus or were, on the other hand, responses to them. But there are good philosophical reasons for thinking of the Epicureans as forcing the discussion. The Epicurean school was already founded when Chrysippus, Stoicism's most anthropocentric teleologist, arrived in Athens. More fundamentally, the recognition of the absence of providence is more important for the Epicurean *to be an Epicurean* than the recognition of its presence is for the Stoic to be a Stoic.

The Epicurean needs to recognize that happiness can be attained only by facing the facts of a senseless cosmos and taking charge of one's life and getting out of harm's way. The Stoic's happiness is independent of her experience. It is achieved not by a change in circumstances (like flight to a garden) but by a change of attitude: "No evil *can* befall a good man; opposites do not mingle."[32] The Stoics gave a number of accounts of evil,[33] but, strictly speaking, they had no need of a doctrine of providence. All the goods to which accounts of providence refer are really but *adiaphora* (indifferents). The core of Stoic ethics is the ideal of the sage, an ideal rarely (perhaps never) attained by any actual human being. As Chrysippus characterized his attitude, it is clear that the sage requires no detailed understanding of the ways of the world:

> As long as the consequences are not clear to me, I cleave ever to what is better adapted to secure those things that are in accordance with nature; for God himself has created me with the faculty of choosing things. But if I really knew that it was ordained for me to be ill at this present moment, I would seek even illness; for the foot also, if it had a mind, would seek to be covered with mud.[34]

"Inconvenience" will happen to him, but he avoids disappointment by properly husbanding his expectations. "Say 'I shall set sail unless something intervenes' and 'I shall become praetor unless something hinders me' and 'my enterprise will be successful unless something interferes,'" Seneca advised. Since "his first thought has been that something might obstruct his plans," the worst that can happen is that things turn out not as the wise man "has wished but as he has thought."[35]

The sage is never surprised and upset by events, and so is never tempted to blame the gods (or anyone else). People who have not attained the ideal of the sage are more put out by unanticipated setbacks to their plans. They may need providential-like explanations to ease them back to *apatheia*. Struggling Stoics need ways of making sense of particular setbacks that will prevent them from slipping into the morally corrosive blame game. This is essentially defense, the marshalling of possibilities to deflect attention from unpromising avenues of thought. Something closer to theodicy arises in response to Epicurean and Skeptical challenges to these concrete but merely therapeutic claims. Only at this point could Stoicism's ability to provide a providential story about every event seem central to its coherence and viability as a philosophical way of life.

It is ultimately only in the arena of polemics between Stoics and their critics that providence matters. However, our sources for the views of the Hellenistic philosophers are almost exclusively reports of debates, or responses to them. This obscuring of the essentially therapeutic moral motivations of both the critics of providence and its defenders is unfortunate – if prophetic of the representation of the similarly therapeutic early modern positions that between them gave rise to the discourse of theodicy. Leibniz's response to Bayle, often seen as reviving Augustine's response to the Manichees, is probably better understood in terms of the Stoics' responses to the arguments of Skeptics and Epicureans. We lose sight of the essentially therapeutic concerns of both Bayle and Leibniz if we present it as a philosophical debate about the problem of evil. Arguably, the texts on "the problem of evil" of Voltaire, Rousseau and Hume are best understood in terms of Hellenistic therapies, too.

2. Theodicy despite Leibniz

Leibniz coined the word "theodicy" in the 1690s.[36] It first appeared in print on the title page of his *Essais de Theodicée sur la Bonté de Dieu, la Liberté de l'Homme et l'Origine du Mal* of 1710 (but nowhere in it). Leibniz did not define the term, perhaps because it never occurred to him that it needed spelling out that "theodicy" means not Milton's justification of the ways of God to man but "the justice of God."[37] The *Theodicy* is not the defense of a divine plaintiff against particular human complaints, although divine and human justice are indeed the same for Leibniz, the greatest of modern antivoluntarists. Patrick Riley has suggested that we understand Leibnizian theodicy as "universal justice," an extension of his "universal jurisprudence."[38]

The *Theodicy* is known primarily as a response to Bayle, but Leibniz had planned to write it before the appearance of Bayle's *Dictionnaire historique et critique* in 1697. A fragment from 1695–7 suggests that Leibniz was intending a continuation of his earlier irenic project, "demonstrationes catholicae," under the new name "THEODICAEA."[39] The *Theodicy* strategically appealed to the authority of Lutheran, Catholic and Reformed authors in proposing a platform for a reunited Christian church to stand down the "libertines" who threatened progress in Europe.[40] As the Preface makes clear, the project of the *Theodicy* is to remove doubts about the goodness of God and the meaningfulness of ethical exertion that result not from Bayle's skepticism but from voluntarist "opinions, apt to do harm," which rest "on confused notions . . . concerning freedom, necessity and destiny."[41] Bayle appears not as an enemy but as the unwitting accomplice of voluntarism. He represents the well-intentioned people at risk if the Christian community doesn't provide a unified front against those who describe a God we cannot love and so undermine religion and morality.

Leibniz's understanding of the task of moral philosophy fits into what Schneewind calls the "Pythagoras story" model of moral philosophy.[42] The fundamental task of the moral philosopher is to remove doubts and distractions.[43] The good exists, and people are by nature oriented to it. They don't need to be *told* to orient themselves to it.

Since morality is more important than arithmetic, God has given to man instincts which lead, straight away and without reasoning, to part of what reason commands. Similarly we walk in conformity with the laws of mechanics without thinking about them; and we eat not only because it is necessary, but also and much more because eating gives us pleasure. But these instincts do not irresistibly impel us: our passions lead us to resist them, our prejudices obscure them, and contrary customs distort them.[44]

Our apprehension of goods can, however, be obstructed. Finitude, sin, bad company and poor habits raise obstacles. People thus need to be *taught* to see goods, especially to see beyond the transient allure of sensory pleasure,[45] and need to be protected against the seductive arguments of voluntarist "libertines" who would give them license to ignore their own moral instincts.

After Bayle, it was necessary also to show why the very real experiences of evil in the world were no reason for doubt or despair. The "best of all possible worlds" argument, an argument Leibniz had espoused for decades, was Leibniz's basic response, but he insisted that it was nothing new. It is the upshot of every worthwhile Western tradition. (Leibniz traced it to Plato.) The best of all possible worlds argument is a priori, and so immune to doubts like those raised by Bayle. Nothing whatever about the contents or nature of this world matters for it. No a posteriori proof or disproof is possible.

Leibniz knew, however, that an a priori argument would not satisfy one convinced by Bayle that the texture of experience calls reason itself into question. Bayle gave dozens of examples of apparent divine negligence, callousness or mismanagement, arguing that in these cases reason forgets its own arguments for the benevolent designer of the world, asserts the opposite and ends in perplexity. Leibniz could not and didn't claim to be able to explain why God permits the particular evils Bayle discussed. All we can manage and all we need, he thought, is defense: an alternative interpretation that is consistent with philosophical theism.[46] Leibniz's "hypotheses" don't have to be plausible to undermine Bayle's claim that only one interpretation is possible.

This is made clearest in the *Theodicy's* "Preliminary Dissertation on the Conformity of Reason and Faith":

> It is the part of the objection to open up the subject, and it is enough for him who answers to say Yes or No. He is not obliged to counter with a distinction: it will do, in case of need, if he denies the universality of some proposition in the objection or criticizes its form, and one may do both these things without penetrating beyond the objection.[47]

An appendix "Summary of the Controversy Reduced to Formal Arguments" makes it clear that the book's purpose is a negative, therapeutic one. The syllogistic arguments it treats are not Leibniz's but the mainly voluntarist arguments to which his work responds. Leibniz responded

to each in good Scholastic fashion with "I reject the major" or "I deny
the minor," providing ways for theologians and philosophers confronted
with the various challenges to cope, *whichever* view they happened to take.
For instance, Leibniz left open the possibility that evils outweigh goods in
the human world, in this world, as well perhaps as in the next. Although
he implied that he thought none of these is the case, he didn't need to
demonstrate this. His responses were thus compatible with many theological accounts, neither enabling nor requiring a choice among them.
All of the particular claims Leibniz invoked – Stoic arguments about the
evils that attend goods, Plotinian arguments about the aesthetic value
of variety and contrast, Augustinian arguments about God's bringing a
greater good out of every evil – were made in a similarly tentative way
and need to be understood as performances of reconcilability, designed
to put to rest the doubts that sometimes threaten to overcome even the
most well-intentioned people.

Like the Stoics (whose philosophy was more like his own than he realized), Leibniz thought one needed no detailed account of providence.

The whole future is doubtless determined: but since we know not what it is, nor
what is foreseen or resolved, we must do our duty, according to the reason that
God has given us and according to the rules that he has prescribed for us; and
thereafter we must have a quiet mind, and leave to God himself the care for the
outcome. It is true that we cannot "render service" to him, for he has need of
nothing: but it is "serving him," in our parlance, when we strive to carry out *his
presumptive will,* co-operating in the good as it is known to us, wherever we can
contribute thereto. For we must always presume that God is prompted towards the
good we know, until the event show us that he had stronger reasons, although
perhaps unknown to us, which have made him subordinate this good that we
sought to some other greater good of his own designing, which he has not failed
or will not fail to effect.[48]

The heart of Leibniz's argument is the claim that God wills the good
"antecedently" and the best "consequently."[49] This has been taken to
be the divine imprimatur for utilitarianism, but only God could know
enough to optimize. The infinite knowledge needed to determine the
best of all possible worlds makes his choice a "mystery" to us.[50] We should
always be attempting to do God's *antecedent* will. In those cases where
the fruits do not materialize, what Leibniz calls the *Fatum Christianum*
(Christian fate) should support us.

Do your duty and be content with that which shall come of it, not only because
you cannot resist divine providence, or the nature of things (which may suffice

for tranquility, but not for contentment), but also because you have to do with a good master.[51]

These flashes of awareness are always of events past, however, and we generalize them at our peril.

Our reference when we look forward, when we deliberate among possible avenues of action, is never – except accidentally – the "reality" of *this* world, but neither is it a distinct realm of freedom, a heavenly city transcending the world of our experience and in which all goods coexist. We refer, rather, to possible worlds, the goods of all of which God wills to realize. We don't know which is the actual until *after* we have done our duty.[52] A religious account of things in the world is brought in only in order to make ethics motivationally maintainable in the face of disappointed moral effort. It does this not by providing a comprehensive account of the way the world is or of the way a moral world would be, but by helping tide us over moments when untoward events (especially the frustration of our good intentions) disorient us and threaten our sense that we know enough to trust our apprehensions of good and evil.

The *Theodicy* seeks to put worries about evil and providence conclusively to rest, as they can only interfere with ethical life, but Leibniz acknowledged that we will continue to experience moments of confusion. At these times, we may need to venture guesses as to the reason for the particular disposition of things in this world, but, as Leibniz thought he had made clear, these neither can nor need to be more than tentative. The a priori argument that this is the best of all possible worlds will support a *Fatum Christianum* best if unencumbered by a posteriori commitments. Nevertheless, the *Theodicy* was soon read as the very paradigm of a posteriori optimism. Leibniz's concerns may have been therapeutic, but the teleological claims he used had their own momentum, fired by the demands of the emerging discourse of theodicy.

Indeed, the very arguments Leibniz made to insist on the tentativeness of his hypotheses had the effect of massively strengthening them. Leibniz's claim that nothing would exist but for a "determining" or "sufficient" reason we cannot hope to comprehend created a void that neither a priori nor a posteriori arguments could fill. This was deliberate. Our job within what Schneewind has felicitously called the "divine corporation"[53] is to pursue goods in possible worlds, not to track God's choice of worlds. The promise of a "sufficient reason" crucial yet undeliverable in this life was Leibniz's attempt to *short-circuit* the nascent discourse of theodicy. The way he made this point was, however, to generate a cosmic legitimation crisis. As we realize that other worlds were really possible, José Ortega y Gassett suggested, "the reality of [this] world loses its firmness, becomes questionable, is converted into an enigma."[54] This only feeds the discourse of theodicy, and through Leibniz's famous two questions (Why is there anything at all? Why this?), nihilism.

Further, precisely to the extent that it succeeds in transcending the dualism of its Platonist forebears by locating the "region of the eternal verities," the source of incompossibilities, in the understanding of God, Leibniz's version of the argument that this is the best of all possible worlds opened a chasm between the attributes of God. While his goodness determines God (morally) to choose only the best of all possible worlds, his understanding contains the possibility of worlds more and less good, and his will could, if only in principle, actualize any of them. Kant, who had a more profound understanding of Leibniz's philosophy than is often supposed, saw the problem already in 1753–4: "Leibniz presents the rules, which aim at perfection, as conflicting with each other in their application."[55]

3. Kant's Invention of Theodicy

If Leibniz was not the inventor of theodicy, who was? Kant's critical turn is often thought to have destroyed the very possibility of theodicy. In fact, however, the pathos of theodicy was established as a challenge to philosophy by the ambivalent anthropocentrism of Kant's sublation of voluntarism and antivoluntarism. Far from weaning people from unfruitful concern over the apparent moral disorder of the world, Kant's philosophy established the problem of evil as one of those questions it is the "peculiar fate" of reason to be unable either to answer or to dismiss.[56] Leibniz hoped people would lose interest in the "problem" of evil. For Kant this would be close to a euthanasia of human prospects. The autonomous agent cannot feel comfortable in her world. By basing his mature ethics and religion on the insolubility of the problem of evil, Kant thus gave the problem of evil an altogether new significance.

Kant discussed theodicy in print at the beginning and at the end of his career. In each case his arguments were untimely. In 1759 he defended Leibnizian optimism against voluntarist critiques that he himself found tempting. In 1791, he declared the "failure of all philosophical attempts in theodicy," whether voluntarist or antivoluntarist. This last essay is sometimes taken as marking the end of the "century of theodicy,"[57] spelling out the implications of the *Critiques* for the project of theodicy. Far from displacing the pathos of theodicy, however, Kant's late view threatens to break under the weight of teleology denied. The 1791 essay's proposed "authentic theodicy" – the practical reason-based recognition of the impossibility of philosophical theodicy – is unstable, and seems even in Kant's thought to cry out for more assurances than the critical philosophy can give.

Hyperteleology

Kant's early views on theodicy oscillated between a voluntarist and an antivoluntarist pole. He wrote notes for, but did not complete, an essay for the 1755 prize competition of the Berlin Academy of Sciences on the difference between the views of Leibniz and Alexander Pope. Leibniz's a priori view (best of all possible worlds) seemed question-begging, Kant noted, but Pope's a posteriori view (whatever is, is right) was vulnerable to the objection of "an Epicurus" about the preponderance of disorder.[58] In his 1759 response to the winning (Popeian) essay, Kant asserted that the Leibnizian argument was not only true but *obviously* so. People stray from it into voluntarism only out of boredom and the desire to appear clever.[59]

If Kant's recent reservations about the Leibnizian position were not even mentioned, however, this may be because Kant took Leibnizian "preestablished harmony" seriously in a whole new way. In other writings, he developed an argument (which he attributed to Pope in 1753–4) that goes beyond voluntarism and antivoluntarism, and gives a kind of answer to the voluntarist charge that the Leibnizian view "deprives" God of his "self-sufficiency." The argument was unveiled in "New Elucidation of the First Principles of Metaphysical Cognition" and in the anonymous *Universal Natural History and Theory of the Heavens* (both of 1755), and is elaborated in 1762's *The Only Possible Argument in Support of a Demonstration of the Existence of God* (published 1763), where much of Kant's critical rejection of metaphysics made its first appearance.

What holds Kant's theism in place here are neither theoretical arguments for the existence of God nor the moral proof he will later develop, but a proof anchored in an ingenious application of Leibniz's mysterious, originally Stoic concept of compossibility. Since "possibility" could only be understood in relation to something actual, Kant argued, God's nature defined possibility. All things possible must be harmonious with God's perfections – and hence with each other. The possibles are thus by nature harmonic, sociable, and one "may expect to find harmony and beauty in the combination of natural things" in *any* possible world.[60] This is the best of all possible worlds, but the claim did a lot less work now that every possible world expressed the source of its possibility, God, and none contained evil.[61]

Kant made the point in a striking way. God is the *"non-moral* source" of everything possible, and the *"moral* cause" of the actual world.[62] Our discovery of harmony and order in nature brings us closer to God, but we must not too quickly conclude that some particular instance of harmony is something for which God is to be praised *as moral.* The antivoluntarist's God, whose actions are intelligible to us and structurally analogous to our own efforts, is here overshadowed by a God whose operations are not even comprehensible to us as agency at all. Kant boasted that far from undermining piety, this view would elevate our "amazement" at the harmoniousness of the creation to an entirely new plane.

> For although it is true that, employing the analogy of human behavior, one can form some concept of how such a Being could be the cause of something real, one cannot form any concept of how that Being should contain the ground of the internal possibility of other things. It is as if this thought rises far higher than mortal creatures can reach.[63]

Kant found the conception of divine "all-sufficiency" *(Allgenugsamkeit)* that includes God as cause *and* source preferable to Leibniz's mere "infinity" in comparing the divine with human attributes. It made clear that the difference between God and man was qualitative, not just quantitative.[64]

Despite the hyperharmonious world order he described, Kant was aware that maintaining faith in God is not always easy. Physico-theology may be philosophically flawed, but it is "much more practical than any other" argument in maintaining a vivid faith in God "even from the point of view of the philosopher."[65] Its real danger is that we tend to distort it anthropocentrically, taking the very real amenability of natural phenomena to our interests to be explanations when their benefits to us may be no more than "ancillary advantages." "One should take care not to incur the legitimate mockery of a Voltaire who . . . asks: 'Why do we have noses?' and then replies: 'No doubt so that we can wear spectacles'."[66] The creation is shot through with teleology. It transcends our two-dimensional conception of teleology. Here is a world in which everything is at once end and means. Everything works at once to achieve its own end *and* to achieve those of others; nothing is a means only.

This God who can do no wrong, because his acts are the "outcome of his own inmost nature," was, Schneewind argues, the first agent to act autonomously.[67] Kant was still some distance from inventing the human autonomy that would turn philosophy on its head, however. Nor had he really agonized over the apparent injustice of human suffering. In the 1760s, however, a Rousseau-strengthened sense both of human worth and of human misery made the problem of the impunity of the wicked and the suffering of the innocent start on its way to becoming a central part of Kant's religious thinking.[68] For the time being, Rousseau's Stoic rejection of theodicy was enough. In his notes to *Observations on the Feeling of the Beautiful and the Sublime* (1765), Kant remarked that it is only because man's desires are "degenerate" that his judgments about God are "wrong [*verkehrt*]"; "luxury" breeds complaints about "the divine government and the government of kings."[69] Echoing Rousseau's Savoyard Vicar, Kant piously remarked: "I who know with certainty that I suffer no evils but those which I draw to myself and [that] it is just up to me to be happy through the goodness of the divine arrangement will never grumble against it."[70] And yet Kant's next book showed that he would have been grateful to see the apparent maldistribution of fortune explained.

The semiserious *Dreams of a Spirit Seer* (1766) commends to us the Socratic view "how many are the things of which I have no need," and ends with Voltaire's Epicurean injunction, "Let us attend to our happiness, and go into the garden and work!"[71] Its core, however, is a dream that the moral world is as well governed by universal laws as is the physical. This is presented in a tongue-in-cheek way as the best one might make of the ideas of the enthusiast Emmanuel Swedenborg, but Kant's main argument for this fantasy view is that it solves the problem of evil.

For in this case, the anomalies seem to vanish which are normally so embarrassingly conspicuous in the contradiction between the moral and the physical circumstances of man here on earth. All the morality of actions, while never having its full effect in the corporeal life of man according to the order of nature, may well do so in the spirit-world, according to pneumatic laws.[72]

This dream would return in Kant's critical philosophy as what we must (or may) hope if our experience is to make sense to us. As the rest of Kant's precritical theology collapsed into the subjective, the impossibility of this dream would become increasingly painful.

Critique and Theodicy

The *Critique of Pure Reason* might be thought to pull the rug out from under philosophical speculation on the problem of evil as effectively as any negative theology. The order of the world of our experience is not traceable to nature or its God but to the structure of our minds. The forms of our understanding make things appear orderly. Whether or not there is comparable order in the *Ding an sich* we can never know.[73] The *Critique* is thus in part at least a defense. The hyperteleological argument having now gone the way of the theoretical arguments for the existence of God, Kant built his "moral proof" precisely on our sense of *missing* harmony between the worlds of our moral and physical experience. In order that anything make sense, we are entitled to believe that God is just and powerful enough to make harmonization of these worlds possible. Belief in a God with any other attributes than the moral ones was no longer warranted.

Kant mentioned the problem of evil only in passing in the *Critique of Pure Reason*, but the "Canon of Pure Reason" suggests that we should take seriously his claim (in 1790) that the *Critique* was "the genuine apology for Leibniz."[74]

If we assume an absolutely perfect cause, we need not be at a loss explaining the purposiveness, order, and vastness which are displayed in the world; but in view of what, judged at least by our concepts, are the obvious deviations and evils, other new hypotheses are required in order to uphold the original hypothesis in the face of the objections which these suggest.[75]

Kant's argument here was like Leibniz's in the "Preliminary Dissertation" to the *Theodicy*, where he made it clear that his responses to Bayle can and need only be tentative. They strengthen moral faith only negatively, by deflating the claims of skepticism.

[A]lthough, in dealing with the merely speculative questions of pure reason, hypotheses are not available for the purposes of basing propositions upon them, they are yet entirely permissible for the purposes of defending propositions; that is to say, they may not be employed in any dogmatic, but only in polemical fashion. By the defence of propositions I do not mean the addition of fresh grounds for their assertion, but merely the nullifying of the sophistical arguments by which our opponent professes to invalidate this assertion.[76]

The only acceptable grounds lie in practical reason, in an argument arrived at without the benefit (or risk) of any interpretation of the course of events. Kant did not permit the application of his entirely general faith to particular cases. And yet, when an Epicurus shows up, we are entitled to deploy hypotheses in defense of the claims of moral faith. Not just Epicurus: "The opponent [*Gegner*] we must always look for in ourselves. For speculative reason in its transcendental employment is *in itself* dialectical."[77] As Hegel was to note with disdain, this changes the whole situation: the problem of evil is generated by reason, not by the world.[78]

If the first *Critique* made theodicy null and void, however, it took Kant some time to realize it. He offered a theodicy in his 1783–4 lectures on the philosophical doctrine of religion,[79] and his essays in the philosophy of history made explicit appeal to the language of theodicy. "Idea for a Universal History with a Cosmopolitan Purpose" (1784) described itself as constituting a *"justification* of nature – or rather perhaps of *providence."*[80] Kant's earnestly playful reinvention of Genesis 2–6:17 in "Conjectural Beginning of Human History" (1786) claimed to have shown the coherence and power of Rousseau's theodicy and even arrived at a philosophically defensible version of original sin:

This, then, is the lesson taught by a philosophical attempt to write the most ancient part of human history: contentment with Providence, and with the course of human affairs, considered as a whole. For this course is not a decline from good to evil, but rather a gradual development from the worse to the better; and nature itself has given the vocation to everyone to contribute as much to this progress as may be within his power.[81]

As late as 1795's *Toward Perpetual Peace,* Kant suggested that no theodicy might be possible, but that providence was "justified in the course of the world" if we assumed the "objectivity" of moral laws.[82]

Kant's philosophy of history has been read as proto-Hegelian, but the 1783–4 lectures aside, Kant was careful not to present the case for progress in human history as closed.[83] The argument already of the "Idea" was presented in a subjunctive mood. What we are presented with is an outline of what would have to be the case in order for man to achieve his end. Everything *else* in our experience achieves its end, so there is no reason to doubt that humankind will, too. But by definition, nature (or God) cannot make man act freely. A series of jokes reminds us that everything may yet end in disaster – most conspicuously the explanation of the title of "Toward Perpetual Peace."[84] All of Kant's considerations of the possibility of moral progress in human history are similarly Janus-faced. What might be called the rhetoric of freedom *requires* that no clear answers be given. Ambiguity is not enough. Only the stalemate of individually compelling cases for *yes* and *no* make possible hope's *maybe.*

The *Critique of Teleological Judgment* might seem to spell a change. Does not the explanatory scandal of organism oblige us to assume that every teleologically ordered thing has a merely "extrinsic purposiveness" except man, the "ultimate purpose of creation"?[85] Chrysippus seems to have returned when Kant notes the felicitous way tropical forests and ocean currents conspire to make the Arctic wastes habitable for human beings,[86] or asserts that even "things we find disagreeable and contrapurposive [*zweckwidrig*] in particular respects" turn out to be useful to us: "For example, we might say that the vermin that plague people in their clothes, hair, or beds are there by a wise provision of nature, namely as an incentive to keep clean."[87] And yet Kant *also* insisted that "in the chain of natural purposes man is never more than a link."[88] Seeing ourselves – or the freedom that humanity may someday achieve – as the only thing able to provide a meaning for the universe is just something *we* need to do, nothing more, and must be grasped as that. The claim is about us, not about the world. The resolution of the "Antinomy of Teleological Judgment" makes sure that we do not let the discovery of teleology stop us from continuing to seek mechanical explanations for everything.

The *Critique of Teleological Judgment* is a kind of confidence trick, the most daring extreme of the rhetoric of freedom. Experiences both of purposiveness and of contrapurposiveness are unpacked to reveal confirmation for our supernatural vocation. The third *Critique* can be read as condoning a view of the cosmos and humanity's place close to Pope's, but it also contains a remarkable description of a world that will drive even the most virtuous atheist to despair through its recalcitrance.

For while he can expect that nature will now and then cooperate contingently with the purpose of his that he feels so obligated and impelled to achieve, he can never expect nature to harmonize with it in a way governed by laws and permanent rules (such as his inner maxims are and must be). Deceit, violence, and envy will always be rife around him, even though he himself is honest, peaceable, and benevolent. Moreover, as concerns the other righteous people he meets: no matter how worthy of happiness they may be, nature, which pays no attention to that, will still subject them to all the evils of deprivation, disease, and untimely death, just like all the other animals on the earth. And they will stay subjected to these evils always, until one vast tomb engulfs them all (honest or not, that makes no difference here) and hurls them, who managed to believe that they were the final purpose of creation, back into the abyss of the purposeless chaos of matter from which they were taken. And so this well meaning person would indeed have to give up as impossible the purpose that the moral laws obligated him to have before his eyes.[89]

Something stronger than hope seems required here, and within a year Kant would write: "the world is *often* a closed book for us, and it is so *every time* we look at it to extract from it God's *final aim* (which is always moral) even though it is an object of experience."[90]

Authentic Theodicy

Kant returned to theodicy in "On the Failure of All Philosophical Attempts in Theodicy" a year later (1791), as he started to develop his view of "radical evil in human nature," the euthanasia of practical reason that comes from the peer-pressured atrophy of self-vigilance but can be accounted for only with reference to an original propensity to evil. Theodicy, defined as "the defense of the highest wisdom of the creator against the charge which reason brings against it for whatever is contrapurposive [*dem Zweckwidrigem*] in the world," is declared impossible.[91] Kant found that every attempt to "defend" the "moral wisdom" of God in the face of sin, pain and the "disproportion of crime and punishment" had failed. None indeed could ever succeed. But Kant was not arguing against *all* theodicy:

[W]e cannot deny the name of "theodicy" also to the mere dismissal of all objections against divine wisdom, if this dismissal is a *divine decree*, or (for in this case it amounts to the same thing) if it is a pronouncement of the same reason through which we form our concept of God – necessarily and prior to all experience – as a moral and wise being.[92]

What Kant called "authentic theodicy" was "honesty in openly admitting one's doubts; repugnance to pretending conviction where one feels none."[93] This is not a "doctrinal" or "philosophical" theodicy, but it is still a response, and tendered in the currency of hope so important to moral philosophy.

Kant announced that he had found "an authentic interpretation" of nature "expressed allegorically in an ancient holy book," the Book of Job.[94] The discussion is interesting because the position taken by Job's comforters is antivoluntarist, while Job's position is an unabashed voluntarism. The friends argue from "that system which explains all ills in the world from God's *justice*," while Job "declares himself for the system of *unconditional divine decision*. 'He has decided,' Job says, 'He does as he wills.'"[95] Kant argued that there was "little worthy of note in the subtle or hypersubtle reasonings" of *either* side.[96] Job's view is honest, what anyone in his situation would say, but not therefore correct. Truthfulness, while better than mendacity, is no guarantee of truth.

In any case, Job's wasn't the last word. God's response to Job is one of the few places in Kant's works where God speaks, and Kant's is one of the few modern interpretations of the Book of Job in which God is seen as presenting an argument and not just flaunting his power. Kant's

God reveals to Job that everything in nature in fact achieves its purpose, but that these purposes interfere with each other.

[God] allowed [Job] glimpses into the beautiful side of creation, where ends comprehensible to the human being bring the wisdom and the benevolent providence of the author of the world unambiguously to light; but also, by contrast, into the horrible side, by calling out to him the products of his might, among which also harmful and fearsome things, each of which appears indeed to be purposively arranged for its own sake and that of its species, yet, with respect to other things and to human beings themselves, as destructive, counterpurposive, and incompatible with a universal plan established with goodness and wisdom. And yet God thereby demonstrates an order and a maintenance of the whole which proclaim a wise creator, even though his ways, inscrutable to us, must at the same time remain hidden – indeed already in the physical order of things, and how much more in the connection of the latter with the moral order (which is all the more impenetrable to our reason).[97]

The authentic interpretation of the world is "made by the law-giver himself,"[98] and it tells us that the universe is ordered but not in a way we will ever understand. We are but one of its many purposes.

We have met this God before. It is not the God we are enjoined to postulate by practical reason, but the "all-sufficient" God of the *Only Possible Argument,* creator of a world in which all aims are achieved together. Facilitating the achievement of our *summum bonum* is one of his projects, but he has others. Justice is only one of his attributes. Kant presented God's attributes – *holiness* as "the author of the world, as law-giver (creator)," justice "as *judge*" and goodness "as *ruler* (preserver)"[99] – as a practical reasoned trinity, but their hierarchy points beyond a God comprehensible as just. God's holiness is higher than and even prior to his justice, in the same way his justice is to his goodness. One of Kant's few other references to Job – here to 9:2 ("how should man be just with God?") – appears in a Reflexion that notes that it is as confusing to assume "goodness and justice in one person" as to see "holiness and justice in one."[100] Kant's claim seems to be that God is *more than* moral, and that this is a fact graspable in the right (negative) way only by a person who, like Job, "did not found his morality on faith, but his faith on morality."[101]

What are we to make of this impossible claim – coming from the mouth of God, no less? The critical Kant can't even gesture in the direction of such a view. Even understood as allegory, the Book of Job points beyond Kant's moral theism. Is Job a proof text for Kant? Kant thinks Scripture can be the source of insights human reason could never have worked out on its own but then make its own. Schneewind has shown that the teachings of the "greatest of the ancient philosophers," Jesus, function this way in Kant's understanding of the history of ethics.[102] *Religion Within the Limits of Reason Alone* makes similar arguments about the nature of human evil, and the possibility of regeneration through the church founded by a God-man. Perhaps fighting the good fight in the face of the moral chaos of the world is something we know is possible only because it was possible for Job. Perhaps the move beyond philosophy is warranted by the rejection of philosophy in the "most philosophical book of the Old Testament."

The 1791 essay is not Kant's last word on evil, although it is his last word on theodicy. Its closing discussion concerns the mendacity exemplified by Job's friends, who did not speak spoke "frankly," as Job did, but "as if they were being secretly listened to by the mighty one."[103] Untruthfulness about one's own motives is the slippery slope that Kant would within a year argue lead toward "radical evil." But can a self-mortification of reason based in an original sin-like doctrine be accepted by agents obliged and entitled by their autonomy to reject revealed religion?

Conclusions

In laying out the evolution of Kant's views against the backdrop of Leibniz and the prehistory of theodicy, I have tried to suggest that there are precedents to the fate of Kant's attempts to displace teleology for the sake of ethics. The most obvious precedent is Leibniz. Both Leibniz and Kant developed an a priori version of providence that – together with hypotheses for responding to internal and external objections – was intended to help ethical agents pick themselves up when their best efforts to do good met with failure. Both undermined their own best efforts, and in related ways. Leibniz asserted that everything has a "sufficient reason," but argued that we can't and needn't ever know even one of these reasons. This generated an appetite for justification which could be satisfied by neither a priori nor a posteriori arguments. Kant generated a similar vacuum from the other side by suggesting that we cannot help seeing the world in teleological terms – nothing can ultimately make sense to us unless everything does – but at the same time warning that none of our teleological judgments could ever be taken literally, and that we must be ever suspicious of our desire to see the world make sense. Both positions hasten the onset of nihilism. By making the unquenchable thirst for theodicy the sign of moral health, however, Kant's is the one that established the problem of evil in modern Western thought.

Kant is often described as the slayer of theodicy, but as I have tried to show, the pathos of theodicy comes into its own as he invents autonomy. Evils have always called for responses, but the forms of moral self-discipline and the open-ended philosophy of history and nature Kant thinks autonomy requires are what anchor evil as a philosophical problem. In the end, Kant's ethical suspension of teleology comes close to collapsing under the weight of frustrated hope, and he finds himself reaching illegitimately to his precritical theology, to the resources of the Bible and to the doctrine of original sin. Kant established the problem of evil as an eternal wound for philosophy to tend, but his awkward solutions satisfied few. Perhaps the juggernaut of theodicy was not to be stopped. In any case, the story of theodicy's shaping of modern thought begins as Fichte, Schelling, Schleiermacher, Hegel, Feuerbach, Schopenhauer, Kierkegaard, Nietzsche, James, Royce, Heidegger and others offered different diagnoses and cures of the wound Kant had made. Contemporary discussions treat theodicy and ethics as unrelated. What would Kant, the inventor of autonomy *and* theodicy, think? Can autonomy survive in an environment that no longer feels the thirst for theodicy?

Notes

1. J. B. Schneewind, *The Invention of Autonomy: A History of Modern Moral Philosophy* (Cambridge University Press, 1997), ch. 22.iii–iv.
2. Ibid., p. 500.
3. Ibid., p. 226.
4. Odo Marquard, "Unburdenings: Theodicy Motives in Modern Philosophy," in *In Defense of the Accidental: Philosophical Studies*, trans. Robert M. Wallace (Oxford University Press, 1991), pp. 8–28, 11. Marquard's most extended discussion appeared in *Schwierigkeiten mit der Geschichtsphilosophie: Aufsatze* (Suhrkamp, 1973). More recently, Marquard assembled the series of articles on "Malum" in *Historisches Wörterbuch der Philosophie*, ed. Joachim Ritter and Karlfried Gründer, vol. 5 (Schwabe and Co., 1980). In English see Kenneth Surin, *Theology and the Problem of Evil* (Basil Blackwell, 1986), and Terrence W. Tilley, *The Evils of Theodicy* (Georgetown University Press, 1991). I have tried to provide sources for a more historically nuanced understanding of responses to evils in my *The Problem of Evil: A Reader* (Blackwell, 2001). Representative selections from many authors mentioned in the following discussion – Plato, Seneca, Sextus Empiricus, Plotinus, Lactantius (for Epicurus), Augustine, Boethius, Aquinas, Milton, Bayle, Leibniz, Pope, Voltaire, Rousseau, Hume, Kant – may be found there.
5. Schneewind, *Invention of Autonomy*, p. 550.
6. Ibid., p. 553.

7. David Hume, *Dialogues Concerning Natural Religion*, ed. Richard H. Popkin (Hackett, 1980), p. 63. The source of Epicurus's questions is Lactantius, who cites an otherwise unknown passage from Epicurus in *De ira dei* 13.20–1. Hume knew the text presumably via the article "Paulicians" in Bayle's *Historical and Critical Dictionary*, the source also of Voltaire's quotation in the article "Bien (tout est)" of his *Philosophical Dictionary*.

8. "Danziger Rationaltheologie nach Baumbach" (1784), *Kants Werke* [hereafter Ak.] 28:1287.

9. Saint Thomas Aquinas, *On the Truth of the Catholic Faith: Summa Contra Gentiles, Book Three: Providence, Part I*, trans. Vernon J. Bourke (Hanover House, 1956), pp. 240–1 (3.71.10).

10. Martin Luther, *On the Bondage of the Will* (De Servo Arbitrio), trans. and ed. Philip S. Watson with B. Drewery, in *Luther and Erasmus: Free Will and Salvation* (Westminster, 1969), p. 330.

11. Michael L. Peterson, *God and Evil: An Introduction to the Issues* (Westview, 1998), p. 33. See, e.g., Alvin Plantinga, "God, Evil, and the Metaphysics of Freedom," in *The Problem of Evil*, ed. Marilyn McCord Adams and Robert Merrihew Adams (Oxford University Press, 1990), p. 10. For the connection to reformed epistemology, see Peterson, *God and Evil*, pp. 60–1.

12. See the Introduction to *The Problem of Evil*, ed. Adams and Adams, pp. 2–3, and Marilyn McCord Adams, *Horrendous Evils and the Goodness of God* (Cornell University Press, 1999), p. 7 and passim.

13. See my *The Problem of Evil*, pp. xii–xviii.

14. Paul Ricoeur, "Evil: A Challenge to Philosophy and Theology," *Journal of the American Academy of Religion* Liii/3 (1985), pp. 635–48, 636.

15. See Tertullian, *Adversus Marcionem*, ed. and trans. Ernest Evans, 2 vols. (Clarendon, 1972), vol. 1, pp. 97–9 (II.5).

16. Augustine, *Confessions* 7:12, trans. R. S. Pine-Coffin (Penguin, 1961), p. 148.

17. Saint Augustine, *Faith, Hope and Charity* [*Enchiridion de fide, spe et caritate*], trans. Bernard M. Peebles (Fathers of the Church, Inc., 1947), pp. 376–7 (3.11).

18. Albert Camus, *The Plague*, trans. Stuart Gilbert (Vintage, 1948), p. 120. Camus's book, a classic of the literature of theodicy, can arrive at its rather simplistic conclusion because there is only one disease in town.

19. Aquinas, *Summa Contra Gentiles* 3.71.10, pp. 240–1.

20. Boethius, *The Consolation of Philosophy*, trans. "I. T." (1609) and revised by H. F. Stewart in Boethius, *The Theological Tractates; The Consolation of Philosophy* (Harvard University Press, 1918; Loeb Classics), pp. 150–1.

21. "Epicurus," rem. S, *The Dictionary Historical and Critical of Mr. Peter Bayle*, 2nd ed., 5 vols. (London 1735), vol. 2, pp. 786–9. Bayle's most important discussions of the problems Christianity and dualism pose for each other are the articles "Manichees" and "Paulicians," and the second "Clarification" to the *Dictionary*. Epicurus is discussed as a virtuous and consistent atheist in many places in Bayle's work.

22. Hans Blumenbach, *The Legitimacy of the Modern Age*, trans. Robert M. Wallace (MIT Press, 1985).

23. See Wilfred Cantwell Smith, *Faith and Belief* (Princeton University Press, 1979), and, for "reticence," William C. Placher, *The Domestication of Transcendence: How Modern Thinking about God Went Wrong* (Westminster John Knox Press, 1996).

24. See Terrence W. Tilley, *The Evils of Theodicy* (Georgetown University Press, 1991), pp. 113–40.

25. *Theology and the Problem of Evil* (Basil Blackwell, 1986), 11. Cf. G. R. Evans, *Augustine on Evil* (Cambridge University Press, 1982), pp. 29–90.

26. Gregory the Great, *Moralia in Iob* 5.1.1; quoted in Susan E. Schreiner, *Where Shall Wisdom Be Found? Calvin's Exegesis of Job from Medieval and Modern Perspectives* (University of Chicago Press, 1994), p. 31.

27. Ernst Cassirer noted that theodicy arose as belief in original sin waned. See *The Philosophy of the Enlightenment*, trans. Fritz C. A. Koelln and James P. Pettegrove (Princeton University Press, 1951), pp. 137–60.

28. Adams, *Horrendous Evils and the Goodness of God*, pp. 11–12.

29. Placher, *The Domestication of Transcendence*, p. 205.

30. See Lucien Febvre, *The Problem of Unbelief in the Sixteenth Century: The Religion of Rabelais*, trans. Beatrice Gottlieb (Harvard University Press, 1982), esp. pp. 335–53.

31. Lucretius, *De rerum natura* 5.199–200, in A. A. Long and D. N. Sedley, eds., *The Hellenistic Philosophers*, 2 vols. (Cambridge University Press, 1987), vol. 1, p. 60. Epicureans weren't the first to deny the gods' care for the world. Plato (*Laws* 887–8) argues against just this view, and Aristotle's view was not far from it. Skeptics, too, questioned the cogency of Stoic arguments. A more complete account of proto-theodicy in Hellenistic philosophy would have to include the ways Skeptics' arguments and prescriptions interacted with those of Stoics and Epicureans.

32. Seneca, "On Providence" 2.1 (Loeb 1:6–7).

33. Long and Sedley mention six major strands of explanation of "cosmic evil": the "principle of opposition," "blessings in disguise," individual suffering for the good of the whole, evil "concomitants" of goods," and – less important – divine oversight and the intervention of evil spirits (*The Hellenistic Philosophers*, vol. 1, pp. 332–3).

34. Epictetus, *Discourses* 2.6; *The Discourses as Reported by Arrian, the Manual, and Fragments*, with an English translation by W. A. Oldfather, in 2 vols. (Loeb 1979), pp. 248–9; for muddy feet, cf. 2.5 (Loeb pp. 244–5).

35. Seneca, *On Peace of Mind* 13.2–3, in *Hellenistic Philosophy: Introductory Readings*, trans. Brad Inwood and L. P. Gerson, 2nd ed. (Hackett, 1997), p. 243.

36. The earliest attested reference is in a letter of September 1697; see G. W. Leibniz, *Philosophische Schriften*, ed. C. I. Gerhardt, 7 vols. (Berlin, 1875–1890), vol. 6, p. 4n.

37. Leibniz's letter to Thomas Burnet of 30 October 1710 (Gerhardt 6:11). English usage is shaped by Milton's project to "justify the ways of God to man" (*Paradise Lost* 1.26) and Alexander Pope's promise to "vindicate the ways of God to man" (*Essay on Man* 1.16). Germans more commonly think of theodicy as a "defense" (*Verteidigung*), following from Kant's 1791 definition cited later.

38. Patrick Riley, *Leibniz's Universal Jurisprudence: Justice as the Charity of the Wise* (Harvard University Press, 1996).

39. Leibniz, *Textes Inédits*, ed. Gaston Grua, 2 vols. (Paris, 1948), vol. 1, pp. 370–1. "Catholic demonstrations" was a description Leibniz had used for his efforts to orchestrate a reconciliation of the Christian churches in 1669 and 1679 (Grua, *Textes Inédits*, p. 370 n.260).

40. See Leroy S. Loemker, *Struggle for Synthesis: The Seventeenth-Century Background of Leibniz's Synthesis of Order and Freedom* (Harvard University Press, 1972).

41. *Theodicy*, Preface; *Philosophische Schriften*, ed. Gerhardt, vol. 6, p. 29; *Theodicy: Essays on the Goodness of God, the Freedom of Man and the Origin of Evil*, trans. E. M. Huggard, ed. with introduction by Austin Farrer (Open Court, 1985), p. 53.

42. Schneewind, *The Invention of Autonomy*, pp. 536–43.

43. Leibniz's is a "problem-solving" moral philosophy. See Stuart Brown, *Leibniz* (Harvester Press, 1984), pp. 197–207, for the argument that Leibniz's whole philosophy is "problem-solving." G. H. R. Parkinson (in "Leibniz's Philosophical Aims: Foundation-Laying or Problem-Solving?" in *Mathesis Rationis: Festschrift für Heinrich Schepers*, ed. Albert Heinekamp, Wolfgang Lenzen and Martin Schneider [Nodus, 1990], pp. 67–78) argues that this is an exaggeration, but I think the bulk of the *Theodicy* would be accepted as problem-solving by both.

44. Leibniz, *New Essays concerning Human Understanding* 1.2.9, trans. and ed. Peter Remnant and Jonathan Bennett (Cambridge University Press, 1981), pp. 92–3.

45. For the wide range of measures Leibniz had in mind, see "Memoir for Enlightened Persons of Good Intention" (also of the mid-1690s) in *Leibniz: Political Writings*, ed. Patrick Riley, 2nd ed. (Cambridge University Press, 1988), pp. 103–10. Michael Seidler has shown the importance of "moral therapy" for Leibniz; see his "Freedom and Moral Therapy in Leibniz," *Studia Leibnitiana* XVII/1 (1985), pp. 15–35.

46. "One is justified in assuming that a thing may be true so long as one does not prove that it is impossible." *Theodicy*, Summary (*Philosophische Schriften*, ed. Gerhardt, vol. 6, p. 378; *Essays*, ed. Farrer, pp. 379–80). Recent interpretations of Leibniz have shown the importance of the legal concept of "presumption" for Leibniz's thinking about theodicy.

47. *Theodicy*, Preliminary Dissertation §72; cf. §§26, 35, 57–8, 81.

48. *Theodicy* §58.

49. *Theodicy* §§23–5, 114–19, and passim.

50. *Theodicy* Preliminary discourse §23. We cannot say of any evil *why* it was permitted; nor may we conclude that its kind will be permitted in the future. Leibniz famously introduced the idea that there is a "sufficient reason" (in the *Theodicy* [I §44] it's called "determining reason") why things exist, but we cannot know what it is *in any case*. Leibniz allows that Christ, the linchpin of Malebranche's theodicy, was the "strongest reason for the choice of the best series of events (namely, our world)," but he offers no *philosophical* argument that this reason was clinching, referring instead to Scripture, for him an a posteriori form of knowledge. See *Theodicy*, "Causa Dei" §49; "A Vindication

8888 *Mark Larrimore*

of God's Justice Reconciled with His Other Perfections and All His Actions," in *Monadology and Other Philosophical Essays*, trans. Paul Schrecker and Anne Martin Schrecker (Bobbs-Merrill/Library of Liberal Arts, 1965), pp. 114–47, 124.

51. *Theodicy*, Preface; *Philosophische Schriften*, ed. Gerhardt, vol. 6, p. 30; *Essays*, ed. Farrer, p. 55.

52. See my "The Moral Import of Possible Worlds," in *Nihil Sine Ratione: Mensch, Natur und Technik im Wirken von G. W. Leibniz, VII. Internationaler Leibniz-Kongreß: Vorträge*, ed. Hans Poser (Technische Universität, 2001), pp. 693–8.

53. See J. B. Schneewind, "The Divine Corporation and the History of Ethics," in *Philosophy in History: Essays in the Historiography of Philosophy*, ed. Richard Rorty, J. B. Schneewind and Quentin Skinner (Cambridge University Press, 1984), pp. 173–91. It is instructive to see that the problem of theodicy is deferred in this kind of view.

54. José Ortega y Gasset, "Concerning Optimism in Leibnitz," appendix to *The Idea of Principle in Leibnitz and the Evolution of Deductive Theory*, trans. Mildred Adams (W. W. Norton, 1971), pp. 343–75, 348.

55. Ak. 17:236; *Theoretical Philosophy*, ed. and trans. David Walford and Ralph Meerbole (Cambridge University Press, 1992), p. 81.

56. *Critique of Pure Reason* A vii, trans. Norman Kemp Smith (St. Martin's Press, 1965), p. 7.

57. See Carl-Friedrich Geyer, "Das 'Jahrhundert der Theodizee'," *Kant-Studien* 73 (1982), pp. 393–405.

58. Kant's reflections seem to me too conflicted to bear the weight of Schneewind's interpretation (*Invention of Autonomy*, pp. 492–4). The a priori Leibnizian position prejudges things by asserting the existence of God from the outset, Kant notes, robbing us of the "most reliable and easiest proof" of God's existence, the actual a posteriori demonstration of the "universal agreement of the arrangements of the world" (Reflexion #3705; Ak. 17:23 8; *Theoretical Philosophy* 82). But Kant's train of thought is derailed by a familiar figure: "It seems to me that an Epicurus would reply to someone building on this [the a posteriori] proof: If the agreement, which you perceive in the world, seems to you to prove the existence of an organizing wisdom as its Creator, then you must admit that most of the world does not depend on that wisdom, for it everywhere contains within it, and that in more than half the cases, absurdities and abhorrent irregularities" (Ak. 17:239; 82). In response, an "I" (Kant?) pledges allegiance to the view that "not all things . . . are subject, in respect of their properties, to the pleasure of that first cause," but this view is presented the way its voluntarist critics describe it, as a kind of dualism that "deprives that power of its all-sufficiency": "I prefer, therefore, to conclude as follows: if the wise first cause was not able to bring all things into a scheme of harmonious beauty, then it follows that not all things, at least, are subject, in respect of their properties, to the pleasure of that first cause. Eternal fate, which so much limits the power of the potent cause, and which extorts from it the agreement to the existence of crude evils, thereby deprives that power of its all-sufficiency, and makes it subject to the necessity of those very evils" (Ak. 17:239; 83). Kant is unable to move beyond

the damning characterization of each side by the other, and the fragment breaks off.

59. Ak. 2:29.

60. Ak. 2:110; see also 1:333–4.

61. Ak. 2: 153–4; *Theoretical Philosophy* 194.

62. Ak. 2: 100; *Theoretical Philosophy* 143.

63. Ak. 2: 152–3; *Theoretical Philosophy* 192–3.

64. Ak. 2:154; *Theoretical Philosophy* 194.

65. Ak. 2: 117; *Theoretical Philosophy* 159. Kant will remain sympathetic to the uses of physico-theology in maintaining subjective certainty; see, for instance, *Critique of Pure Reason* A 624–5/B 652–3.

66. Ak. 2:131; *Theoretical Philosophy* 172. The reference is to the article "Causes finales" in Voltaire's *Philosophical Dictionary*.

67. Schneewind, *Invention of Autonomy*, p. 497. Schneewind makes Kant seem more voluntarist than he is at this point: "A state of affairs can be good, Kant now holds, only if someone wills or desires it" (*Invention of Autonomy*, p. 496). But Kant's is a claim only about the perfect being; this is not a *general* point about agents or goods. While this is one of the templates for Kant's later idea of human autonomy, at this stage Kant goes out of his way to stress how *unlike* human willing it is.

68. Kant's "Bemerkungen" suggest that Rousseau answered an important question for Kant: "Newton was the first to see order and regularity connected with great simplicity where before disorder and poorly paired multiplicity were and since then comets move in geometrical tracks. Rousseau was the first to discover beneath the multiplicity of human forms the deeply buried nature of the same and the hidden law according to which providence is justified through his observations. Before them the objection of Alphonsus and Manes still held. After Newton and Rousseau God is justified and now Pope's proposition is true." See *Bemerkungen in den »Beobachtungen über das Schöne und Erhabenen«*, ed. Marie Rischmüller (Felix Meiner, 1991), p. 48.

69. Kant, *Bemerkungen in den »Beobachtungen«*, pp. 47, 35.

70. Ibid., p. 54. Cf. Jean-Jacques Rousseau, *Emile, or On Education*, trans. Allan Bloom (Basic Books, 1979), p. 282: "Man, seek the author of evil no longer. It is yourself. No evil exists other than that which you do or suffer, and both come to you from yourself. General evil can exist only in disorder, and I see in the system of the world an unfailing order."

71. Ak. 2:3 69, 373; *Theoretical Philosophy* 355, 359, referring to Diogenes Laertius 2:25 and to the end of Voltaire's *Candide*.

72. Ak. 2:335–6; *Theoretical Philosophy* 323.

73. This is what Odo Marquard has in mind in arguing that idealism displaced theodicy; see "Idealismus und Theodizee" in *Schwierigkeiten mit der Geschichtsphilosophie*, esp. p. 58.

74. Ak. 8:250; cf. Henry E. Allison, *The Kant–Eberhard Controversy* (Johns Hopkins University Press, 1973), p. 160.

75. A 774/B 802; Kemp Smith, p. 616.

76. A 776/B 804; Kemp Smith, p. 617.

77. A 777/B 806, Kemp Smith, p. 618.
78. Hegel arraigns Kant for "tenderness for things; it would be a shame if they contradicted each other," and so antinomy stays "in our minds [*Gemüte*] as once it was God who had to take everything contradictory into himself." See G. W. F. Hegel, *Vorlesungen über die Geschichte der Philosophie III, Werke,* 20 vols. (Suhrkamp), vol. 20, p. 359.
79. Ak. 28:1078–82.
80. Ak. 8:30.
81. Ak. 8: 123; I've used Emil L. Fackenheim's translation from Immanuel Kant, *On History,* ed. Lewis White Back (Bobbs-Merrill, 1963), pp. 53–68.
82. Ak. 8:360–2, 380.
83. For the proto-Hegelian reading, see Yirmiyahu Yovel, *Kant and the Philosophy of History* (Princeton University Press, 1980). That Kant scrupulously avoids dogmatic philosophy of history is shown by Pauline Kleingeld, *Fortschritt und Vernunft: Zur Geschichtsphilosophie Kants* (Konigshausen and Neumann, 1995).
84. William James Booth is one of the few scholars to take these jokes seriously; see *Interpreting the World: Kant's Philosophy of History and Politics* (University of Toronto Press, 1986).
85. Cf. *Critique of Judgment* §84; Ak. 5:434–6, trans. Werner Pluhar (Hackell, 1987), pp. 322–3.
86. §63; Ak. 5:369; cf. "Perpetual Peace," Ak. 8:363–5.
87. §67; Ak. 5:379, Pluhar, p. 259.
88. §83; Ak. 5:430, Pluhar, p. 318.
89. §87; Ak. 5:452, Pluhar, p. 342.
90. Ak. 8:264.
91. Ak. 8:255. Kant originally planned a less ambitious point, suggesting that he was only going to discuss the impossibility of *constructive* accounts; see the "Vorarbeit" at Ak. 23:85.
92. Ak. 8:264.
93. Ak. 8:266.
94. Ak. 8:264. Since at least the 1770s, Kant had thought of Job as exemplary for refusing to say that things made sense when he didn't see how. In a well-known letter to Lavater of 28 April 1775, Kant described himself as "A man who believes that, in the final moment, only the purest candor concerning our most hidden inner convictions can stand the test and who, like Job, takes it to be a crime to flatter God and make inner confessions, perhaps forced out by fear, that fail to agree with what we freely believe" (Ak. 10:167–8, in *Philosophical Correspondence,* trans. Arnulf Zweig (University of Chicago Press, 1967), pp. 79–80.
   Aloysius Winter suggests that Kant's discussion of Job in 1791 is influenced by the German translation of Shaftesbury's *Letter concerning Enthusiasm.* In his campaign against religious melancholy, Shaftesbury recommended "good humour" and "freedom" of inquiry and found "a notable instance of this freedom in one of our sacred authors" – the Book of Job. In the German translation, "freedom" was rendered "Freymütigkeit" (38), which becomes "frankness" in the new English translation (Ak. 8:266). See Anton Ashley Cooper, *Grafens von Shaftesbury, Characteristicks, oder Schilderungen von Menschen,*

Sitten, Meynungen, und Zeiten, ... (Heinsius, 1768), pp. 38–9, and Aloysius Winter, "Theologiegeschichtliche und literarische Hintergrunde der Religionsphilosophie Kants," in *Kant über Religion,* ed. Friedo Ricken and François Marty (Kohlhammer, 1992), pp. 17–51, 48.

An older related use of Job 13:7 appeared in Francis Bacon, *Novum Organum* Book I: Aphorism 89, where those who argue that "if intermediate causes are unknown, everything can more readily be referred to the divine hand and wand" are likened to Job's friends (*Novum Organum. With Other Parts of The Great Instauration,* trans. and ed. Peter Urbach and John Gibson [Open Court, 1994], p. 99) – a usage echoed by Kant in the *Critique of Pure Reason* A 738/B766 and A 750/B778; Kemp Smith, pp. 593, 600.

95. Ak. 8:265, referring to Job 23:13.
96. Ak. 8:265.
97. Ak. 8:266.
98. Ak. 8:264.
99. Ak. 8:257.
100. Reflexion #6095, Ak. 18:450.
101. Ak. 8:267.
102. Schneewind, *The Invention of Autonomy,* p. 544.
103. Ak. 8:265.

4

Protestant Natural Law Theory

A General Interpretation

Knud Haakonssen

[Kant] believed that in the unique experience of the moral ought we are 'given' a 'fact of reason' that unquestionably shows us that we possess such [contracausal] freedom as members of a noumenal realm. Readers who hold, as I do, that our experience of the moral ought shows us no such thing will think of his version of autonomy as an invention rather than an explanation.[1]

The first point to make when considering the significance of the Protestant natural law tradition is that it was not a tradition in the sense of a coherent body of doctrine unfolding during the early modern period. It is more adequately described as a genre in moral and political philosophy, characterized by the attempt to account for morals and politics by means of juridical concepts derived from Roman law and its medieval and early modern commentators. The central concepts were those of law, duty, obligation, right, contract, property and their many subdivisions. But this apparatus of juridical concepts was in the service of fundamentally different philosophies, and one may say that the tradition was as much characterized by disputes between opposing theoretical standpoints as by the coherence of its concepts. In other words, "the tradition" is an artifact that has to be analyzed before we can begin to assess its various components. A full account, however, would require much more

This essay originated as my contribution to the Hester Seminar at Wake Forest University in November 1997 and I owe a great debt of gratitude to the organizer of that seminar, Professor Win Chat-Lee, for commissioning the paper. A revised version was read to the conference in honour of Professor Jerome B. Schneewind at The Johns Hopkins University in March 2000. I am grateful to participants in both events as well as to Aaron Garrett, Tim Hochstrasser, Ian Hunter and Michael Seidler, for their comments.

than a conceptual analysis, for the different natural law theories were potent weapons in a variety of moral, theological and political battles, and they were, in large measure, shaped for such purposes. A brief synoptic account, such as the present one, can at best gesture towards this multiplicity of contexts.[2]

We can underline these points through a different consideration. During the seventeenth and eighteenth centuries, natural law became established as an academic subject, a discipline or subdiscipline, in nearly all universities and colleges in Protestant Europe. Like philosophy of law in the twentieth century, it was taught both as a "liberal arts" subject in colleges and the philosophical faculties of universities, often as part of moral philosophy, and in the law faculties as a "foundation course" (and, in some cases, as part of courses on Roman law). Sometimes there were bitter ideological disputes between faculties concerning the appropriate place for the teaching of natural law, and these, again, were extensions of ideological disputes in and between church and state. As an academic discipline, natural law harboured many different schools of thought both concerning the philosophical basis for natural law and concerning its practical role in morals and politics. Considered as a genre and as an academic subject, natural law is a striking, in fact a dominant, feature of early modern thought, but it is exactly this prominence that easily gives the misleading impression that it was a much more coherent phenomenon than in fact it was.

The fault lines in modern natural law are many and intersecting; they do not form any simple pattern. They are philosophical, theological, political and institutional in nature, and, as might be expected, they vary profoundly from place to place and shift significantly over the roughly two centuries in question, namely, from the last significant "scholastic" thinker, Francisco Suárez, and the first "modern" natural lawyer, Hugo Grotius, to the post-Kantian debates about the foundation of justice and law. In order to account for what I consider some of the most significant contributions to modern thought that emerged from this composite tradition of natural law, I will concentrate on just a few, mainly philosophical disputes, though these cannot be discussed without reference to several other problem areas, as we shall see.

A traditional way of looking at modern natural law is as a prolonged debate about the ontological status of moral values, a debate in which the two sides commonly have been referred to as "realists" and "voluntarists." In the following, I will first look in turn at both and suggest that each of these strands of Protestant natural law theory has had a shaping influence on modern moral philosophy, though not entirely in the ways sometimes assumed. I will then turn my attention to voluntarism as a philosophy of convention that in a way sidesteps the whole issue of ontology.

The main representatives of the realist tradition were Gottfried Wilhelm Leibniz and Christian Wolff in Germany, the so-called Cambridge Platonists (especially Benjamin Whichcote, Henry More and Ralph Cudworth) in England. These thinkers drew self-consciously on ancient and medieval theories of values as ontologically inherent in the natural world. In the case of Leibniz the inspiration was mainly, though not exclusively, neo-Platonist; in the case of Wolff, it was neo-Thomist. The Englishmen, despite the label given them in the late nineteenth century, drew on Aristotelian as well as Platonist sources, an eclecticism epitomized in Nathaniel Culverwell and cultivated in the so-called ethical rationalists, such as Samuel Clarke and William Wollaston.

While philosophically multifarious, these thinkers have a number of basic features in common. Their approach is metaphysical in the sense that both the theory of knowledge and the theory of action are dependent upon a view of how the mind and the community of agents are positioned and function in the universal system of being. They are, therefore, "rationalists" in the sense that they assume a structure to be inherent in reality that is consonant with and, hence, accessible to reason, including human reason. Further, as far as the active side of human nature is concerned, they insist that actions must be understood and evaluated in terms of their position in, or contribution to, the *communities* of activity in which they occur, ultimately the system of moral beings as a whole. As a consequence, natural law is seen as an explication and prescription of that which is inherently good by this criterion.

This metaphysical, realist tradition is now often seen as a last outpost of scholasticism and as the casualty that defines its victor, namely, the modernity of voluntarist natural law and its empiricist heirs, or, in other words, individualistic rights theory and, eventually, utilitarianism. This is not, however, a plausible interpretation of the trajectory of moral and political thought from the Reformation to the end of the nineteenth century. The realist and rationalist tradition was clearly a prominent form of practical philosophy well into the eighteenth century, as seen in the popularity of ethical rationalism.[3] Furthermore, the mainstream of British moral philosophy in the Enlightenment, namely, moral-sense and common-sense theories, is best seen as elaborate attempts at making a basic realism, or objectivism, in morals compatible with the new approach through theories of the individual person's moral sentiments.

From Joseph Butler, Francis Hutcheson and George Turnbull to Richard Price, Thomas Reid and Dugald Stewart, there is no danger that the emphasis on individual moral perception will lead to a questioning of the objectivity of morals.[4] Nor do these thinkers cease to see morals within a metaphysical framework, though this has been transformed into a naturalistic providentialism.[5] This type of moral philosophy remained a potent force far into the nineteenth century, as we may gauge from the constant need of the utilitarians to assail it. The common-sense philosophy of Reid and Stewart, in particular, was of the first importance for basic philosophical education in France and in America for decades.

As far as Germany is concerned, it is commonly recognized that the metaphysical tradition in moral philosophy was a dominant force through the eighteenth century. In fact, here the greater danger is that we forget the opposition that, thanks to Pufendorf, Thomasius and their followers at the new universities of Halle and Göttingen, made voluntarist natural law theory into a formidable presence. Nevertheless, Wolffianism eventually won the war for control of the universities and, hence, the education of the governing elite, and the history of eighteenth-century German philosophy has largely been written from the perspective of the winners ever since.[6] What is more, the metaphysical approach to ethics went far beyond the Wolffians. While interpretation of Kant's ethics for a long time, not least in Anglo-American scholarship, has been dominated by the theme of personal autonomy and the epistemology of individual moral judgement, Kant was also a metaphysician, not least in morals, where the metaphysical postulate of the two worlds inhabited by humanity is fundamental to everything.[7] Beyond Kant, idealism – German, British and American – has perpetuated the main features of metaphysical realism in morals.

In other words, a main point in the significance of Protestant natural law in the early modern period is that it harboured a realist and antiindividualist strand that provided some basic continuity between scholastic and nineteenth-century moral and social thought. Within this historical mainstream, voluntarist individualism crops up as little more than floating islands. These have, however, come to assume quite disproportionate dimensions in the contemporary search for the ancestry of human rights ideas and, in a different key, as objects of vilification in the criticism of the "Enlightenment project." The rest of this essay is devoted to giving a more adequate picture of the so-called voluntarist tradition.

It was a line of argument that was mainly developed by Thomas Hobbes, Samuel Pufendorf and Christian Thomasius. While these thinkers were very well versed in ancient and, to some extent, in scholastic thought, and while they were aware of the similarities between their standpoint and some aspects of Epicureanism, they did not support their actual voluntarism by reference to the most obvious medieval precursors of this line of argument, especially William of Ockham. Whether rightly or wrongly, they seem to have considered their argument to be significantly different from that of Ockham and his followers. They clearly shared with the medieval thinker a divine voluntarism according to which the existence of values in the world ultimately is due to an act of God's will. That is to say, the natural world can be distinguished from the realm of values, and the latter is superimposed upon nature through divine willing. However, this was not the important point for the seventeenth-century philosophers; their emphasis was on human voluntarism.

The central point for the voluntarists was that humanity has no access to the divine mind by means of reason, as opposed to revelation, except through the world of experience. However, the use of allegedly empirical facts of nature and history to interpret divine providence, that is, to find prescriptions for human behaviour, was seen by these thinkers as the main source – apart from the even more contentious use of revelation – of the religious divisions and thus of the wars that had rent Europe since the Reformation. Basic to their intellectual enterprise, therefore, was an effort to understand what orderliness human nature is capable of without other assumptions about divine intentions than the absolutely minimalist claims of natural religion. They reduced the sum of the law of nature to 'seek peace' (Hobbes) or 'be sociable' (Pufendorf), because they saw it as a universal lesson of experience that human existence could not be solitary, but they took this existence itself as a natural fact and did not see it as part of their philosophical enterprise to interpret it in terms of any telos beyond the purposes set by human beings themselves. This does not question the sincerity of their religious beliefs; their ambition was to close off religion and philosophy from each other and pursue them as entirely separate human endeavours; they did not want to replace one with the other.

The logic of their argumentative situation was, therefore, to focus on the human will as the key explanatory factor in understanding the value schemes that make up humanity's cultural world. And this is the point where the question of the ontological status of values crosses another line of inquiry that divided not only natural law theory but also early modern philosophy over a much wider front. I am referring to what is sometimes seen as an epistemological turn that made the question 'What can we know?' into the centre of philosophical endeavour. However, this way of characterizing the development in question is something of an anachronism deriving from Kant's rewriting of the history of philosophy as a set of premises for his own critical philosophy. It distorts some of the major features of early modern philosophy, and the casualties include the true nature of the voluntarists' moral theory. In order to get closer to the latter, therefore, we have to widen our inquiry, even though this can be done only in briefest outline in the present context.[8]

The problem with the Kantian interpretation is that it suggests that early modern philosophy saw knowledge primarily as propositional in character and subject to assessment in terms of truth value. Setting to one side, for present purposes, the question of how far this might be true of Descartes' view, it seems clearly to be a distortion and streamlining of much post-Cartesian thought, that is, of the late seventeenth and main part of the eighteenth centuries. The central point in the Lockean revolution was to ask 'What does knowledge do to the knower?' or 'What are the conditions under which a knowing subject holds knowledge?' That is to say, the primary object of attention was the subject as such, and knowledge was only one of the conditioning factors of the subject. The person became seen as a crossroads for environmental factors, and in order to analyze personality, philosophers had to use such factors as central parts of their explanans. The turn towards the subject led to the invocation of the situational factors forming the subject, and personhood in effect was transformed into a notion of situationally reactive powers, most obviously shown by the fact that the *passions* – streamlined as desire – became the focus for explanation of *action*.[9] It is within this broad development that we have to place the many new attempts to conceive of conscience, the moral sense, the active powers and so on. The overall result may be called a 'performative notion' of knowledge according to which knowledge first of all was to be seen as part of the total behavioural scope of the individual, and it was the task of philosophical inquiry correctly to portray this scope.[10]

Like most Enlightenment science, these efforts to create a science of human nature distinguished themselves from most of their seventeenth-century predecessors by having an even more pronounced teleological twist. The various features and functions of human nature, including the powers of the mind, were generally understood in the eighteenth century within a providential framework for which science was supposed to provide empirical evidence. In the case of the moral powers, their providential goal was to guide human behaviour so that it contributed to some divinely appointed system of moral perfection or happiness or beatitude. As indicated earlier, for a great many philosophers, this providentialist view of the moral powers in effect replaced a straightforward realism in morals with which they were uncomfortable for metaphysical and theological reasons, seeing it as scholastic essentialism. Without making such metaphysical commitments, the teleology of Providence lent a transcendent objectivity to moral values that was needed to stave off scepticism – or, as we would call it, relativism. The transition from moral realism proper to providentially guaranteed objectivism is well exemplified in Britain by the passage from Cambridge Platonism to Hutcheson's moral sense theory, and in Germany by the transformation of Wolffianism into the 'Popularphilosophie' of Johann Georg Heinrich Feder or Christian Garve.

It has often appeared difficult to pinpoint the difference between the mainstream idea of a science of human nature in providentialist *régie* and the voluntarism in morals with which we are particularly concerned here. The voluntarists were clearly, as I have already indicated, part of the turn towards theories of the subject and the associated adoption of a performative view of knowledge as a condition or quality exhibited by the subject in its behaviour. However, the argumentative logic of their standpoint meant that they were inclined to be radically reductivist in their approach. The crux of the matter may be put as follows. Since, on their view, the human mind has no access to the divine mind, it is impossible to know whether the *functions* of the former, such as moral judgements and moral and social institutions, are evidence of the *meaning* or *intentions* of the latter. Accordingly the philosopher, as distinct from the religionist, has no other recourse than to search for efficient causes since final causes are not accessible.

Now whether or not this train of reasoning was clearly articulated by anyone before David Hume, it was the underlying rationale for the classic voluntarists' shying away from ad hoc acceptance of cognitive powers, including moral powers, whose veridical performance, or objectivity, was supposed to be certified by their providential telos. Instead, Hobbes, Pufendorf and Thomasius concentrated their efforts on a theory of human nature as primarily characterized by its exertion of will. By reducing the assumptions made about the powers of the mind, they increased the explanatory demands on environmental factors. If the various types of human behaviour were not to be explained as springing from a will informed by cognitive powers designated to judge the behaviour in question, then the shaping of the will would have to be accounted for by reference to factors external to the mind's naturally provided equipment. The most elaborate attempt among the thinkers referred to here is Hobbes's well-known explanation of the act of willing as the last swing of the pendulum of attraction and repulsion that characterizes the relation between a person's biologically given vital motion and any particular object of possible action. This may be simple psychology, but the very simplicity of it helped force one of the most interesting developments in early modern philosophy, namely, theories of language as the mediator of the causal influences on the mind. Pufendorf in particular felt the need to account for mental operations, including deliberations about action, as linguistic in nature, but the language that was required for such inner dialogue must derive from external dialogue, that is, from the social interaction between people.[11] This idea of knowledge as sociolinguistic performance is at the core of the performative notion of knowledge that I referred to earlier, and it was an idea that reached a high point when Condillac liberated language from its (supposedly) Lockean slavery of labeling 'ideas.'[12]

If the voluntarists were headed into a social theory of the mind and of its language, we need to ask how they could provide social explanations, that is, explanations in which the primary explanans was the interaction between individuals considered simply as agents of will. The standard metaphor for this interaction was that of the contract or covenant between two or more individuals, and the natural lawyers provided contractarian accounts of, so to speak, all aspects of human culture. The question is, then, how they, within their reductionist scheme, could account for ties between individual wills or, as they would say in their juridical language, for obligation. Commonly they have been seen either as subscribing to a hopeless, pure 'will theory' of obligation, or as harbingers of game-theoretical accounts of rational choice.[13] Neither approach seems accurately to capture what is important in their enterprise.

The central issue is one that was completely clarified only when David Hume reflected upon nearly a century's attempts to shape a language adequate to the conventionalist theory of culture that the voluntarists were trying to establish. How can a voluntary agreement create a moral bond, or an obligation, unless people already have the idea that voluntary agreement is the sort of thing that creates obligation, in which case obligation is not a moral feature of the world that is introduced by such acts of will? Or to put it differently, how can an act of will – considered as purposive behaviour – create an obligation without having obligation as its purpose, that is, without assuming that obligation already is part of humanity's moral culture? While there were many false starts on the way

from Hobbes via Pufendorf to Hume, all the voluntarists were trying to
get clear about – and to find a language in which to express – one line of
argument. They needed an account of social behaviour that people engaged in out of simple, 'natural' motives, that is, motives relating to each
individual's immediate ways of being in the world (eventually Hume's
'natural virtues') but behaviour that had collective results that post hoc
were perceived as socially functional, that is, as having a function and,
in that sense, a point or meaning not originally intended by the participants but that subsequently could be used as a reason for maintaining
the behavior in question.

The natural motives ranged from Hobbes' idea of humanity's unavoidable need for cognitive order in moral matters, through Pufendorf's combination of self-interest and spontaneous sociability, to Hume's similar
ensemble of limited self-love and confined benevolence. In the case of
Hobbes, the social result was a linguistic performance in which members
of any accidental, or historically given, group would assure each other of
their allegiance to some centre of authority – the would-be sovereign –
provided that the allegiance was mutual. The usual criticism of Hobbes
has been that no rationally self-interested individual would be the first
performer of such an agreement because it would expose such a person to the possibility that the other parties to the contract would not
perform and, thus, that there would be no sovereign and hence no protection against these others. But that is clearly not Hobbes' problem for
the simple reason that there is nothing to perform – other than the act of
promising itself. If the act of promising, or 'contracting,' is an act done in
common within the group, then the situation of any would-be defaulter
is that of contemplating defection from the collectivity of those who are
promising – and thus from the sovereign power. Now, promising as something that is 'done in common' in a group can be understood in many
different ways, ranging from the simultaneous voting of the assembled
people (as in the literal interpretation of a founding contract that takes
individuals out of the state of nature), through the voting of one or more
layers of representatives of the members of the group, to the historically
constituted "common act" of traditional allegiance (e.g. Hume's idea of
"opinion" as the foundation for authority).[14] Whatever makes a number of individual actions 'common,' whether literal simultaneity or the
drift of history, the collective effect of naturally motivated (e.g., spontaneously benevolent or self-interested) individual acts, transforms the
nature of these individual acts so that they have a hold on each person, a
hold that was not there before or in abstraction from the commonality.

The situation in which the individual exerts his or her natural motives has been transformed by the make-believe of the other person's words.[15]

The crucial factor in this transformation is, of course, language, whether language in the literal sense of a contractual promise or language in the wider sense of traditional meanings of individuals' behaviour in a group. It is as figures of speech that individuals make up a social group, for it is through what they say, irrespective of what they 'really' *are*, that they become a social presence in each other's lives. When I think that 'all the others' are signaling allegiance to the party or the king, the party or the king becomes a factor in my life as an effect of the 'linguistic' or signaling performances – whether literal or metaphorical – of my fellows. As a consequence, the natural persons of my fellows – the persons whom otherwise I interpret in terms of shared natural motives, such as love or self-interest – are, for the purposes of social intercourse, hidden behind the sociolinguistic mask of the 'party member' or the 'subject.'

This separation of the public or social persona from the private and 'natural' was of immense importance, and it was Pufendorf's merit to pursue it with particular clarity. His idea was that culture as such, not just the central political institution of government, had to be analyzed in terms of the many different social personae that individuals undertake in the flow of life. Life in its moral, that is, interpersonal or social, aspect consists in the performance of such *officia* that arise in the interchange between people, and it is in the discharge of the offices – or duties – that come one's way that one obeys the basic natural law of being sociable. From this we can see that the performative notion of knowledge outlined earlier is at its most radical in this voluntarist theory. Here the central issue in practical knowledge, knowledge of what should be done, including moral knowledge, is not whether such knowledge can be formulated in propositions that are true in some absolute sense. The real interest is in knowing what sort of social persona you adopt – 'become' – by the signs you send to your fellows. In order to know what to do in the world, you have to know what the use of a uniform or a title or a form of words or the occupancy of a job or position tell others that you 'are,' socially speaking. It was Thomasius who saw the full meaning of this for education and its role in political society. For him, the fundamental philosophical discipline had to be moral philosophy in the sense of the general theory of practice indicated here, while any discipline – meaning here especially theology – that laid claim to being foundational because of its teaching of 'true' doctrine had to be put in its place. The faculty of theology in universities had to accept that its appropriate role was to teach social discipline to pastors for propagation in the population at large, just as the law faculty had to educate lawyers to the practical service of government.[16]

This is not to say that Hobbes, Pufendorf or Thomasius were disbelievers in the absolute truth of the Christian faith, but the implication of their theological doctrine of the divine mind's inaccessibility to humanity was that such belief was irrelevant to the foundation of practical knowledge and social action. To the modern charge of relativism, they would likely answer that this begs the question by assuming an absolute standard of practical truth as something that is being denied by the changing standards thrown up by social conventions. Driving home the logical conclusion of their position, one may say that these thinkers were agnostics in the matter of absolute standards for social life in this world and that their whole endeavour was to sort out what makes practical debate and its institutionalization in social life possible in the absence of such certainty.

This profoundly conventionalist view of the moral life of the species virtually demanded an historical interpretation, that is to say, a theory of history as the record of how humanity had engaged in conventions – or, in the language used earlier, had reached common views that subsequently achieved prescriptive force. The seventeenth-century voluntarists already had a deep understanding of the importance of history to their enterprise, demonstrated not only by the fact that they all wrote extensively on the past but also by their keen sense of the contemporary context in which they themselves argued. However, it was mainly in the eighteenth century, and especially in the works of David Hume and Adam Smith, that the idea of the historicity of the moral world was fully appreciated and worked out in detail. These works are commonly seen as part of a wider Enlightenment historicism, but this can easily mislead. It is important to distinguish between two different kinds of historicism in the period. On the one hand, there was the mainstream view that history was the record of how native moral powers had scored over time in making true or false moral judgements and that this provided the empirical evidence for the march of Providence in the world. On the other hand, there was the conventionalist approach outlined earlier, according to which history simply was the record of the moral beliefs that humanity has happened to hold under different circumstances.

These two bases for an historical view were run together already in the eighteenth century, and this is a clear indication of how difficult it was fully to understand the conventionalist view of morality and, as a consequence, how unclear it was that the great seventeenth-century voluntarist natural lawyers, by supplementing the revival of scepticism and Epicureanism, had prepared the way for Mandeville, Hume and Smith. We have already pointed to some of the crosscurrents that help explain this lack of clarity, especially the vagueness of the notion of moral powers. To these we must now add one more, namely, the development of a theory of rights, for then as now, no other concept had as much potential for creating conceptual chaos as this notion.

The 'father' of modern natural law, Hugo Grotius, had argued that the primary characteristic of being a moral agent was to have basic rights in one's person and its claims on the world, but exactly because they were the individual's rights, they could be given up.[17] The history of humankind was the record of the rights that people had given up, ranging from the whole of their liberty (in slavery) via their political freedom (in the absolutist state) to the retention of such freedom (in republican government).[18] Hobbes took this general approach further with his theory of the *necessity* of giving up all rights in order to secure life. But in the case of Grotius, there were other sides to the idea of rights. First, he thought that rights conceptually presupposed relations of justice.[19] Second, the idea that some right or rights were so tied up with moral personality that they could not be given up at all seems at least to be implied by Grotius's argument. When this idea was matched with the traditional Calvinist notion of the inviolability of conscience, the idea of a basic right as not only 'natural' but also inalienable had become clear.

In most Calvinist theory, conscientious self-judgement was the unavoidable core of humanity's moral existence, for only in the private conscience could the individual find evidence as to whether he or she was among the divinely elect, indeed, whether there was reason for believing that there is a divinity at all. Conscientiousness was, therefore, at one and the same time the basic law of nature and the basic natural right. 'Judge for yourself in matters of conscience!' was both God's command to each individual and His grant of a liberty from interference by anybody else. Since the exercise of this right was demanded by God – and unavoidable even if God's existence was denied – it was considered *inalienable*, and this is an important root of the idea that became so significant in the much later rights ideologies of the American and the French revolutions.

This idea of inalienable right arose out of debates about the legitimacy of resistance to the French king among the intellectual leaders of the French Huguenots who had been exiled by the revocation of the Edict of Nantes in 1685, the most prominent of these leaders being Pierre Jurieu and Pierre Bayle. But from the point of view of natural law theory, the crucial figure was a man of the next generation, Jean Barbeyrac, who in effect transformed the older Grotian theory of rights as an argument for absolutism into a theory of the right of resistance.[20] It should be stressed, however, that Barbeyrac himself and most of the other Huguenots by no means saw their theory of rights as a revolutionary doctrine. Exactly because each person had to judge for himself, citizens could not judge for each other or for the magistrate, except in ultimate self-defence of the right of self-judgement.

These ideas of inalienable rights were taken up for debate in Scotland by Francis Hutcheson and others,[21] but the radical potential in this debate was largely muted by the idea of overriding duty to the common good.[22] Much the same applies to the most interesting of the French-language natural lawyers in the generation after Barbeyrac, the Swiss Jean-Jacques Burlamaqui.[23] And it was in this less than clarified state that the theory of a natural right reached the American colonists and combined with traditional English ideas of political rights. While this combination did not contribute to conceptual clarification, it did accentuate the radical potential of the whole idea of a natural right.[24]

The development of the notion of natural right was not central to early modern natural law. It was not only in Scottish, Swiss and American thinking that the concept remained derivative from the natural law duty to promote the common good. The same was, of course, the case with moral realist theories such as Christian Wolff's.[25] However, the most confusing aspect of the historiography of rights is that they played a similarly secondary role in the voluntarist theories of Pufendorf and Thomasius. One might have expected that these thinkers in this, as in so many other respects, would have developed the basic idea of Hobbes, in this case that rights were the aspects of life that could be alienated, that is, put outside each individual's control through contracts. The reason for the two Germans' rejection of such a fundamental role for rights was that their Lutheran sensibilities led them to see rights as theologically dangerous. While they had no difficulties with natural rights to the means of performing the duties imposed by the natural law of sociability, the Hobbesian idea of natural right as morally justified freedom and conceptually independent of natural law duty was in their eyes tantamount to a claim to know God's moral intention with human life. They found confirmation of such suspicion in Grotius's idea that rights could be understood as moral abilities, a suggestion over which Pufendorf accused the Dutch master outright of scholastic essentialism.[26] In other words, the Lutheran voluntarists would undoubtedly have been as unsurprised as they would have been unimpressed with the Huguenot rights debate and its issue in the idea of inalienable rights. They would have seen it as little more than a rephrasing of scholastic realism.

As I have suggested elsewhere, we can take Hume's studied avoidance of the theory of rights as a continuation of this voluntarist tradition.[27] The other great heir to that line of thought, Adam Smith, forged his own original compromise when he replaced the metaphysical (theological) basis of rights with a sociopsychological theory according to which rights always are socially embedded and have to be understood historically, except for a minimal, empirically established content of rights that seems to be definitive of any recognizably human form of life (and that accordingly can be called 'natural' and 'inalienable').[28] However, Smith only left this theory in the minds of his students and not in print. Consequently Jeremy Bentham's slash-and-burn rhetoric about natural rights as "nonsense upon stilts" has been – and is still being – allowed to stand as the great break with natural law theory in English-language moral and political theory. In fact, Bentham was, in this regard, firmly in a long tradition of voluntarist natural lawyers with a deep-seated suspiciousness of rights considered as ultimate or inalienable. When he rejected first the American declarations and then the French, it was precisely with reference to their metaphysical foundation.[29] It is very likely that he himself did not understand this tradition, for he clearly was instrumental in creating the subsequent idea of 'natural law' as a monolithic metaphysical monstrosity in which all the distinctions and divisions outlined earlier were either ignored or downplayed. Ironically, Bentham thus helped create one of the most considerable 'fictions' in modern thought, one deserving of Benthamite deconstruction.

In sum, with Hume's agnosticism and Bentham's atheism, the fundamental voluntarist thesis about the gulf between the divine and the human mind reaches new depths, and this serves to reinforce and radicalize the rejection, begun by Pufendorf, of Grotian rights theory as the appropriate means of formulating the conventionalist theory of the moral life. As long as the notion of rights had connotations of a divine legacy in the human mind, it could not be used as the explanans in theories of mutual adaptation between individuals ('contracts') without begging the question, namely, the central voluntarist thesis that morals are *instituted* by such adaptations. Only Adam Smith's much deeper take on the problem could supply a nonmetaphysical notion of rights that was based on a Humean theory of the mind.

Hopefully, enough of a sketch has now been given to indicate why
Protestant natural law theory had a significance in the history of early
modern philosophy that went far beyond being a phase in the emergence
of the Kantian notion of autonomy. Modern natural law was not simply
one phenomenon but, rather, a genre within which the most profound
differences in moral thought were set out. On the one hand, natural
law theory sustained the continuous development of a metaphysically
based realism and objectivism as the dominant force in moral theory
from late scholasticism to the nineteenth century. On the other hand,
natural law in an entirely different vein, that of voluntarism, which has
been my main concern here, simultaneously provided all the elements
of an antimetaphysical conventionalism in morals that, while repeatedly
drowned out, eventually helped undermine the religious foundation of
moral theory and foster empirical study of the moral conventions by
which the species lives.

Notes

1. J. B. Schneewind, *The Invention of Autonomy: A History of Modern Moral Philosophy*
(Cambridge University Press, 1998), p. 3.
2. See Knud Haakonssen, *Natural Law and Moral Philosophy: From Grotius to
the Scottish Enlightenment* (Cambridge University Press, 1996); Haakonssen,
"German Natural Law," in *Cambridge History of Eighteenth-Century Political
Thought*, ed. Mark Goldie and Robert Wokler (Cambridge University Press,
forthcoming); Tim Hochstrasser, *Natural Law Theories in the Early Enlightenment* (Cambridge University Press, 2000); Ian Hunter, *Rival Enlightenments:
Civil and Metaphysical Philosophy in Early Modern Germany* (Cambridge University Press, 2001); Gerald Hartung, *Die Naturrechtsdebatte: Geschichte der Obligatio
vom 17. bis 20. Jarhhundert* (Verlag Karl Alber, 1998); and Richard Tuck, *The
Rights of War and Peace: Political Thought and the International Order from Grotius
to Kant* (Oxford University Press), 1999.
3. See Frederick C. Beiser, *The Sovereignty of Reason: The Defense of Rationality in
the Early English Enlightenment* (Princeton University Press, 1996).
4. See Haakonssen, *Natural Law and Moral Philosophy*, chs. 2 and 6–8.
5. See Isabel Rivers, *Reason, Grace, and Sentiment: A Study of the Language of Religion
and Ethics in England 1660–1780*, vol. 2: *Shaftesbury to Hume* (Cambridge University Press, 2000), and the discussions of Hutcheson, Turnbull and Kames in
David Fate Norton, *David Hume: Common-Sense Moralist, Sceptical Metaphysician*
(Princeton University Press, 1982).
6. For important recent attempts to redress the balance, see Hochstrasser, *Natural Law Theories*, and Hunter, *Rival Enlightenments*. Concerning the dominance
of Wolffianism, see Eckhart Hellmuth, *Naturrechtsphilosophie und bürokratischer
Werthorizont: Studien zur preußischen Geistes und Sozialgeschichte des 18. Jahrhun-
derts* (Vandenhoeck and Ruprecht, 1985).
7. See above all Hunter, *Rival Enlightenments*, ch. 6.

8. For further consideration of what Kant's rewriting of the history of philosophy meant to our perception of early modern philosophy, see Hochstrasser, *Natural Law Theories*; Haakonssen, The History of the History of Eighteenth-Century Philosophy," in *The Cambridge History of Eighteenth-Century Philosophy*, ed. Knud Haakonssen (Cambridge University Press, 2005); Richard Tuck, "The 'Modern' Theory of Natural Law," in *The Languages of Political Theory in Early-Modern Europe*, ed. Anthony Pagden (Cambridge University Press, 1987), pp. 99–109.

9. For the seventeenth-century background to this development, see Susan James, *Passion and Action: The Emotions in Seventeenth-Century Philosophy* (Oxford University Press, 1997).

10. I am here indebted to a similar perspective on early modern ideas of language; see Hans Aarsleff, "Philosphy of Language," ch. 16 of *The Cambridge History of Eighteenth-Century Philosophy*, ed. Haakonssen.

11. Pufendorf, *De iure naturae et gentium* (1672), translated as *The Law of Nature and Nations* by B. Kennet (5th ed. London, 1739), reedited with an introduction and commentary by Knud Haakonssen (Liberty Fund, forthcoming), 11.4.13 and IV.1; 'Apologia pro se et suo libro . . . ', para. 24, in *Ens Scandica* (Frankfurt a.M., 1705), pp. 33–5. See especially the discussion in Hochstrasser, *Natural Law Theories*, 87–95.

12. See Etienne Bonnot de Condillac, *Essay on the Origin of Human Knowledge*, trans. and ed. by Hans Aarsleff (Cambridge University Press 2001); Aarsleff, *From Locke to Saussure: Essays on the Study of Language and Intellectual History* (University of Minnesota Press, 1982), pp. 146–224; Aarsleff, "Language" (see note 10). As Aarsleff explains, Locke's own view of language was considerably more sophisticated than allowed by the common interpretation gestured towards in my text.

13. The former is particularly well represented by James Gordley's sharp criticism in the neo-Thomist vein, *The Philosophical Origins of Modern Contract Doctrine* (Clarendon Press, 1991). The latter is well known from prominent lines of interpreting Hobbes, such as David Gauthier, *The Logic of Leviathan* (Clarendon Press, 1969); Gregory S. Kavka, *Hobbesian Moral and Political Thought* (Princeton University Press, 1986); and Jean Hampton, *Hobbes and the Social Contract Tradition* (Cambridge University Press, 1986).

14. Hume, "Of the first principles of government," in *Political Essays*, ed. K. Haakonssen (Cambridge University Press, 1994), pp. 16–19.

15. This argument can be made much more effectively if one rejects the whole tradition of seeing the contract as a transaction or process, but that requires a much lengthier analysis than can be afforded here; hence my attempt to state the argument in the usual process terminology. But see Bernd Ludwig, *Die Wiederentdeckung des Epikureischen Naturrechts: Zu Thomas Hobbes' philosophischer Entwicklung von 'De Cive' zum 'Leviathan' im Pariser Exil 1640–1651* (Vittorio Klostermann, 1998).

16. For a splendid analysis of Thomasius in this regard, see Hunter, *Rival. Rival Enlightenments*, Chapter 5.

17. Hugo Grotius, *Dc iure belli ac pacis* (1625), anonymously translated as *The Rights of War and Peace* (London, 1738), reedited with an introduction and commentary by Richard Tuck (Liberty Fund, 2005), I.1.

18. See Richard Tuck, *Natural Rights Theories: Their Origin and Development* (Cambridge University Press, 1979), chapter 3; Tuck, *Philosophy and Government, 1572–1651* (Cambridge University Press, 1993), chapter 5; Tuck, *The Rights of War and Peace. Political Order and the International Order from Grotius to Kant* (Oxford University Press 1999), chapter 3; Schneewind, *Invention of Autonomy*, pp. 66–81; and, for criticism, Brian Tierney, *The Idea of Natural Rights: Studies on Natural Rights, Natural Law and Church Law 1150–1625* (Scholars Press, 1997), chapter 13.

19. See Knud Haakonssen, "The Moral Conservatism of Natural Rights," in *Natural Law and Civil Sovereignty: Moral Right and State Authority in Early Modern Political Thought*, ed. Ian Hunter and David Saunders (Palgrave Macmillan, 2002), pp. 27–42.

20. See Elisabeth Labrousse, "The Political Ideas of the Huguenot Diaspora (Bayle and Jurieu)," in *Church, State, and Society under the Bourbon Kings*, ed. R. M. Golden (Coronado Press, 1982), pp. 222–83; Tim Hochstrasser, "Conscience and Reason: The Natural Law Theory of Jean Barbeyrac," in *Grotius, Pufendorf and Modern Natural Law*, ed. Knud Haakonssen (Dartmouth Publishing Co., International Library of Critical Essays in the History of Philosophy, 1998), pp. 381–400.

21. Hutcheson, *An Inquiry into the Original of our Ideas of Beauty and Virtue* (1725), ed. Wolfgang Leidhold (2004), Section 7; *Short Introduction to Moral Philosophy* (1747), ed. Luigi Turco (forthcoming), 11.2; *A System of Moral Philosophy* (1755), ed. Knud Haakonssen (forthcoming), 11.3; all in *The Works and Correspondence of Francis Hutcheson*, gen. ed. Knud Haakonssen, 7 vols. (Liberty Fund, 2003–). Concerning the important contribution of Hutcheson's predecessor, Gershom Carmichael, see *Natural Rights on the Threshold of the Scottish Enlightenment: The Writings of Gershom Carmichael*, ed. James Moore and Michael Silverthorne, (Liberty Fund, 2002); James Moore and Michael Silverthorne, "Gershom Carmichael and the Natural Jurisprudence Tradition in Eighteenth-Century Scotland," in *Wealth and Virtue: The Shaping of Political Economy in the Scottish Enlightenment*, ed. I. Hont and M. Ignatieff (Cambridge University Press, 1983), pp. 73–87; Moore and Silverthorne, "Natural Sociability and Natural Rights in the Moral Philosophy of Gerschom Carmichael," in *Philosophers of the Scottish Enlightenment*, ed. V. Hope (Edinburgh University Press, 1984), pp. 1–12.

22. Haakonssen, *Natural Law and Moral Philosophy*, chapter 2. For different perspectives see James Moore, "The Two Systems of Francis Hutcheson: On the Origins of the Scottish Enlightenment," in *Studies in the Philosophy of the Scottish Enlightenment*, ed. M. A. Stewart (Clarendon Press, 1990), pp. 37–59; Moore, "Natural Law in the Scottish Enlightenment," in *Cambridge History of Eighteenth-Century Political Thought*, ed. Mark Goldie and Robert Wokier (Cambridge University Press, forthcoming).

23. For this interpretation of Burlamaqui's *Principes du droit naturel* (1747) and *Principes du droit politique* (1751), see Haakonssen, "Moral Conservatism of Natural Rights" (cf. note 19), where Burlamaqui's dependence upon Hutcheson is also referred to.

24. Haakonssen, *Natural Law and Moral Philosophy*, chapter 10; Morton White, *The Philosophy of the American Revolution* (Oxford University Press, 1978); Terrance McConnell, "The Inalienable Right of Conscience: A Madisonian Argument," *Social Theory and Practice* 22 (1996), pp. 397–416.

25. See Haakonssen, "German Natural Law," chapter 9 in *Cambridge History of Eighteenth-Century Political Thought*, ed. Goldie and Wokler.

26. Pufendorf, *De iure*, 1.2.6 and 1.6.4. Significantly Hutcheson explicitly took up Grotius's suggestion when he developed his own theory of the moral sense. See Haakonssen, *Natural Law and Moral Philosophy*, pp. 80–1, and, concerning Pufendorf, ibid., pp. 35–43.

27. See Haakonssen, *Natural Law and Moral Philosophy*, pp. 117–20.

28. Adam Smith, *The Theory of Moral Sentiments*, ed. K. Haakonssen (Cambridge University Press, 2002), II.ii; *Lectures on Jurisprudence*, eds. R. L. Meek, D. D. Raphael and P. G. Stein (Clarendon Press, 1978), (A) I, 1–25 and (B) 5–11. Cf. Haakonssen, *Natural Law and Moral Philosophy*, chapter 4; Haakonssen, *The Science of a Legislator: The Natural Jurisprudence of David Hume and Adam Smith* (Cambridge University Press, 1981), pp. 99–114; Haakonssen, Introduction to *Theory of Moral Sentiments*.

29. Jeremy Bentham, *An Introduction to the Principles of Morals and Legislation*, ed. J. H. Burns and H. L. A. Hart (The Athione Press, 1970), "Concluding Note," especially pp. 309–10; and "Anarchical Fallacies" in *The Works of Jeremy Bentham*, ed. John Bowring, 11 vols. Edinburgh, 1838–43, vol. II.

5

Autonomy in Modern Natural Law

Stephen Darwall

Morality seems to bind us in a special way. In part, this is because it can *require* us to do things, and not just recommend them. But our ends can generate a kind of requirement too. If I am bent on driving to Brighton and the only way of getting there is via US 23, there is a sense in which I am required to take that route. Still, this requirement is escapable or optional, since it arises only relative to my choice of end. I can avoid it entirely if I decide to drive to Chelsea rather than Brighton.[1] Maybe what is special about morality, then, is that its requirements are inescapable or nonoptional. However, there are plenty of requirements, not themselves moral, that I cannot escape at my option. If I drive to Brighton, the law says I must carry a valid license with me, whether I want to or not. This requirement of Michigan law is not itself a requirement of morality, even if morality normally requires me to obey it. Philippa Foot famously made a similar point about etiquette. The prohibition on eating peas with a knife is not suspended if I want to impress my hosts with my digital dexterity or, perhaps especially, if I want to shock their socks off.[2]

Philosophers frequently seek to capture the special character of moral requirements with the Kantian claim that they are categorical imperatives. This thesis has three parts: (a) fundamental moral requirements apply to all rational agents (they are *universal*); (b) these requirements give

In addition to the 2000 conference at Johns Hopkins University honoring J. B. Schneewind, an earlier version of this essay was presented at the 2000 meetings of the Pacific Division of the American Philosophical Association in Albuquerque, New Mexico. I am indebted to other participants and audience members on both occasions, but especially to Terence Irwin, who saved me from some significant errors regarding Suárez, as well as to Tamar Schapiro and J. B. Schneewind.

agents to whom they apply reasons to act, regardless of the agent's aims or interests (they are *categorical*); and (c) these reasons invariably override or silence countervailing reasons (they are *conclusive*).

This gets to the bottom of *part* of what is special about moral requirements, but only part, since we might, after all, say something similar about logic. If a conclusion follows from true premises, then we are under a requirement to infer it that purports to apply to all rational beings and to give them conclusive reasons, considerations to the contrary notwithstanding. What has been left out (and helps to explain the contrast with logic) is morality's essential involvement with *accountability*. If I am morally required to do something, then I am accountable or answerable for doing it in a way that I am not, automatically anyway, for drawing logical inferences. The whole apparatus of charge, excuse, culpability, and so on, seems part and parcel of morality in a way that it isn't of logic. Anyone who feels guilty about logical errors has a "moralized" sense of the logical, to say the least.

According to what I shall presumptuously call "our" contemporary conception, morality is a system of *mutual accountability* of free and equal persons, structured by categorical norms that apply to each of us as one person among others. Although this obviously has a Kantian, neo-Kantian, or contractualist ring, versions can also be found in the utilitarian tradition from Mill to Brandt, as, for example, when Mill famously remarks that we do not call something wrong unless we believe it apt for punishment or reproach, whether by others or by conscience.[3] No doubt this idea has many roots, and one aspect or another can be traced back very far, for example, to the Stoic idea of a law of nature. In large measure, though, it is with the modern natural law tradition (from Grotius on) that the main elements of this conception begin to be formulated and the project of defending and accounting for them originates. Specifically, the modern natural lawyers are concerned to describe and explicate a distinctive way in which morality can *obligate* us (to our mutual advantage) to act in ways that are contrary to our individual personal goods. This was not simply a matter of discerning the contours of a concept found ready to hand. To some extent, the thinkers of this period were involved in philosophical invention, as, to some degree, we continue to be now. In what follows, I will be interested in certain key aspects of their philosophical work that has continuing significance for ours today.

J. B. Schneewind has taught us that the modern natural law tradition arose in reaction to problems that first took shape in Europe in the second half of the sixteenth and the first half of the seventeenth centuries owing to fundamental changes in politics, science and religion. As Schneewind tells the story, it was Montaigne who first explored "the consequences for daily life of the loss of publicly acknowledged moral authority in a religiously divided world."[4]

The intellectual framework against which Montaigne and the modern natural lawyers were reacting was the classical tradition of natural law, forged by Aquinas in the thirteenth century and carried into the seventeenth by writers such as Francisco Suárez. Suárez, like the early modern voluntarists yet to come, gave greater stress than Aquinas to a conception of moral *obligation* as resting on God's authoritative *will*. But Suárez accepted the main tenet of Aquinas's synthesis of Christianity and Aristotle, namely, that the content of natural law is fixed by what Aquinas called "eternal law": a teleological archetype that specifies every natural being's "due end" or good. Since good and right are codetermined to be identical, this makes it metaphysically impossible for individuals to benefit by doing wrong. Each must do best by realizing the common good.

In seventeenth-century Europe, however, this position had worn thin as a basis for public moral and political order, Suárez to the contrary notwithstanding. Antagonistic, sometimes violent, religious division undermined its currency both internationally and intranationally, as in Montaigne's France. In 1625, when Hugo Grotius came to write his famous treatise on international law, he confronted what Schneewind calls the "Grotian problematic." Lacking the classical tradition's "thick" common good rooted in a shared religious outlook, Grotius attempted to articulate a conception of moral and political order that could be convincing to people lacking a common, harmonious vision of the good life.

According to Schneewind, the Grotian problematic consisted of the acceptance of "an enduring tension" between our social and antisocial "dispositions or needs" together with the project of grounding natural law within broadly empiricist constraints and independently of any "substantive conception of the highest good."[5] Important as these were, however, they were not perhaps the most philosophically significant feature of the situation that confronted Grotius. Sidgwick perceptively remarked that "the most fundamental difference" between modern and ancient ethical thought is that, whereas the ancients believed that there is only one "regulative and governing faculty" to be "recognized under the name of Reason," "in the modern view, when it has worked itself clear, there are found to be two – Universal Reason and Egoistic Reason, or Conscience and Self-love."[6] In this respect, although Aquinas's and especially Suárez's ideas of natural law encoded a conception of morality and moral obligation that was far from anything in Aristotle, they were nonetheless fully within the ancient framework, since they allowed only one fundamental principle. For them, eternal law's teleological archetype simultaneously determined the agent's good and natural law so that these necessarily prescribed the same actions.

Grotius, however, entertains the challenge that it might be "supreme folly" to do what is just, since following natural law might sometimes do "violence to [one's] own interests."[7] And he responds to this challenge not by arguing that following natural law is actually advantageous (contrary to appearances), but by claiming that we have a reason to be just that is different from self-interest, one based on "an impelling desire for society."[8] Thus Grotius seeks to ground natural law's normativity in something that is independent of the agent's good, *and* he takes the relation of natural law to the agent's good to be entirely contingent. For Aquinas and Suárez, natural law and the agent's good both derive from the agent's "due end." For practical purposes, therefore, they reduce to the same principle. With Grotius, however, we get the beginnings of the modern conception of morality as a body of universal norms (natural laws) whose claim on us differs from that of our own good, indeed, whose prescriptions can conflict with our good and still bind nonetheless.[9]

Disagreement about a common good – or worse, agreement about irresolvable conflict between individuals' goods – is the source of collective action problems: situations in which all may do worse by acting for their individual goods than they might by following some alternative, collective strategy. This, I think, was the most important feature of the problematic that Grotius and his contemporaries faced, to which they proposed the modern conception of natural law as solution. Lacking the confidence that a sufficiently rich conception of common good could gain sufficiently wide acceptance among reasonable persons for unconstrained prudence to govern without significant, mutually disadvantageous conflict, they needed a conception of mutually advantageous, prudence-constraining norms (natural law or morality) to solve the otherwise inevitable problems of collective action. As a consequence, they faced the philosophical issue of defending and explicating the normativity of a second "regulative and governing faculty" intrinsically related to these moral norms.

Perhaps no philosopher is more closely associated with the thesis that morality is intrinsically connected to a "regulative" faculty of practical reason than Kant. A second theme of Schneewind's is that Kant's moral philosophy can fruitfully be viewed as a response to problems that were originally posed within the modern natural law tradition and as developing ideas that were first formulated there. This can seem quite surprising and remarkable, since morality for natural lawyers like Pufendorf and Locke essentially concerns obedience to superior authority, whereas for Kant, it is self-legislated by free rational agents. On the one view, morality is external, imposed by another's will; on the other, it is internal, arising within the agent's own deliberations. For the early modern voluntarists morality is fundamentally about *subjection*, whereas for Kant it has to do with what it is to be a free moral *subject*.

However, elements of the Kantian picture can be found in the voluntarist natural lawyers from the start. For example, it was important to Pufendorf, as it had been indeed also to Suárez, that although moral obligations derive from commands of superior Divine authority, these commands are *addressed to free rational agents to govern their conduct*. The category of moral subject thus carried the implications *both* of subjection to a superior and of free rational subjecthood. In a phrase, only free and rational subjects can be morally subjected.

In what follows, I shall be discussing aspects of the voluntarist conception that lead in the direction of Kant. I prefer to discuss these, however, not in terms that are specific to the Kantian system. Rather, I want to consider voluntarist natural law from the perspective of our contemporary conception of morality as a system of mutual accountability of free and equal rational persons. Putting it this way may seem no less puzzling than the Schneewindian claim about the early modern natural lawyers' relation to Kant. What can this idea of mutual accountability owe to the early modern idea of morality as subjection to the will of superior authority? I shall argue that, from the outset, the voluntarist natural lawyers combined two ideas of central importance for the claim that morality concerns mutual accountability. First, and most obviously, they held that morality essentially involves accountability. Moral norms don't just say what we are required to do, but what we are *answerable* for doing. Or, to put it another way, morality includes second-order, procedural norms that can require us to *account* for our conduct in light of the first-order norms, and unexcused violations can be imputed to our account. Of course, Pufendorf and Locke believed that morality essentially involves accountability to superior authority, to God. But, as we shall see, they also believed that being thus accountable is possible only for free rational agents who are able to govern themselves appropriately in light of the norms. I shall argue that this idea exerts a pressure on their thought in the direction of a conception of morality as a system of accountability between equals, though this is not a conception they accepted or would have accepted on reflection.

The second idea is that moral norms derive from a demand or claim that one will can address *to* or make *on* another, and that moral obligations would not exist but for the possibility of reasons that can arise through, or that are assumed by, this relationship between wills. Again, the modern natural lawyers stress that the requisite relationship is asymmetric: morality is, in its nature, incumbent on beings who are subject to the demands of a superior will. We become moral subjects by being *subjected* to God's will. At the same time, however, it is essential to their view that the relevant form of subjection is a relation *between rational wills*, one that differs from intimidation or other forms of nonrational control. In addressing demands to us, God gives us a distinctive kind of reason for acting that we would not otherwise have had. This view requires Pufendorf and Locke to think about the nature of these reasons and about the nature of a free rational agent that can be guided by them. Here again, I shall argue that doing so exerts a pressure on their thought in the direction of a conception of morality as a system of accountability between equals, even if, again, this is not a conception they accepted or would have accepted on reflection.

What is common to both of these ideas is the notion of a "second-personal" perspective or standpoint that is taken up in *interaction between rational agents*. Accountability is always *to* some other or others. It involves the addressing and receiving of charges, justifications, excuses, blame, condemnation, reproach, punishment, and so on. Similarly, the voluntarists believe that God creates natural law by addressing commands *to* rational beings. It is by entering into this relation to us that He is able, by His will, to lay us under moral obligations.

I will be arguing that the second-personal standpoint involved in these forms of interaction carries presuppositions that push in the direction of a conception of morality as mutual accountability between free and equal persons. Inherent in the idea that morality consists of claims or demands that are *addressed* by a (superior) will in a way that aims to be intrinsically reason-giving are implications concerning the nature of these reasons and those to whom they can be given by a second-personal address. And inherent in the idea that addressees are, by virtue of these claims or demands, *accountable* or answerable for complying with the reasons thereby addressed, are further implications concerning the capacity of addressees freely to guide themselves by these reasons as a result of being given them. Although certainly not a matter of simple entailment, I shall argue that these implications suggest a line of thought that is capable of issuing in the conclusion that obligating moral reasons are motives that arise through the exercise of the capacity for free rational deliberation, specifically, through a form of "codeliberation" involved in second-personal interaction in which one person attempts to *give* a distinctive kind of reason to another.[10] Roughly speaking, there can be such a thing as morality only if free and rational subjects can be accountable for guiding themselves by reasons addressed to them by a rational will. And free and rational subjects can be thus accountable only if the exercise of their capacity for free and rational deliberation (including free and rational codeliberation) involves guidance by such reasons. It follows that there can be such a thing as morality only if the exercise of this capacity leads to guidance by moral reasons. Consequently, if there is such a thing as morality, a system of mutual accountability of free and equal persons is what it would have to be.

I am not suggesting, I should again stress, that Locke and Pufendorf accepted this conception or that they would have on reflection. What they *did* accept, however, are certain ideas that can be seen to lead toward this conception when, to adapt Sidgwick's remark, the ideas work themselves "clear." What I shall try to do is to identify both these ideas and the lines along which they might be clarified.

1. Suárez

It will be useful to begin with Suárez so that we can see what he shared with Pufendorf (and Locke) in these respects and what he did not. Where Suárez departs from the Thomist tradition is in arguing that Thomas failed to appreciate the *distinctively* lawlike character of moral *obligation*. Suárez complains that Thomas's definition of law as "a certain rule and measure in accordance with which one is induced to act or is restrained from acting" (Suárez's rendering) is too broad, since it is applicable to any being, not just to "rational creatures." "Everything," Suárez says, "has its own rule and measure" that can "induce" or "restrain" it from acting."[11] In making this latter claim, he affirms the Thomist doctrine of "eternal law," according to which every being has an end that serves as its normative standard or "law" and that, for human beings, is the basis of natural law. This leaves out, Suárez thinks, morality's distinctive power to bind or *obligate* those subject to it.[12] Telling falsehoods may be "repugnant" to rational nature and inconsistent with divine perfection, but this repugnancy is insufficient to lay us, and a fortiori God, under a moral obligation to tell the truth.[13] Morality cannot be identified with any teleological structure like Thomist eternal law, therefore, because nothing like this could explain morality's power to obligate.

To understand morality as binding, Suárez believes, it is necessary to see its laws as commands addressed to us by a superior authority, by God. Several ideas are packed into this. First, because "ordering pertains to the will," moral norms or laws must issue from a superior will.[14] Only thus can morality have a "binding force" and create a "necessity" for acting here and now, which would not exist under other circumstances and per se.[15] Second, moral norms are God's will as *addressed to us*. Suárez's idea is not that God simply wants or wills us to act in certain ways. If *that* were His will, we could not fail to comply ("all these precepts would be executed"), since God is omnipotent.[16] Rather God wills "to bind" His subjects by addressing them in a certain way, by commanding them.[17] Third, the commands that create morality are addressed to human beings *as free and rational*. Morality can exist "only in view of some rational creature; for law is imposed only upon a nature that is free, and has for its subject-matter free acts alone."[18] So, fourth, although moral norms "provid[e] motive force and impe[l]," they do so by providing a distinctive kind of *reason* that wouldn't have existed but for God's will's having been addressed to ours in this distinctive way.[19] Fifth, this second-personal address makes morality something we are *accountable* for complying with. If we do not "voluntarily observe the law," therefore, we are *culpable* ("legal culprits in the sight of God").[20] Finally, sixth, morality brings with it a distinctive variety of goodness that consists in acting on the distinctive reasons created by God's commands. To be morally good, one must, he says, "act for righteousness's sake."[21]

It is thus essential to Suárez's picture of moral obligation that it derives from a distinctive second-personal relationship between one rational will and another. Moral obligations derive from claims that are made will to will and that purport to give the second, the addressee, a distinctive reason for acting he wouldn't otherwise have had, and to place him in the position of accountability for so acting. Of course, it is no less essential to Suárez's view that the requisite second-personal relation is asymmetric, that of a superior to an inferior will. There can be "moral government," he thinks, only through the existence of rational *creatures*, that is, rational beings who, because they are created, are (in their nature) subject to the authority of their Creator.[22] Still, if the more abstract proposition were put to Suárez, he would be committed to accepting it. Moral obligation exists only through the possibility of a second-personal address in which one rational agent can give another a distinctive kind of reason she wouldn't have had but for the possibility of second-personal address and that she is, thereby, accountable for acting on.

Suárez says very little about how this is supposed to work as a matter of moral psychology. What must rational agents be like if they are to be guaranteed the ability to recognize and act on such reasons? And what must such reasons be like if they are guaranteed the ability to guide free agents' rational deliberations? It is simply unclear how Suárez thinks that moral "necessity" and obligation can enter into the deliberations of a rational agent. He never explicitly rejects the traditional Thomist picture of the will as inherently aiming at the good, and he clearly accepts the Thomist doctrine of eternal law, according to which whatever morality dictates necessarily accords with the agent's good, properly understood. Thus, in spite of the stress Suárez lays on morality's creation of a distinctive kind of reason, it remains unclear how he thinks this is to be located within a free agent's practical reasoning in deliberation.

2. Pufendorf

We find these same themes in Pufendorf, but put more sharply and without the Thomist doctrine of eternal law. The increased acuity comes from Pufendorf's distinction between physical and moral "entities": the difference, he claims, between how things stand in nature without the address of a commanding will, on the one hand, and the "superadded" moral changes that result from this form of address, on the other.[23] "The way . . . moral entities are produced," Pufendorf tells us, cannot be better expressed "than by the word *imposition*."[24] Without God imposing His will through command, all beings (including human beings) stand "physically complete," their respective physical natures fixing "their ability directly to produce any physical motion or change in any thing."[25] With God's command, however, "moral entities" are superadded to the physical realm – moral law and moral reasons are created. It takes God's second-personal address to give free and rational human beings moral reasons for acting.

Pufendorf's moral conception is modern in Sidgwick's sense. To regulate or avoid human conflict for mutual advantage, we require a conception of a distinctively obligating reason for acting that can be grounded independently of the agent's own good. "Moral entities" make possible the "orderliness and decorum of civilized life."[26] Without the moral law, "men should spend their lives like beasts."[27]

Pufendorf defines what he calls the "active force" of moral entities as its being "made clear to men along what line they should govern their liberty of action, and that in a special way men are made capable of receiving good or evil and of directing certain actions towards other persons with a particular effect."[28] We shall return to how Pufendorf sees the moral law entering into rational deliberation presently. But first, we should understand what he means by the "special way" men can receive good or evil and can direct "certain actions towards other persons with a particular effect." What Pufendorf is talking about here is accountability, specifically, the standing to bring and receive *sanctions*.

The key idea here is that the distinctive second-personal character of God's relation to those He commands makes addressees *accountable* for obedience. Once God addresses us in this way, our actions and various of their effects are imputable to our account. When, consequently, God threatens evil if we violate His commands, He is not merely threatening or coercing us. His punishment is but a further expression of the same second-personal accountability relation that God establishes in commanding us in the first place. It is what His holding us accountable consists in.

When God addresses His will to free and rational beings, He makes us "moral causes," agents to whom actions and their effects can be *imputed* and for which we are thereby accountable. Of course, He must also have made us free and rational, since this is necessary for imputability. But it is not sufficient, since imputability, as Pufendorf thinks of it, entails accountability, and that, he believes, requires imposition. The formal nature of a moral action, he says, "consists of its 'imputativity'," "whereby the effect of a voluntary action can be imputed to an agent." Whether the effects be "good or evil," Pufendorf continues, "he must be responsible for both."[29] This is the "primary axiom in morals": "a man can be asked for a reckoning" for anything in his power. Or, equivalently, "any action controllable according to a moral law, the accomplishment or avoidance of which is within the power of a man, may be imputed to him."[30] According to Pufendorf, then, when God addresses His will to free and rational beings, He simultaneously creates the moral law and makes them "moral causes" by making them accountable for following it.

Being under moral obligations, then, is not simply a matter of standing under categorical oughts, but, as well, of being obligated *to* (answerable to) someone for complying with these oughts. Moral obligation, consequently, can only result from a form of second-personal address that can generate the requisite accountability relations, as Pufendorf believes, to God. Pufendorf agrees with Suárez (and, he points out, with Hobbes) that this can only come from a *will*. He quotes with approval Hobbes' definition of law as "a precept in which the reason for obedience is drawn from the will of the person prescribing it."[31] And he also agrees that law can only be imposed on free and rational wills and by a form of second-personal address.[32] "A law is a decree by which a superior obligates a subject." And a "decree," he emphasizes, comes into existence only in "being communicated to the subject in such a way that he recognizes he must bend himself to it."[33] Morality, with its distinctive form of accountability, therefore, can only exist because of the distinctive demands that one kind of will can make on another that is free and rational.

As Pufendorf's critics, notably Leibniz, pointed out, however, and as Pufendorf himself affirmed, even God's commands cannot create the whole structure of accountability *ex nihilo*. Cudworth put the point this way: "it was never heard of, that any one founded all his Authority of Commanding others, and others Obligation or Duty to Obey his Commands, in a Law of his own making, that men should be Required, Obliged, or Bound to Obey him."[34] Without its already being true that we should obey God's commands, these cannot obligate us to perform specific actions. Pufendorf actually agrees with this point. We could not be obligated by God's command, he says, unless "we owed beforehand obedience to its author."[35]

But what, according to Pufendorf, can make this the case? The terms in which Pufendorf draws the distinction between moral and physical entities apparently prevent him from holding, with Suárez, that *created* rational beings are *in their nature*, and independently of imposition, the Creator's moral subjects in the sense of being rightly ruled by Him. Moral entities "do not arise out of the intrinsic nature of the physical properties of things, but . . . are superadded *at the will of intelligent entities*," specifically by imposition.[36] So there can't be a more fundamental obligation or accountability relation grounded in the natures of these different kinds of rational beings from which God's imposed will draws its authority over us. But without that, it remains unclear, by Pufendorf's own admission, how God's impositions can have the background authority needed to impose obligations.

In spite of the distinction between physical and moral entities, Pufendorf tries to fix this problem by arguing that we are obligated to obey God out of gratitude, since we are indebted to Him for our "very being."[37] However, this creates problems of its own. Gratitude is, for Pufendorf, an imperfect rather than a perfect duty, and so it is insufficient to generate the accountability relations needed for perfect duties.[38] Moreover, if we are permitted to help ourselves to an independently standing duty of gratitude to give moral force to the structure of command, then why suppose that other duties require command for their moral force? What is special about gratitude? Once a voluntarist makes a concession on this duty, why should he not make it also on others?

This was perhaps the most fundamental problem that voluntarists like Pufendorf ultimately faced. They wanted to hold that morality requires a distinctive form of accountability that derives from one kind of will's addressing a demand to another. But they also held that this is insufficient. It is necessary as well that the two wills be related already as superior to inferior, independently of any second-personal interaction (or anything presupposed in such interaction per se). This is what makes the relevant demand an *order*, obligating the inferior to obey as the superior's subject. But assuming this prior moral relation creates two kinds of problems. First, assuming *any* prior moral relation raises the question of why other relations can't be taken for granted also, for example, promiser to promisee or parent to child. This is the problem we encountered earlier. Second, in holding that any rational agent whom God addresses is thereby accountable for obedience, the voluntarists made their views subject to pressure from the idea of rational accountability in ways that can seem to cut against theological voluntarism. God can hold free and rational agents accountable for following His commands, Pufendorf and Locke held, only if exercising the capacity for free and rational deliberation would lead agents to recognize reasons for obedience deriving from this second-personal address. But this requires that free and rational deliberation necessarily leads to an acknowledgment of the moral relation of inferior to superior, which gives God's commands authority in the first place. And what might guarantee that?

3. Accountability, Freedom and Moral Reasons

We shall return to considering how the voluntarist ambition to underwrite a conception of morality as accountability might be developed in the final section. In this section, I shall discuss the voluntarists' own attempts to assure the connection between moral reasons and freedom that is necessary for accountability. I have argued elsewhere that this was an important element in Locke's later moral thought, which he fully articulated only in the second edition of the *Essay*.[39] Like Pufendorf, Locke held that moral notions are fashioned rather than discovered – in his terms, "archetypal" rather than "ectypal." In particular, the categories of 'man' and 'person', as they operate in moral thought, are not natural kinds; they have " "nominal" rather than "real essences." "When we say that *Man is subject to Law*," Locke says, "[W]e mean nothing by *Man*, but a corporeal rational Creature."[40] And "'Person' is a Forensick Term appropriating Actions and their Merit; and so belongs only to intelligent Agents capable of a Law."[41] Specifically, Locke holds, we fashion the concept of person in such a way as to ensure accountability (Pufendorf's 'imputativity'). This is evident, in ways frequently unappreciated, in Locke's famous discussion of personal identity, which, he says, is that whereby a person "becomes . . . accountable," thus presupposing an agent who consciously "owns or imputes to it *self* past Actions" on the same grounds "that it does the present."[42]

These claims require Locke to develop an account of freedom and the will that can fit with such a concept of (accountable) persons, so that violations of the law can be accounted for as a "neglect or abuse" of this liberty and "imputed to [the agent's] own election."[43] This is a major aim of Locke's massively revised chapter on power (II.xxi) in the *Essay*. Specifically, Locke develops a new theory of the will as self-conscious self-command and a theory of a different kind of liberty from the power to do what one wills: self-determination or the agent's power to form the will him self or herself. Agents have the power to step back from their current desires, examine their objects "on all sides," and by this means form a genuinely practical "*judgment*," which, because of the way it is formed, has motivational strength in proportion to the value that is judged.[44]

What, however, links the exercise of the capacity for self-determining deliberation to the moral law? Locke is both a psychological and a rational egoistic hedonist, so he thinks that agents can desire only their own pleasure and that only this gives them reasons for acting. But Locke also believes that the whole point of the moral law is to *restrict* the pursuit of individual pleasure for mutual advantage.[45] So it is a consequence of Locke's hedonism that God does not give human beings motivation to follow His law *directly*. "Moral rectitude . . . considered barely in it self is not good or evill nor in any way moves the will."[46] God must therefore give us special reasons of egoistic pleasure and pain that are conditional on our following His law; that is, He must create sanctions. It is considering *these* that enables self-determining agents to follow natural law when they exercise their capacity for free and rational deliberation.

This leaves Locke in an unhappy position. On the one hand, he holds emphatically that "every man's own interest" is not the basis of the law of nature and that "all obligation binds conscience and lays a bond on the mind itself, so that not fear of punishment but a rational apprehension of what is right, puts us under an obligation."[47] On the other hand, according to Locke's moral psychology, no consideration other than one relating to the agent's happiness can provide a motive to action. Thus, whereas for Locke the moral law lays a "bond on the mind," it apparently can lay no bond on the will.

Pufendorf faces a version of this same problem, and it seems to tie him in even greater knots. Unlike Locke, Pufendorf holds that morally good action must not simply conform to the moral law but have a "determinative relation" to the law as a "directing rule."[48] It must not be performed "for any other cause than that of offering the law its required obedience."[49] This commits Pufendorf to thinking it possible to act on moral reasons. Conscience, he says, takes "cognizance of laws for the direction of human action," and "whatever we do from obligation" we do from "an intrinsic impulse of the mind."[50,51] At the same time, it is a corollary of Pufendorf's theory of the will that "nothing can constrain the human mind, as it deliberates on the future, to do or to avoid anything, except reflection on the good and evil which will befall others or ourselves from what we do."[52] It seems, then, that Pufendorf, like Locke, has no way of assuring a connection between the moral law and the rational motives necessary to make us accountable for following it other than Divine sanctions.

4. Accountability, Moral Reasons and the Second-Person Standpoint

We should look more carefully, however, at the distinctive evils that Pufendorf believes attend moral violations, since he holds that these differ from other evils in significant ways. Many things can "influence the will to turn to one side" or the other, but other evils "bear down the will as by some natural weight, and on their removal [the will] returns of itself to its former indifference."[53] Obligation, however, "affects the will morally," so that it "is forced of itself to weigh its own actions, and to judge itself worthy of some censure, unless it conforms to a prescribed rule."[54] Obligation thus "differs in a special way from coercion." Although "both ultimately point out some object of terror, the latter only shakes the will with an external force," since what moves the will is only "the sense of the impending evil." "An obligation," however, "forces a man to acknowledge of himself that the evil, which has been pointed out to the person who deviates from an announced rule, falls upon him justly."[55]

It may not be obvious how this can help. If only good or evil can move the will, how does it help to explain obligation's ability to move the will directly, differently from coercion, to know that the evil that is threatened if we violate the moral law falls on us "justly"? To see what Pufendorf must be getting at, we need to distinguish between merely external censure or blame and internal blame. Blame is purely external when it comes from outside and is not accepted. When, however, one accepts blame or censure, sees oneself through the eyes of the censuring person, and credits that imputation, one also blames oneself. What Pufendorf evidently believes is that violating the moral law does not merely threaten evils that are only externally related to the violation, but also the evil of internal blame, one's own censure. But cannot even internal blame be externalized? Is the worry supposed to be that I cannot avoid my own gaze, and so my own blame, in a way that I can avoid others, if I stay out of their sight? What if I could take a pill that would wipe out the memory of the violation?

What Pufendorf must mean here, I think, is that although a pill might expunge the psychic state of internal blame, it couldn't expunge one's being *to blame, as one judges here and now one would be.* In making this judgment, one is, in effect, holding oneself accountable for one's future conduct with respect to the relevant law. Moreover, it seems implicit in the judgment one now makes that one has conclusive reasons against violation. It seems incoherent to judge that someone is to blame for an action that there were (or she had) conclusive reasons for doing. When, consequently, a free and rational deliberating agent acknowledges that she would be to blame for doing something, she thereby acknowledges conclusive reasons not to do it and, in a sense, holds herself accountable.

This picture links accountability more centrally to the reasons free and rational beings have for living by the moral law. They are no longer, as with Locke, props for a system of accountability that are imposed externally. Rather, on this picture, recognizing moral reasons is itself part of moral agents' active participation in a scheme of accountability, part of their holding themselves accountable for guidance by the relevant norms. But once we view things this way, some significant pressures develop on the sort of voluntarism that Pufendorf and Locke put forward. Most obviously, accountability is no longer simply to God, but also, in a sense, to oneself. It may still be, of course, that God rightly claims, uniquely, the right to punish and to judge. But this idea may also come under pressure if this punishment itself includes self-condemnation and a sense of guilt, since these involve internal, and not just external, blame.

To the extent that we conceive of moral agents as capable of internal blame, we must think of them as capable of taking part in a second-personal moral community. For Pufendorf, each agent forms such a community with God alone, with God being accountable to no one. But Pufendorf also thinks that agents can form such a community with God only if they are capable of *accepting* God's censure internally, hence only if they can be in this way accountable also to themselves. Moreover, since such an assessment is of oneself *as a person*, one will have this capacity only if one is capable of entering into a community of mutually accountable persons. Pufendorf does not himself draw the conclusion, of course, but it follows that only beings capable of entering into relations of mutual accountability can be moral agents.

We should return now to voluntarism's fundamental problem. Pufendorf simply helps himself to the assumption that free and rational agents will accept the background juridical relation of superior to inferior necessary to make God's demands into orders. But what in the capacity of free and rational beings to enter into relations of accountability guarantees the recognition of this moral obligation? At this point, Pufendorf runs up against what appears to be an insoluble problem. Mere imposition, the actual addressing of a claim by one rational will (God) to others, is normatively impotent without a presupposed normative background that is not itself imposed. But Pufendorf also holds that the very existence of moral entities, and thus of relations of moral accountability, itself depends on this form of second-personal address.

Suppose, however, that we were to view the voluntarists as putting forward but one *conception* of a more general *concept* of morality as accountability. Any interpretation of this general concept, we might think, must see morality as grounded in the possibility of second-personal community and moral reasons as rooted in demands that one free and rational will can make on another. What characterizes a voluntarist conception, in particular, is its taking a moral hierarchy for granted and then deriving the rest of morality (by fiat) from that. As we have seen, however, tendencies within the general idea of morality as accountability put heavy pressure on a voluntarist interpretation of that idea. To distinguish between moral obligation and coercion, Pufendorf must provide an analysis of moral agents' distinctive capacity for self-censure and its role in deliberation. However, this effectively assumes that agents can be accountable not just to God but also to themselves. And Pufendorf provides no account whatsoever of how the capacity for second-personal, accountable community might imply a recognition of the kind of commanding moral authority that voluntarism assumes God to have.

Once, however, we have identified the more general idea of morality as accountability, we might ask whether there are other ways in which, to recall Sidgwick's phrase, this idea can "work itself clear." It seems implicit in the very idea of one free and rational will making a claim on another (as free and rational) that the former must take the latter to be capable of accepting this claim and being guided by it, thereby being accountable to the other by holding himself accountable. Further, the addresser of the claim must apparently also take the addressee to share this understanding. In other words, this shared understanding seems a *presupposition of any such claim.* But if moral community requires such a shared understanding, what could morality be? What claims might one free and rational will make on another and reasonably expect reciprocation? The very logic of the question suggests a line of response that we find developed in different ways in Kant and post-Kantian German idealism, especially in Fichte and Hegel (and before that, I would argue, in Adam Smith), and in our own time in, among others, Rawls and Scanlon. If we take no particular moral relationship for granted and simply ask what demands one free and rational will might make on another (expecting reciprocation), a natural answer would seem to be: whatever demand *any* free and rational being would make on any other, since it will be sensible to make the demand only if it would be sensible to accept it. And it will be sensible to accept it only if one would make it also oneself. These are ideas that lead in the direction of Kant's Categorical Imperative, Fichte and Hegel on reciprocal recognition (*Anerkennung*), Rawls' original position and "rightness as fairness," and Scanlon's contractualism.

Obviously, these ideas are in many ways far from anything in voluntarism. They can, however, be seen as attempts to develop and clarify two central claims the voluntarists made: first, that morality derives from a kind of demand that one free and rational will can make on another and, second, that morality essentially involves the accountability of free and rational wills. The voluntarists interpreted these ideas within a conception of morality as subjection to a superior will. Working them clear, however, may lead to a conception of morality as the mutual accountability of free and equal moral subjects.

Notes

1. Strictly speaking, what I am required to do is *either* to take these (necessary) means or give up the end (assuming that my belief that the only way of getting to Brighton is US-23 stays put).
2. "Morality as a System of Hypothetical Imperatives," *The Philosophical Review* 81 (1972), pp. 305–16. (Phillipa Foot

3. "We do not call anything wrong, unless we mean to imply that a person ought to be punished in some way or other for doing it; if not by law, by the opinion of his fellow creatures; if not by opinion, by the reproaches of his own conscience. This seems the real turning point of the distinction between morality and simple expediency.... There are other things ... which we wish that people should do, which we like or admire them for doing, perhaps dislike or despise them for not doing, but yet admit that they are not bound to do; it is not a case of moral obligation; we do not blame them, that is, we do not think that they are proper objects of punishment. How we come by these ideas of deserving and not deserving punishment, will appear, perhaps, in the sequel; but I think there is no doubt that this distinction lies at the bottom of the notions of right and wrong; that we call any conduct wrong, or employ, instead, some other term of dislike or disparagement, according as we think that the person ought, or ought not, to be punished for it; and we say that it would be right to do so and so, or merely that it would be desirable or laudable, according as we would wish to see the person whom it concerns, compelled, or only persuaded and exhorted, to act in that manner." (John Stuart Mill, *Utilitarianism*, ed. George Sher [Hackett, 1979], Ch. V, pp. 47–8). On the conceptual tie between wrong and blame and guilt, see also Allan Gibbard, *Wise Choices, Apt Feelings* (Harvard University Press, 1990), p. 42; and John Skorupski, *Ethical Explorations* (Oxford University Press, 1999), e.g., p. 142. For a moral theory that stresses the role of accountability, see T. M. Scanlon, *What We Owe to Each Other* (Harvard University Press, 1998).

4. J. B. Schneewind, *The Invention of Autonomy* (Cambridge University Press, 1999), p. 44.

5. Ibid., pp. 119–20.

6. Henry Sidgwick, *Outlines of the History of Ethics for English Readers*, 6th ed., enlarged (Beacon Press, 1964), pp. 197–8. As befits his subject in that book, Sidgwick confines his remark to modern English thought. For a discussion of this claim, see William Frankena, "Sidgwick and the History of Ethical Dualism," in *Essays on Henry Sidgwick*, ed. Bart Schultz (Cambridge University Press, 1992). Compare also Sidgwick's claim that the difference between ancient and modern ethics is that between a system whose fundamental guiding notion is "attractive" and one whose fundamental guide is "imperative" (i.e., that one must act in a certain way despite the existence of more attractive alternatives) (*Outlines of the History of Ethics*, pp. 1–20; *The Methods of Ethics*, 7th ed. [Macmillan, 1967], pp. 105–6). For commentary, see Charles Larmore, *The Morals of Modernity* (Cambridge University Press, 1996); and Nicholas White, "Attractives and Imperatives: Sidgwick's View of Ancient and Modern Ethics," in *Essays on Henry Sidgwick*, ed. Schultz, pp. 311–30.

7. Hugo Grotius, *The Law of War and Peace*, trans. Francis W. Kelsey (New Carnegie Endowment for International Peace, 1925), pp. 10–11.

8. Ibid., p. 11.

9. See note 1.

10. I take the term 'co-deliberation' from Scanlon, *What We Owe to Each Other*, p. 268.

11. Francisco Suarez, *De Legibus ac Deo Legislatore* (1612), translated as *A Treatise on Laws and God the Lawgiver* by Gwladys L. Williams, Ammi Brown and John Waldron, with certain revisions by Henry Davis, S.J., and an introduction by James Brown Scott, in *Selections from Three Works of Francisco Suarez, S.J.*, vol. 2 (Clarendon Press, 1944), reprinted as vol. 20 of *Classics of International Law* by the Carnegie Endowment for International Peace, Bk. I, Ch. I, §1, p. 21.

12. Of course, Aquinas also distinguished between "eternal law" and "natural law," holding that it is because rational beings can know the eternal law that they are subject to natural law. What this still leaves out, however, is the idea that what makes it law is that it is (known to be) addressed to rational beings as an expression of God's will making a claim on ours.

13. Ibid., Bk. II, Ch. V, §7–8, 181–3.

14. Ibid., Bk. I, Ch. V, §13, 66.

15. Ibid., Bk. I, Ch. V, §15, 66, 67.

16. Ibid., Bk. I, Ch. IV, §7, 55.

17. Ibid., Bk. I, Ch. IV, §8, 55.

18. Ibid., Bk. I, Ch. III, §2, 37.

19. Ibid., Bk. I, Ch. IV, §7, 54.

20. Ibid., Bk. I, Ch. XVIII, §3, 132.

21. Ibid., Bk. II, Ch. X, §11, 241. It is necessary "in order that observance of the precept may be moral, that it may be the effect of the law or precept, and that this fact may be attributed to the man himself" (Bk. II, Ch. X, §5, 235)

22. Ibid., Bk. I, Ch. III, §3, 37–8.

23. Samuel Pufendorf, *De Jure Naturae et Gentium Libri Octo* (1688), *On the Law of Nature and Nations*, trans. C. H. Oldfather and W. A. Oldfather (Clarendon Press, 1934), I.i.§2–6, pp. 4–7.

24. Ibid., I.i.§3, p. 5.

25. Ibid., I.i.§4, p. 6.

26. Ibid., I.i.§3, p. 5.

27. Ibid.

28. Ibid., I.i.§4, p. 6.

29. Ibid., I.v.§3, p. 68.

30. Ibid., I.v.§5, p. 70.

31. Ibid., I.vi.§1, p. 88.

32. That law can only bind free rational wills is a major theme of Chapter IV of Book I, pp. 52–65.

33. Ibid., I.vi.§4, p. 89.

34. Ralph Cudworth, *A Treatise on Eternal and Immutable Morality*, ed. Sarah Hutton (Cambridge University Press, 1996), I.ii.§3. This was first published posthumously in 1731; Cudworth died in 1688. Leibniz made similar arguments against Pufendorf explicitly in his *Opinion on the Principles of Pufendorf* in Gottfried Wilhelm Leibniz, *Political Writings*, ed. Patrick Riley, 2nd ed. (Cambridge University Press, 1989), pp. 70–5.

35. *On the Law of Nature and Nations*, I.vi,§4, p. 89.

36. Ibid., I.i.§4, pp. 5–6 (emphasis added).

37. Ibid., I.vi.§12, p. 101.

38. I am indebted to J. B. Schneewind for this point.

39. *The British Moralists and the Internal 'Ought': 1640–1740* (Cambridge University Press, 1995), Ch. 6, pp. 149–75. I argue there that Locke's views on freedom and accountability drew heavily on those advanced by Ralph Cudworth in his manuscripts on freedom of the will.

40. John Locke, *An Essay Concerning Human Understanding* (London, 1690; 2nd ed., 1694), Peter H. Nidditch, ed. (Oxford University Press, 1975), p. 516.

41. Ibid., p. 346.

42. Ibid.

43. Ibid., p. 271.

44. Ibid., pp. 262–4.

45. I discuss this aspect of Locke's views in *British Moralists*, pp. 36–44.

46. This is an entry in Locke's 1693 Commonplace Book titled "Voluntas" (Lovelace Ms. C28, fol. 114).

47. *Essays on the Law of Nature*, ed. and trans. from the Latin by W. von Leyden (Clarendon Press, 1954), p. 185.

48. *On the Law of Nature and Nations*, I.vii.§3, p. 114. Compare Locke: "*Morally Good and Evil*...is only the Conformity or Disagreement of our Voluntary Actions to some Law, whereby Good or Evil is drawn on us, from the Will and Power of the Law-Maker." *Essay on Human Nature*, p. 351.

49. *On the Law of Nature and Nations*, I.vii.§4, p. 115.

50. *On the Law of Nature and Nations*, I.iii.§4, p. 41.

51. *On the Law of Nature and Nations*, III.iv.§6. Also, obligations "do not have any efficacy in action until a man knows how to regulate his actions to some norm" (I.i.§7, p. 8).

52. *On the Law of Nature and Nations*, I.vi.§5, p. 91.

53. Ibid.

54. Ibid.

55. Ibid.

PART TWO

AUTONOMY IN PRACTICE

6

Pythagoras Enlightened

Kant on the Effect of Moral Philosophy

Larry Krasnoff

In the intriguing epilogue to *The Invention of Autonomy*, J. B. Schneewind distinguishes two very different conceptions of the aim of moral philosophy.[1] For us, he tells us, the dominant conception is likely to be the one that traces its origins back to Socrates' quest for definitions of the virtues – or more precisely, to Socrates' claim that without such definitions, the moral beliefs held by his interlocutors lacked rational grounding. Moral philosophy thus proceeds from the thought that we are not in contact with moral truth until we have found a set of moral beliefs that could be given a systematic philosophical justification. Thus, according to this view, moral philosophy is just an ongoing Socratic search – not necessarily for definitions of the virtues, but certainly for some kind of rationally grounded answer to the question of how we ought to live.[2]

However, Schneewind shows us, a very different view has enjoyed considerable influence throughout the history of philosophy, and especially in the early modern period. According to this second view, the question of how to live has been definitively answered by Judeo-Christian revelation: the ethical claims implicit in the Bible have already shown us what we ought to do. Moral philosophy, then, cannot search for some new set of moral principles, assuming, as Socrates seems to, that the true set of principles is yet to be found. What, then, is the moral point of the philosophical reasoning that was pursued by the ancient Greeks and is now pursued by their contemporary successors? According to Schneewind, moral philosophers committed to this second conception tend to point to human sinfulness, which has pulled us away from what we ought to know about what we ought to do.[3] The Fall weakened not just the strength of our moral commitment but also our rational capacities themselves, leaving us unsure of how to act rightly. The task of moral philosophy, then, is to revive our commitment to biblical morality through rational accounts of its principles and authority. On this conception, moral philosophy plays a kind of therapeutic role; philosophical reasoning about morality helps fallen human beings to recover the original moral clarity of biblical revelation.

As Schneewind amusingly reminds us, moral philosophers committed to this view had a historical problem: they needed to connect the seemingly secular (or even pagan) inquiries of the ancient Greeks with Jewish and Christian revelation. If the point of moral philosophy is to restore the moral clarity of the biblical text, it is hard to see how the Greeks could have engaged in moral philosophizing while being ignorant of that text. This problem was rather neatly solved by tracing the origins of Greek moral philosophy not to Socrates but back beyond him to Pythagoras, and then by citing the supposed fact that Pythagoras was, if not a Jew himself, a Greek who had an intimate acquaintance with Jewish doctrines.[4] And so Schneewind comes to call this second account of the goal of moral philosophy "the Pythagoras story."

What is the relationship between these two accounts and the substantive history of *The Invention of Autonomy*? Clearly Schneewind wants to disabuse us of the idea that moral philosophy has a single aim: the whole point of his history is to show that Kant's theory of autonomy was not an answer to some set of timeless philosophical questions, but a specific response to problems specific to the history of modern moral philosophy.[5] But if we are to be open to this sort of view, we need to get beyond the idea that moral philosophy conceives itself in the same way at all places and all times. And this means that we need to free ourselves from the grip of the Socrates story as the only way of looking at moral philosophy. Hence Schneewind needs to remind us of the prevalence of the Pythagoras story in the modern period, and he is especially concerned to show us that Kant himself accepted a version of that story. It is this last claim that will concern me in this essay. For while I agree with Schneewind that Kant cannot be understood as primarily committed to the Socrates story, the manner in which Kant rejects that story makes it rather difficult to attribute to him a version of the Pythagoras story. To deal with this difficulty, we will need to look much more closely at Kant's conception of the role of moral philosophy than Schneewind is able to do in his epilogue.

1. As Schneewind suggests, the Socrates story will not work for a moral theorist who, like Kant, holds that moral truths are already available

to ordinary human beings. If that is so, then Schneewind is right that "[w]hatever moral philosophy is, therefore, it is not a search for hitherto unknown scientific knowledge."[6] The best moral philosophy can do, then, is to deal with the human frailties that can prevent us from doing what we ought to do. Now if one of these frailties is the weakness of our rational capacities, then it is easy to see how moral philosophy can help. As we have already seen, the Pythagorean moral philosopher can tell us that we need philosophical reasoning to perceive better what is right. The problem is that this kind of view is not available to Kant, who holds not only that ordinary moral agents are self-governing, but also that they are self-governing through the exercise of their rational capacities. The Kantian moral truths that are always already available to ordinary agents do not come from revelation or from a native moral sense – both of which could be tutored by reason – but from our capacity for making universal law, which is already the work of our own reason. There is nothing that philosophy can do to make us better moral reasoners.[7]

Of course, this does not mean that human beings always act rightly, that no barriers stand between them and the moral good. Kant has his own account of human frailty and even depravity, which he understands as the result of our natural inclinations. More precisely, human sinfulness is our tendency to place our desires above the commands of the moral law, and thus to allow ourselves to do what we know we ought not to do.[8] But while there may be a great deal to do before we can bring ourselves to act rightly, it is not clear that philosophy can or should do this work.[9] If our rational capacities are already in good working order, and if our moral frailty is mainly the effect of our nonrational desires, then it is hard to see how any philosophical advance, any improvement in our reasoning, could improve our moral behavior. It is difficult to see how Kantian moral philosophy could have any practical effect at all.

But perhaps Kantian moral philosophy is not intended to have a practical effect. This thought may be problematic for the Pythagoras story, but it does not seem problematic for Kant, at least as he is standardly understood. On the most familiar readings of Kant, his moral philosophy is intended to have only a theoretical effect. This view is alien to both the Socrates and the Pythagoras stories, but it is hardly alien to moral philosophy in our time. Ultimately I believe the view gets Kant wrong, but it is not difficult to see why one might want to attribute it to him. For a long time, that the task of moral philosophy was essentially theoretical was exactly what Kant thought.

Recall that there was originally to be only one *Critique*, the critique of theoretical reason. In the *Critique of Pure Reason*, as is well known, Kant sought to vindicate reason by showing that though it has always been entangled in a series of insoluble metaphysical conflicts, it is equally capable of disciplining itself to avoid these self-made conflicts. The key to reason's self-discipline, of course, is the distinction between appearances and things in themselves, together with the relativization of claims to knowledge to appearances. By limiting its pretensions to constitutive metaphysical knowledge, by limiting itself to a regulative role in the pursuit of empirical knowledge, theoretical reason is able to end its fruitless struggle to transcend experience.

No such struggle, however, seems to hinder reason in its practical use. Since Kant thinks that reason is able to legislate its own principle of moral conduct without reference to experience, there is no need for a critique of pure practical reason.[10] This does not mean, however, that morality requires no support from philosophy. Since the idea that all moral agents are equally capable of acting on a purely rational principle requires the claim that human beings are free, we need a philosophical defense of this claim. But Kant understands that defense to have already been provided by the first *Critique* and its distinction between appearances and things in themselves. Since the claim that the will is free is a claim about things in themselves, and since the first *Critique* has already suggested that such a claim can neither be proven nor disproven, moral philosophy can offer no further defense of human freedom. All Kant does, and all he can do, is to use the metaphysical space provided by the first *Critique* to place the moral claims already advanced as certain by ordinary agents. On this view, we are free not because philosophy has proven us to be free, but because we already do take ourselves to be free in moral deliberation, and because no philosophical argument can disrupt this claim. In this sense moral philosophy has no practical effect; it leaves morality exactly as it always was. The only effect moral philosophy can have is theoretical, fending off the metaphysical objections to morality's own assertion of our free and rational nature.

This conception of the role of moral philosophy ought to seem familiar, and not just because it is the conception standardly ascribed to Kant. It is also the conception of moral philosophy that dominated Anglo-American philosophy throughout the twentieth century and that continues to dominate in our time. One can see it at work in some of the most influential big-picture works in contemporary moral philosophy, in books like Christine Korsgaard's *The Sources of Normativity* and Michael Smith's

The Moral Problem.[11] Following Schneewind's usage, I will give this conception the name of the philosopher who originated this way of thinking about moral philosophy, and call it "the Hobbes story."

According to the Hobbes story, the point of moral philosophy is to account for claims to value in what is objectively a valueless world. Hobbes begins *Leviathan* with the claim that the world can be understood mechanically, and this claim is in no way defended in what follows.[12] The idea that the world is purely physical is simply taken for granted, as belonging to the privileged perspective of natural science. From this perspective, what exists in the world is neither good nor bad; there are simply physical objects obeying physical laws. For Hobbes, claims about good and evil are simply subjective expressions of our tendencies as bodies to pursue (or avoid) other physical objects.[13] Moral claims, however, seem to have a kind of objectivity; Hobbes wants to agree, for instance, with the commonsense thoughts that lying and killing are presumptively wrong. The task of Hobbesian moral philosophy, then, is to show how such claims to value, though originally only subjective, can acquire a kind of pseudo-objectivity through our shared desires for physical security and social cooperation (and, later, through our mutual submission to a sovereign power).[14] What is essentially subjective can come to seem to us objective because we all desire the same things.

Not everyone, of course, has accepted Hobbes' solution to the problem of value in a valueless world, or even the supposed improvements on this solution offered by Hume and contemporary noncognitivists like Allan Gibbard and Simon Blackburn.[15] Their opponents, often but not always Kantian, regard the pseudo-objectivity constructed by noncognitivism as insufficient to capture the normativity of moral claims. Even on this opposing view, however, the task of moral philosophy is to show how we can make the moral claims we already do, given our commitment to the physicalism implied by modern science. Here a popular strategy, much influenced by Kant, is to assert that the normativity of scientific claims, the objectivity of physicalism itself, depends on a deeper conception of rationality that is also at work in ethics. But even here, the agenda of moral philosophy is decisively set by the theoretical outlook of modern science, not by any practical issues in ethics or politics. Moral claims themselves are left entirely to the side; on these views, moral philosophy is wholly metaethical. For cognitivists and noncognitivists alike, the task of moral philosophy is to reconcile the seeming objectivity of moral claims with the valueless world of the physical scientist. The most influential issues in twentieth-century moral philosophy, from the early debates about the meaning of ethical utterances to more recent debates about the relationship between reasons and desires, have derived their influence from this larger problem of reconciliation that owes its origin to Hobbes.

Now perhaps the most striking feature of *The Invention of Autonomy*, and indeed of all of Schneewind's work, is its almost total indifference to the Hobbes story. Schneewind has never been interested in the metaethical debates of the twentieth century, and he flatly denies that the agenda of modern moral philosophy was decisively set by the development of the modern scientific outlook.[16] Hobbes and Hume, he is fond of reminding us, have been a great deal more influential in the past century than they ever were in their own time or even in the nineteenth century.[17] While scientific discoveries may have influenced the development of modern moral philosophy, Schneewind says, the decisive factors were developments in politics and religion. Culture, not science, is what really matters in the history of moral philosophy.[18] With that initial declaration – on the third page of the book – Schneewind plunges into more than five hundred densely argued pages of history in which modern science and the Hobbes story matter hardly at all. But if this kind of history is to make sense, and to make sense of Kant in particular, we need a reading of Kant that enables him to leave the Hobbes story behind as well. And this, I have suggested, is not provided by Schneewind's brief appeal to the Pythagoras story. We still need a way of showing that Kantian moral philosophy can have a practical effect.

2. I have already noted that applying the Hobbes story to Kant is closely bound up with the idea that there needed to be only one *Critique*, the theoretical critique. If moral philosophy requires only that we clear the metaphysical space for morality's assertion of our freedom, then the substantive work of moral philosophy was already accomplished in the *Critique of Pure Reason*. All a work like the *Groundwork of the Metaphysic of Morals* can do is to tie ordinary morality to the idea of freedom that was already shown to be possible in the first *Critique*. This kind of view meshes perfectly with the way Anglo-American philosophy has always liked to look at Kant: respectful of the first *Critique* and of the moral philosophy (especially the *Groundwork*) considered independently, but deeply suspicious of the systematizing, proto-Hegelian tendencies of the second and especially the third *Critique*. But these later works are essential to Kant's thinking, particularly his thinking about the task of philosophy, and so we need to set this kind of suspicion to the side. After a century of Anglo-American

philosophy, we ought to be able to think about Kant's claim that there needed to be a second and a third *Critique* without fearing, with Russell and Moore, that we will lose our way in the fog of metaphysics. In fact this kind of fear is especially unfounded, because what Kant is primarily concerned with in the last two *Critiques* is not the pure needs of metaphysics, but the way reason can and must accommodate the fact of our empirical nature.

To understand this, we need to look more closely at Kant's reasons for expanding the critical project. The Introduction to the second *Critique* begins with the claim that there is no need for a critique of pure practical reason; in the practical realm, as we have already noted, pure reason is able to set out its own principle of conduct, binding on all rational agents at all places and times. What needs to be criticized is not pure but empirical practical reason; we need to restrain empirical practical reason from overstepping its limits by proclaiming its own "supremacy." But this claim ought to seem puzzling. If pure practical reason is truly legislative, its claims are supremely authoritative; if the principle of universal law has its source in our own reason, we cannot fail to recognize its authority over our nonrational desires. How, then, can empirical practical reason claim to assert its supremacy? Isn't that supremacy already denied by the legislative work of pure practical reason? If we recognize the fact of reason that is asserted in the Analytic of the second *Critique*, the Dialectic cannot entertain the possibility that our desire for happiness might override the claims of duty. So in what sense can the Dialectic provide a critique of the pretensions of empirical practical reason? What pretensions remain to be criticized?

Kant's Introduction does not provide much guidance here. But the opening of the Dialectic itself helps by reminding us that reason falls into antinomy, and thus stands in need of critique, not merely by seeking the unconditioned, but more precisely by seeking the unconditioned within the realm of the conditioned.[19] Thus, in the theoretical sphere, the problem is not that reason develops and is thus interested in the idea of a first beginning, but rather that it tries to find this first beginning within the series of empirically conditioned events. So the problem in the practical sphere must be not that practical reason sets out a pure or unconditioned principle of conduct, but that it attempts to apply this principle to the realm of the conditioned, to the empirical world.

Now by this application to experience Kant cannot mean the task of determining whether or not a given action was produced by a purely

rational motive. Kant has previously and repeatedly declared this problem to be insoluble, and he does not return to it here.[20] The Analytic's
doctrine of the fact of reason has already asserted that even though we
do not and will not ever know if we or anyone else has acted out of duty,
we still take ourselves to be required to act rightly, and thus capable of so
acting, no matter what desires we happen to have. Kant has thus already
set aside the problem of determining whether observable actions are or
are not evidence of pure morality; this kind of explanation is irrelevant to
the deliberative task of determining what we ought to do. The problem
is rather that if we do accept the deliberative authority of pure practical
reason, we are nonetheless led to seek this deliberative authority even for
our empirically motivated actions. We want to see our actions, even when
they are prompted by our nonrational desires, as susceptible to rational
justification.

It is essential to see that this drive to justify our desire-based actions is
not just permitted but is in a crucial sense required by Kant's claim that the
categorical imperative (hereafter simply the CI) serves as the principle of
pure practical reason. The CI is not derived from pure practical reason
in the sense that it is shown to be the unique principle to which every
rational agent is committed. Kant's argument for the CI is rather that if
there is to be a principle of action valid for every rational agent, it cannot
come from any desire or anything else specific to any particular agent, but
only from something that is potentially available to every agent.[21] The CI
then arises from Kant's suggestion that we take this condition of potential
universality (i.e., universalizability), itself only a necessary condition for a
principle of pure practical reason, to be also a sufficient condition. That
is, he suggests that we allow the fact that a particular agent's principle
conforms to universal law to count as justifying the principle to all rational
beings, even if that principle is ultimately dependent on a desire that not
all agents share. If we did not allow this, then we would be left with the
unanswered question of what could serve as a justified principle for all
rational agents.[22] We would have to produce some thicker standard of
rational justification, and show that it was itself justified to all agents. Kant
does not attempt to produce such a thicker standard; instead he suggests
that we allow any standard of justification to count, so long as it could be
consistently adopted by all agents. Any desire, then, can count as a reason
for action, so long as all agents could consistently pursue it.

In this sense the legislative work of pure practical reason, its successful construction of a purely rational principle of action, depends on the
empirical side of our nature. Without the presence of desires to serve as

potential reasons, the idea that the formal condition of universalizability could itself serve as a principle of pure practical reason would make no sense. Once this point is granted, the critical project of the Dialectic should seem far more plausible. If pure practical reason could provide its own legislative principle, in every sense independent of desire, then the claims of empirical practical reason could be set entirely to the side. But the CI is independent of desire only in the sense that it does not depend on any particular desire. The CI does depend, however, on the fact of desire in general, on the presence of desires as potential candidates for universal law. In this sense the legislative authority of the CI itself implies the legitimacy of the claims of empirical practical reason. Our desires, when universalizable, are fully justified reasons for action. We have a legitimate, rational demand for our own happiness. By (necessarily) legitimating this demand, the CI does indeed seek the unconditioned in what is itself empirically conditioned.

But the claim to find the unconditioned within the empirically conditioned is as problematic in the practical realm as it was in the theoretical realm. Pure practical reason declares that the demand for happiness is legitimated by the principle of universal law. But the empirical world shows us something very different: that happiness has no necessary relation to the willingness to obey the moral law. Agents who pursue only their own desires are not necessarily restrained by any law, and they can even flourish. Rather than finding the effect of the unconditioned moral law within the empirically conditioned world, we find the actual attainment of happiness unconstrained by morality. It is for this reason that practical reason falls into antinomy, and stands in need of critique.

Again, if the principle of practical reason were in every sense independent of desire, this antinomy would not arise. The pure law of practical reason could stand entirely on its own, independent of the nature of human happiness. But our situation is not like that. The CI can serve as a principle of pure practical reason only insofar as it has the material of our desires, which it claims to rationalize. If happiness still stands on its own, however, unconstrained by the CI, those desires are not necessarily rationalized at all. The CI's claim to legislate to desire is threatened, and without this legislation, the CI itself is in danger. It is in this sense that despite the absolute claims of duty, empirical practical reason seems to suggest, if not its own supremacy, then at least its independence. Kant's candidate for a principle of duty depends on its ability to constrain empirical practical reason. But the world shows us empirical practical reason unconstrained by law.

The critical solution to this antinomy of practical reason depends on projecting the rationalization of desire, which we fail to observe in our world, into the indefinite future. That is, even if the empirical world is not yet rational, it might still become so through our efforts. There is a close parallel here to the solution of the theoretical antinomies. Though theoretical reason cannot answer any of its questions about the ultimate causes of empirical events, it can agree to set these questions aside if it can accept the regulative role of spurring us on to further empirical research. Here the search for the unconditioned is reconceived as a task: reason's goal is always a deeper, more comprehensive set of empirical laws. Of course, because theoretical reason's goal is merely regulative, this task will never be complete; we will never advance beyond empirical knowledge to constitutive metaphysical truth. Theoretical reason's drive for the unconditioned is thus subordinated to the structure of the empirical world. In the practical realm, the situation is and must be very different. In setting out its own legislative principle, reason makes an unconditional demand on empirical reality. Were reason to subordinate its claims to the empirical world, the thought of a pure principle of duty would come to nothing. Rather, empirical reality must come to subordinate itself to pure practical reason, and this means that we must be able to see the task of practical reason not as indefinite but as potentially capable of completion. That is, we must be able to specify an end, set out by practical reason but achievable in the empirical world, that would constitute the rationalization of desire. Until we understand this end of practical reason as both coherent and capable of realization, the supremacy of pure over empirical practical reason is yet to be assured.

3. Kant's account of the end or object of practical reason is complicated by the fact that he has two parallel, and perhaps competing, candidates for that end.[23] On the one hand, there is the religious, otherworldly end of the highest good, a world in which happiness is perfectly proportioned to virtue. On the other hand, there is the secularized, historical end of the cosmopolitan state, a world federation of republics united by international law. I am not going to go into the differences and potential tensions between these accounts here. Like many others, I prefer to stress the secular, political end, but for present purposes it is enough to note that each end has the required structure of subordinating our empirical ends to a purely rational law. In the highest good, happiness is achieved only by those committed to the moral law, and in a republican condition, the pursuit of an empirical end is permitted only when the freedom to pursue

it is compatible with similar freedom for all others. And both these ends are understood as objects of human moral agency, ends we might bring about through our efforts. Of course, the successful completion of our task will benefit from, and perhaps even require, certain favorable external conditions, like the existence of God or broader historical progress. To the extent that we are interested in pursuing our moral end(s), we will be very much interested in these external conditions, and will even see them as purposive features of nature, as if the world were set up to aid our moral willing. To legitimate these purposive claims, to render them consistent with the account of the empirical world that emerged from the first *Critique*, Kant needed to write a third and final critical work.

And that brings us back to our main topic, which is the role and the effect of a Kantian moral philosophy. According to the standard view, decisively influenced by the Hobbes story, the task of Kantian moral philosophy is to legitimate the appeal to nonempirical moral claims in a world conceived according to scientific naturalism. This might be done if we could show that morality required such claims, and that the claims did nothing to disrupt the naturalistic account of the world. So much Kant claimed to have accomplished in the first *Critique* and in the Analytic to the second *Critique*. But I have been suggesting that in the later stages of his critical project, Kant came to believe that more was required to legitimate morality than to provide it with theoretical or metaphysical space. We need to know more than that a purely rational morality will not endanger scientific naturalism. Specifically, we need to know that this purely rational morality is capable of transforming the potentially indifferent world according to a coherent and realizable end. Not only do we need to repel the naturalistic skeptic's claim that moral freedom is impossible; we also need to repel the world-weary cynic's claim that a better world will never come into being. Notice that this is a specifically practical worry: the cynic does not appeal to science or to metaphysics, but to the moral and/or political failings of human beings.

Kant answers both theoretical skepticism and practical cynicism with claims about possibility, not about actuality. We know only that there might be human freedom, and morality itself asserts that there is such freedom. Similarly, morality itself asserts that there are specific moral ends that we are to realize in the empirical world, and all we need to know is that these ends are possible through our efforts. Moral agents do not need philosophical assurance – their assurance, again, comes from their own ordinary moral reason – but they do need philosophical reassurance, both theoretical and practical. The specifically practical reassurance is possible if philosophy can show us a way of thinking about the world in which we can coherently conceive ourselves as achieving what the skeptic says we cannot. Again, Kant has two accounts of this kind of practical coherence. The first is his philosophical reconstruction of Christian religious belief, in which faith in God and in immortality allows us to believe that the highest good is possible through our moral agency. The second is his conception of an enlightened politics, in which the collective, vocal judgment of a morally engaged public will force authorities to comply with the justified claims of our own political agency. Since I am mainly interested in this second account, I will focus here on Kant's account of political agency, and the way it can be understood as completing the work of a philosophical justification of morality.[24]

We have already seen that the problem for the later stages of Kant's moral philosophy is not the vindication of the legislative power of practical reason. That, again, is already assured by the moral commitment of the ordinary agent, and the space for that commitment provided by Kant's theoretical philosophy. What is now at issue is what might be called the "isolation" of practical reason: the possibility that its legislative work might have no effect on the surrounding world. It is not that morality requires a fully hospitable world: indeed, Kant insists that if the world was already structured to grant our wishes, we would never have advanced beyond the end of happiness to an independent morality.[25] But we have also seen that the principle that we use to express that independent morality, the CI, is meant to do more than satisfy the condition of independence; it is meant to transform the alien material of the empirical world according to its own principle. The unit of moral independence is the isolated individual, autonomously legislating her own principles of practical reason. But such an isolated individual, expressing her own autonomy, is ill suited to transform the world. The situation of such an individual is perfectly illustrated by the solitary political agent: set over against the unchecked claims of powerful authorities, with only her own power and rhetoric to support her moral demands. But the conditions of the modern world, Kant tells us in his well-known essay on the French Revolution, have changed this situation.[26] It is now possible for an ordinary moral agent to understand herself as a member of a larger public of citizens, whose collective approval is itself a force for political change. As a potential member of this public, an individual agent can understand her own moral agency as reflected in a political body that is both collective and effective, in which individual moral demands are echoed and amplified into political practice.

It is not that the actual public is always right, or that it will always speak out against injustice. The point is rather a subjective one, internal to the perspective of the morally committed agent. What we are looking for is a way for the individual agent to overcome her isolation, to translate her moral commitment into worldly effect. By speaking out politically as a Kantian citizen, the individual agent presumes (and must presume) both the justice of her cause and the moral agreement of the wider public. Without these assumptions, the project of political action makes no sense. But with them, the individual agent understands herself as no longer isolated in her moral commitment. An enormous gap, of course, remains between this subjective understanding and the realization of justice as an actual agreement of free citizens. But closing this gap – or rather working to close it, for full agreement will never come – is the task of actual politics. Political philosophy, as the last stage of practical philosophy, is not meant – as in the familiar "Kantian" political theories of our day – to supplant political practice by issuing a set of hypothetically generated moral demands.[27] Rather, the task of a properly Kantian political philosophy is to theorize the standpoint from which political agents can issue their own moral demands, to show that this standpoint has both normative privilege and practical force. The normative privilege comes from the presupposition of free and equal citizenship that characterizes participation in the Kantian public; the practical force comes from the response of approval that the political agent, animated by the experience of modern politics, expects from the rest of the public. If we understand the standpoint of Kantian political agency to include a presumption of both normative and historical force, then we have found a standpoint from which the individual agent can understand her moral agency as working to transform the world. Political philosophy thus completes the work of moral philosophy, by showing that the principles of practical reason can in fact speak to the empirical agency that they require in order to command.

Is this a Pythagorean view of the task of moral philosophy? In the traditional sense, the answer must be no: it is not a rational reconstruction of what we once saw clearly and now need to see again. The practical project of Kantian moral philosophy, as embodied in the turn to political philosophy, is meant to provide a new standpoint for the moral agent, whose commitments already have rational justification, but who also needs to understand those commitments as empirically effective. But in a deeper sense, the parallel is there. Recall that on the traditional view, the task of the Pythagorean view is to compensate for the effects of the Fall, which leaves the Christian believer suspended between two incompatible realms. On the one hand, there is the fallen world, with its characteristic disorder and evil. On the other hand, there is the promise of revelation, holding out the possibility of escape. The fallen human being may dimly perceive the authority of revelation, but her sinfulness alienates her from it: unable to understand the full meaning of revelation, she counts herself as belonging essentially to this empirical world. Exactly the same predicament confronts the isolated Kantian moral agent: she recognizes the rational authority of the moral law, but does not see how to reconcile it with the empirical world, which fails to conform to reason's demands. The difference, of course, is that the traditional Pythagorean philosopher seeks to provide a rationale through which the believer can come to hold fast to the message of revelation, thus taking leave of the actual world. By contrast, Kant, at least in his historical/political account, takes the familiar Enlightenment path of secularizing the ultimate ends of human action. Rather than providing us with the reasons that we can and should abandon this world, Kant seeks to provide us with a standpoint within which we can understand this world as susceptible to the transformative power of our own reason. But on both accounts, the fallen, essentially irrational character of the actual world is the appropriate problem for philosophical treatment.

4. The most difficult and ultimately the most interesting question about this sort of enlightened Pythagorean account is whether it could have anything valuable to contribute to the moral philosophy of our time. Given the power of the Hobbes story and the prestige of metaethics in analytic philosophy, and given the postmodernist critique of the Enlightenment as merely a rationalist reprisal of religious dogmatism, it may seem that I have stressed exactly the worst aspects of Kant's practical philosophy. Could the goal of a contemporary moral philosophy really be to provide a secular theodicy through which we could understand the world as rationalizable through our efforts?

To see that the answer to this question really is yes, we need to remember that the aims of Kantian moral philosophy, and indeed of any Pythagorean moral philosophy, are much more strictly limited than the notion of secular theodicy might at first suggest. What makes this notion objectionable is the thought of philosophy's claiming to legislate from a kind of Promethean standpoint, seeking to bring the contingencies of the empirical world under the firm direction of reason. The claim to such a standpoint offends both the metaphysical sensibility of analytic moral philosophy, which demands the naturalistic warrant for this perspective, and the political sensibility of postmodernism, which sees in this perspective the putative justification for a violently imposed order. But here the role of a Kantian practical philosophy is not the legislative or constitutive one that such critics fear. The legislative or constitutive stage of Kant's practical philosophy takes place earlier, in the construction of the principle of universal law. At this later stage, however, the task of practical philosophy is essentially empirical, with reason playing only an orientative role. The problem is to find within experience, within the diversity of historical phenomena, the sorts of events or developments that will allow committed moral agents to understand their transformative efforts as capable of success. The particular historical phenomenon that Kant himself fastened on, the development of a vocal and powerful public sentiment in the aftermath of the French Revolution, can be described in wholly empirical terms, and Kant issues no philosophical demand that this phenomenon must be taken as evidence of the march of reason through history. What is at stake is not the necessity but the possibility of a moral perspective on history and politics, and it is only from within this standpoint that the belief in progress acquires its meaning and force.

What is more, the need to reformulate this kind of standpoint is in an important sense unending, since political, economic and technological developments are constantly thrown up in our path, posing new challenges to a stable and just political order. The same cannot be said, however, for the dominant projects in analytic and Continental philosophy, for scientific naturalism and postmodernism. Both of these projects are finally parasitic on the corpse of religious dogmatism, on the ghostly objections of their endlessly imagined rationalist critics. Meanwhile, the moral and political struggles that they respectively ignore or disdain go on. But why would these struggles, even new ones, require any help from philosophy? Even if philosophy needs something to do after it has finally decided that it has made the world safe for science, even if a Kantian philosophical perspective on politics and history can escape the charge of metaphysical dogmatism, in what sense do we as moral and political agents need Kantian philosophical support?

Recall that the point of the second, empirically oriented stage of Kant's practical philosophy is to overcome the isolation of practical reason that threatens even after the first, rationally legislative practical philosophy is complete. The worry here is that morality, which proceeds originally from an individual agent's own commitment to make universality into the justifying principle her actions, could come to seem like a kind of private metaphysical fantasy, imagined in the agent's own deliberations but having no effect on the surrounding world. A coherent and rational conception of moral agency demands that we see moral action as capable of some kind of empirical realization. And this realization is especially threatened by the economic and technological developments that are characteristic of the modern world. These historical developments decisively influence our lives, and yet they appear to us as potentially alien forces over which we as agents have no control. Again, Kant's favored solution to this problem is not a kind of Marxist fantasy in which these alien historical forces are subordinated to a kind of total rational planning.[28] Rather the problem is to find, within the empirical, historical trends themselves, some way of understanding them as pointing toward the results that reason and morality would demand, and thus of closing the gap that can threatens to leave us stranded as agents between the larger public trends and the potentially private hopes of our own reason. In itself, again, the modern development of a politics of public opinion is a purely empirical trend, entirely explicable in economic and technological terms. But it is philosophy, within its characteristic concern with rational justification, that can bring us to understand the way in which this politics can be understood as having a kind of normative privilege, as allowing us to bring about, within history, the outcomes that morality prefers.

It may help to end with a contemporary example. A great many recent commentators have noted that the political institutions of the modern nation-state no longer seem adequate to handle the political problems that have followed in the wake of what has come to be called "globalization": problems such as the fair regulation of trade, the protection of the environment, and the proper taxation of commerce and the safeguarding of privacy on the Internet. These political problems will not go away, despite the constant refrain of many of those same commentators – optimists and pessimists alike – that the economic and technological forces that have created them are too powerful for anyone to control. That is certainly right in a very vague sense, but obviously wrong in general, as the politics of this century have already shown. Only the most crazed libertarians would fail to distinguish between the regulation that every decent nation-state applies to its economy and the centralized planning that so dismally failed under communism. The problem is not the intrinsic power of the market and technology, but the inability of individual governments to deal with them under conditions of globalization. That ability, obviously, will require new mechanisms of international coordination and regulation. Obviously those new political mechanisms, to the extent that they are emerging and will continue to emerge, will originally be driven by economic self-interest of various kinds. Just as obviously, the protests and criticisms that are and will be directed against these new political mechanisms will be driven by economic demands and cultural fears. The clash of these motivations will often be morally and politically ugly, as recent protests in Seattle, Genoa, and elsewhere have shown. But only something like political philosophy can sort out the morally legitimate hopes and grievances in these debates and distinguish them from the baser motivations that surround them. The goal is not to replace the process of globalization with some sort of rational control, but to identify those elements within it that are worthy of moral approval, and then to direct our efforts to ensuring that those come to the fore. In practice, that will mean deciding which of the various nascent forms of international governance can be used to promote the right political ends. And this requires not just political but also moral judgment, which only political philosophy is able to provide.

One of the most interesting aspects of *The Invention of Autonomy* is Schneewind's effort to show how the secular moral philosophy of Kant emerged from a series of problems and debates within Christian theology. What is misleadingly, and dismissively, called the "Enlightenment project" was not the private fantasy of secular rationalists, invented in theoretical isolation and then imposed on the ordinary people of the West, who were merely trying to live simple and God-fearing lives in their happy, organic communities. That view is the private fantasy of liberalism's conservative critics. The reality of liberalism was and is far different: a complex series of developments within the Christian tradition of the West that, for good internal reasons, produced a secularism that could stand entirely apart from Christianity. No doubt the development of international political institutions will take a similar form: a complex series of developments within the history of nation-states that will, for good internal (i.e., nationalist) reasons, produce a kind of international political structure that will stand independent by of the nation-state. When this happens – if indeed it is it not happening already – there will be works in political philosophy that can convince us of the moral legitimacy of this new kind of political structure, and after that, works in the history of philosophy that show us how the focus of liberal theory was able to shift from a nationalist to an internationalist perspective. It is my view that these works, like Kant's and like the sort of philosophical history provided by J. B. Schneewind, will be of historical and philosophical interest long after the urgent naturalizing of Hobbes and his contemporary successors has come to seem anything but urgent.

Notes

1. J. B. Schneewind, *The Invention of Autonomy* (Cambridge University Press, 1998), pp. 533–54. Hereafter simply IA.
2. "According to what I shall call the Socrates story of the history of moral philosophy, the situation we are in is as follows. Although we have not reached agreement about the basis of morality, we know the tasks that we moral philosophers should undertake. We are trying to answer the question Socrates raised: how to live. People have always had opinions on the matter, but it is very hard to get an indubitable answer based on an undeniable foundation." Schneewind, IA, pp. 535–6.
3. Schneewind, IA, p. 537.
4. Schneewind, IA, pp. 537–40.
5. Schneewind, IA, pp. 3–13 and 548–50.
6. Schneewind, IA, p. 536.
7. After his initial derivation of the categorical imperative in the first chapter of the *Groundwork*, Kant writes: "In studying the moral knowledge of ordinary human reason we have now arrived at its first principle. This principle it admittedly does not conceive thus abstractly in its universal form; but it does always have it actually before its eyes and does use it as a norm of judgement." Kant, *Groundwork of the Metaphysic of Morals*, trans. H. J. Paton (Harper & Row, 1964), pp. 403–4. (All page references to Kant refer to the edition of the Prussian Academy.) The key point here is that Kant holds not only that ordinary agents are already aware of the categorical imperative, but also that they already use it to reason morally. In that sense, moral philosophy can do little to improve their moral reasoning.
8. In *Religion Within the Limits of Reason Alone*, Kant stresses that our immoral actions are not the result of our natural inclinations, but of our willingness to place them above the commands of duty. Evil is thus an act of the will, not simply the result of the power of inclination. But since Kant identifies the will with practical reason (G 412), there is no way to explain how we can truly will the bad. We cannot rationally choose to follow our inclinations over the commands of duty. In that sense, all we can say about our immoral actions is: somehow we let our inclinations win out. Our rationality was too weak, but at the same time, we know it was not really too weak: to say that we were wrong is to know we could do what we ought to have done. Evil can be explained empirically, but not morally or rationally. See Christine Korsgaard, "Morality as Freedom," in *Creating the Kingdom of Ends* (Cambridge University Press, 1996), pp. 171–3.
9. After deriving the categorical imperative and locating it in ordinary human reason, Kant immediately identifies the inclinations as the chief obstacle to

morally good conduct (Kant, *Groundwork*, 405). He then goes on to explain that philosophical support is required, because under the influence of inclination, we are disposed to "quibble" with the strict laws of duty and to prefer more general accounts of morality that will allow us some exceptions in the interest of inclination. We thus need a philosophical defense of the strict, purely rational principle of duty.

But this passage raises a good many questions, especially because Kant also tells us here that a loose, inclination-based account of morality is one that "even ordinary human reason is unable to approve." For ordinary agents, then, the situation is this: they are at least partially motivated to prefer a different moral theory, but they also know already that this preference is itself morally wrong. It is merely their weakness that leads them to consider an alternate account. How, then, can philosophy be of any help? We cannot say that philosophy should provide a rational conviction, because ordinary agents already *have* the relevant rational conviction, and simply stray from it in the interests of inclination. Philosophy, or the lack of it, is not the problem here. To show that philosophy is relevant, Kant must hold not just that we have a (natural, nonrational) disposition to quibble with morality, but also that a certain (bad) sort of philosophy can do something, or has done something, to help us in our quibbling, and thus to weaken our original rational conviction. So we now need to know what sorts of problems philosophy can raise for morality, but this Kant does not explain in the passage at 405. Both the theoretical worries I discuss next, and the practical worries I try to emphasize later on should be seen as accounts of what philosophy (as opposed simply to inclination) can do to threaten morality.

10. Kant, *Critique of Practical Reason*, trans. L. W. Beck (Macmillan, 1993), 15–16.
11. Christine Korsgaard, *The Sources of Normativity* (Cambridge University Press, 1996); and Michael Smith, *The Moral Problem* (Blackwell, 1995).
12. Hobbes, *Leviathan*, ed. E. Curley (Hackett, 1994), Introduction. That human beings and their commonwealths can be understood mechanically is simply asserted by Hobbes: "What is the *heart*, but a *spring* and the *nerves*, but so many *strings*, and the *joints*, but so many *wheels*, giving motion to the whole body . . . a COMMONWEALTH, or STATE (in Latin CIVITAS), which is but an artificial man, for whose protection and defense it was intended; and in which the *sovereignty* is an artificial soul, as giving life and motion to the whole body" (Introduction, p. 3). Hobbes's project is not to argue for a mechanistic account of human beings and their commonwealths, but only to supply and fill in the details of such an account. The only sense in which his book can be considered an argument for mechanism is as a reply to those who would suggest that a mechanistic account of these phenomena cannot be given.
13. Hobbes, *Leviathan*, Chapter 6, pp. 28–9.
14. Hobbes, *Leviathan*, Chapters 13–14. I say that Hobbes's moral principles, the laws of nature, are pseudo-objective because they depend on the subjective desires of agents and their subjective attitudes toward one another. Were it not that we fear our own death and that we see other human beings as possible causes of death, we would not have moral obligations to others (or at least certainly not to all others). Moral claims are thus not objective in the

sense that they exist independently of our minds in the ways that physical objects do. And although Hobbes calls them "theorems of reason" (p. 100), the laws of nature lack the credentials for principles of reason that Hobbes sets out in his account of rationality in Chapter 5. There reason is defined as the "addition and subtraction of names," the reflection on the logical relations between the words or concepts we human beings have invented to describe physical objects. In this sense "No squares are round" could be a theorem of reason, and so can "No sovereign can be unjust," because to be unjust for Hobbes is to break a contract, and there can be no contract with the sovereign. But our obligation to keep our contract does not depend just on the concept of a contract; it requires additional beliefs and desires. In fact we are *not* obliged to keep our contract if we have any reasonable suspicion that others will not keep theirs. In this sense Hobbes agrees with the Humean claim that principles of reason are not in themselves motivating.

15. Allan Gibbard, *Wise Choices, Apt Feelings: A Theory of Normative Judgment* (Harvard University Press, 1990); Simon Blackburn, *Ruling Passions: A Theory of Practical Reasoning* (Oxford University Press, 1998).
16. Schneewind, IA, pp. 6–8.
17. See Schneewind, IA, pp. 83 n.3 and 355.
18. Schneewind, IA, p. 5.
19. Kant, *Critique of Practical Reason*, 107–8.
20. See, for instance, Kant, *Groundwork*, 407.
21. I argue more fully for this view in my "How Kantian Is Constructivism?," *Kant-Studien* 90(4), 1999, pp. 385–409 (see especially pp. 402–3), and at greater length in a still unpublished paper, "Rawlsian Stability and Kantian Teleology." The account I give is my contribution to a debate about the derivation of the categorical imperative, a debate that centers on the question: can Kant legitimately derive the formula of universal law (and only the formula of universal law) from one or more of his formal starting points (the pure motive of duty, the concept of a categorical imperative or practical law, or the idea of a free will)? For the skeptical view, see Allan Wood, "Kant on the Rationality of Morals," *Proceedings of the Ottawa Congress on Kant in the Anglo-American and Continental Traditions* (University of Ottawa Press, 1976) and *Hegel's Ethical Theory* (Cambridge University Press, 1990), pp. 361–7. For a positive defense of Kant, see Henry Allison, "On a Presumed Gap in the Derivation of the Categorical Imperative," *Philosophical Topics* 19:(1), 1991, pp. 1–15; Allison, "Kant on Freedom: A Reply to My Critics," *Inquiry* 36 (1995), pp. 443–64; and Allison, *Kant's Theory of Freedom* (Cambridge University Press, 1990), pp. 205–6. For a general discussion of the debate and a quite different defense of Kant's derivation, see Samuel J. Kerstein, *Kant's Search for the Supreme Principle of Morality* (Cambridge University Press, 2002).

    Roughly, Allison is defending the claim that the formula of universal law is the unique principle of a purely rational will, while Wood, defending Hegel's criticism that Kant's starting point is empty, denies this claim. My own view is that Wood is right if the debate is framed in this way. But we can nonetheless make sense of Kant's view if we see the formula of universal law not as the unique principle of a purely rational agent (as Allison would have it), but as the unique practical expression of an agent who believes that *there ought to be* a principle of pure practical reason.

22. Kant's derivations of the categorical imperative, then, do not establish that this principle is a fully justified principle of practical reason, but that it is the only principle that could serve us as such a principle. That this is his argument is evident in the disjunctive way he concludes his derivation in the first chapter of the *Groundwork*: "Here bare conformity to universal law as such (without having as its base any law prescribing particular actions) is what serves the will, and what must so serve it if duty is not to be everywhere an empty delusion and a chimerical concept" (402).

23. See Andrews Reath, "Two Conceptions of the Highest Good in Kant," *Journal of the History of Philosophy* 26(4), 1988, pp. 593–619. Reath defends the secular/political conception against the religious conception. For another account along these lines, see Thomas Pogge, "Kant on Ends and the Meaning of Life," in *Reclaiming the History of Ethics: Essays for John Rawls* (Cambridge University Press, 1997). For a defense of the religious conception, see Stephen Engstrom, "The Concept of the Highest Good in Kant's Moral Theory," *Philosophy and Phenomenological Research* 52(4), 1992, pp. 747–80.

24. In what follows, I draw on the account of Kantian political agency developed in my "The Fact of Politics: History and Teleology in Kant," *European Journal of Philosophy* 2(1), 1994, pp. 22–40; "Formal Liberalism and the Justice of Publicity," *Proceedings of the Eighth International Kant Congress*, Volume II, 1995, pp. 61–9; and "Enlightenment and Agency in Kant," *Proceedings of the Ninth International Kant Congress*, Volume IV, 2001, pp. 28–34.

25. Kant, *Critique of Practical Reason*, 146–8, and "Speculative Beginning of Human History," in *Perpetual Peace and Other Essays*, ed. and trans. T. Humphrey (Hackett, 1983), especially 114–15.

26. Kant, "An Old Question Raised Again: Is the Human Race Constantly Progressing?," in *The Conflict of the Faculties*, ed. and trans. M. Gregor (University of Nebraska Press, 1992).

27. I discuss this further in "How Kantian Is Constructivism?"

28. This kind of fantasy is not something that was foisted upon Marx by his followers or interpreters: the idea that humanity has become a slave to economic and technological forces, and now needs to achieve a kind of total mastery of them, is one that is already central to the early, "humanist" Marx. See, for instance, the conclusion of Part One of *The German Ideology*, ed. C. J. Arthur (International Publishers, 1988), especially pp. 91–5.

7

What Is Disorientation in Thinking?

Natalie Brender

In the final chapters of *The Invention of Autonomy*, J. B. Schneewind argues for a twofold interpretive approach to Kant's philosophical project. Firstly, he holds, we must grasp Kant's understanding of himself as a philosopher seeking to illuminate eternal moral truths and thereby to advance humanity's progress toward rationality and enlightenment. Yet even as we pursue this 'internalist' insight into Kant's philosophical presuppositions and intentions, we cannot expect to share them; for pace Kant, there are no historically and culturally timeless human truths susceptible to philosophical articulation. Because our self-understanding is always bound up with the discourse of particular cultures, any conceptualization of morality is tied to the historical and cultural context of its articulation. As Schneewind puts it, in "moral, political, and religious aspects of life. . . . [W]e can only be what we can think and say we are."[1]

If an extrahistorical and extracultural 'view from nowhere' is impossible, then Kant's understanding of moral philosophy and its development cannot be correct. Instead, according to Schneewind, philosophy should be regarded both as a cultural product and as one of the constitutive sources of a culture's conceptual vocabulary and self-understanding. To study the philosophy of a particular period with due attention to its sociohistorical context is to learn what cultural agendas it reflects and promotes. This approach sees a philosopher's work as applying conceptual reformulations to social, political and religious problems of his or her era. Since Kant must be understood through this historicist lens, Schneewind urges that we study the practical issues Kant addresses, the inherited conceptual vocabularies he draws on and the innovations he makes in doing so.

The value of studying the history of moral philosophy through this paradigm, Schneewind holds, is that by gaining insight into the historical formation of Kant's thought, we thereby come to understand how the terrain of modern Western morality took the shape it did. Central to this present-day terrain is the Kantian notion of persons as self-governing moral agents, a concept that in myriad ways pervades formal and informal relationships. Schneewind's point is that insight into the reasons why a Kantian paradigm of moral selfhood has resonated so powerfully – both in its immediate historical context and subsequently – reveals "how we came to a distinctively modern way of understanding ourselves as moral agents."[2] The worth of this much-disputed legacy can be assessed only through a philosophical critique engaged with past and present cultural realities. Since moral philosophy is an enterprise of practical problem solving, it is possible that Kant's conceptual solutions to the problems of his own age could turn out to be useful for current efforts to address our own pressing social problems and agendas. Just as Kant adapted inherited concepts and vocabularies, by drawing on his thought we can hope to "reformulate [our] problems in more manageable ways."[3] *The Invention of Autonomy* concludes with Schneewind's invocation of this potential:

Although we may hold that our time presents its own problems to moral philos-ophy, we may also think that the answers Kant worked out for his problems are useful in coping with ours. And if we share his passionate conviction concerning the equal moral capacity of all normal human beings and their equal dignity, we may well think that something like his basic moral principle is more likely to yield an adequate solution to our problems than any other principle yet invented.[4]

If Kant's moral philosophy offers conceptual resources to us in virtue of what we still share with him, just what are these problems and premises that we share? Presumably Schneewind takes them to include what he identifies as central Kantian assumptions about the human condition: the fact of unsocial sociability, the existence of an irreducible plurality of creeds and religions, the variability in individuals' conceptions of hap-piness, and the resulting need to define socially acknowledged norms of conduct capable of fostering peaceful and just coexistence.[5] Exactly which conceptual commitments this agenda presupposes, however, is not settled. After two centuries in which Kant's theory has permeated Western thought, it may well be unnecessary to advance the philosophical thesis of contracausal autonomy in order to buttress a "passionate conviction" of equal human moral capacity and worth; for as Schneewind notes, these notions "have come to be widely accepted – so widely that most moral

philosophy now starts by assuming them."[6] Yet there are other conceptual resources in Kant's thought, Schneewind presumes, that we can still
usefully draw on in our engagement with current practical issues.

As a sympathizer with Schneewind's vision of moral philosophy, I shall
try in what follows to develop his suggestion that Kant be looked to as a
resource for contemporary thought. The terrain I shall explore concerns
the difficulties agents encounter in pursuing lofty moral ideals in a world
that is grossly discordant with the one they seek to realize. A useful approach to this terrain can be found in Kant's conceptually linked notions
of practical orientation in thinking, moral belief and historical teleology.
After examining what Kant takes practical orientation to be, I shall consider some other contexts in which he identifies potential impasses of
moral agency that can be understood as modes of *disorientation* in practical thought. These contexts, I shall argue, suggest a vision of Kantian
moral agency that sees agents' moral efforts as being sustained partially
through interpretations of experience that bridge the gulf between ideals
and reality. I will conclude by noting some current challenges of practical
reflection in which the threat of disorientation may be particularly acute,
and particularly in need of special interpretive modes of response.

1. About Ideals

Reflection on moral ideals can become caught up in a dialectic of inspira-
tional and deflationary 'moments.' As Mary Midgley has remarked, some
people regard far-reaching ideals as 'humbug' or mere fantasy, believing
that their emptiness is exposed by the vast scope and difficulty of the
changes they propose. Midgeley retorts to this charge by noting what she
takes to be self-evident:

> The whole point of having ideals at all is to criticise current practice.... Ideals,
> then, do not become inert or unreal merely because they are far above us or
> ahead of us and are not likely to be reached in our time. That is their nature.
> They exercise their pull all the time by indicating a direction.[7]

Those sympathetic with this affirmation that ideals have a legitimate role
in guiding practice might nonetheless find Midgeley's remarks to misrep-
resent lived experience. Her declaration that ideals "exercise their pull
all the time" implies that this pull is a phenomenologically consistent
reality as well as a normative claim. Yet for many persons who feel the
demands of moral ideals in daily life, ideals sometimes seem remote and
abstract even to the point of potential irrelevance. Living immersed in
immediate realities as we do, we can suffer from the sense that the ideals

we affirm are not quite as vivid or compelling as other empirical realities that inform our practical reflections.

It might be thought that Kant's rationalism would surely make him oblivious to the possibility of experientially based qualms about the relevance of ideals to lived practical reflection. After all, his theory holds that both subjective moral motivation and the objective content of morality – its formal rules as well as its substantive ideals – are grounded in pure practical reason alone. It is precisely because ideals are abstractions of pure reason that they "exercise their pull all the time," to echo Midgeley, and provide a steady motivational impetus amid the ambiguities and inadequacies of the empirical world. In light of this fact, Kant often asserts, examples or instantiations of realized ideals are relevant only for educating and exercising moral judgment.[8]

Yet notwithstanding these austerely rationalist strands of Kant's thought, in certain respects he intimates a more complex view of the relationship of ideals and observed reality within human moral agency. As recent scholarship has begun to recognize, Kant is concerned not just with the objective content and justification of morality, but also with the subjective conditions in which human beings can realize moral ideals in daily practice.[9] Under the latter heading fall the difficulties agents encounter in reconciling lofty abstract ideals with empirical realities of lived experience. As I shall aim to show in this essay, some of Kant's practical writings manifest an awareness that under certain circumstances, rational ideals could cease to seem relevant to the world we live in, and hence could cease to exercise their pull on us. In what follows, I explicate this dimension of his thought as a concern with the possibility of *disorientation* in moral thinking – that is, the possibility that we might lose our cognitive bearings if we do not perceive a sufficient degree of coherence between the deliverances of experience and those of pure reason. We can fail to grasp how the moral ideal of the highest good could be realizable in the world as we know it. We can be so struck with evidence of human viciousness that we have difficulty in affirming humanity's a priori status as a morally capable and worthy species. We can fail to find sufficient resonance between the abstractions of morality and the rich concreteness of religious experience. And we can fail to see how bringing our moral efforts to bear on present conditions could have any effective long-term role in bringing about a peaceful and just world. Kant responds to these all-too-human confusions by addressing agents' need to find coherence between reason and experience. His doctrine of rational faith legitimizes the introduction of theistic belief into the cognitive framework of morality for the sake of producing this coherence. Parallel considerations shape his discussions of the role of examples in moral life, of the rational interpretation of religious scripture and of the necessity of belief in historical progress. In each of these contexts, Kant holds that agents must engage in interpretations of lived experience in order to demonstrate that rationally affirmed ideals are indeed relevant to the actual human world.

2. Kant's Concern with Disorientation

A narrowly rationalist 'official' construal of Kant's practical philosophy would likely place the fact of reason at the front and center of human moral consciousness. According to the fact of reason, agents are always conscious of being obligated to act in ways that are formally correct and embody substantive moral ends. In knowing this, they know that they can do as they ought; and along with this knowledge comes the rationally produced feeling of respect that gives motivation for moral willing. What makes a philosophical critique of practical reason necessary is not any insufficiency in human moral rationality per se, but the tendency of human reasoning to be corrupted by the passion and self-interest that come with our embodied nature.

The fact of reason also reveals the substantive obligation we have to promote ends such as a just and peaceful world. Yet here is where experiential complications begin: for while reason reveals the certainty of our own autonomy to us, it does not directly guarantee that the empirical world is amenable to the moral transformation we must attempt to realize. This lacuna opens up a potential weakness in the cognitive framework of a Kantian agent's practical reflection. Even an agent who is perfectly virtuous (in the sense of subordinating inclination to reason) could falter in her moral efforts if she came to doubt that substantive moral ends could actually be realized. The possibility of such a breakdown in moral agency is a logical corollary of Kant's theory of rationality, which holds that willing presupposes an agent's belief in the possibility of accomplishing what she proposes to do. If she does not believe that her efforts can produce a given change in world, she cannot coherently undertake the effort to do so. On such logic, an agent who disbelieves the possibility of attaining moral ends thereby rejects the coherence of morality itself. The consequent possibility of despairing quietude has been noted by Onora O'Neill:

Kant does not, of course, claim that despair is impossible. His claim is conditional: commitment to action and morality, that is, commitment to acting morally within a causally ordered world, demands that we hope that our commitments are to some extent realisable in that world. He aims to show not simply that lack of hope is psychologically hard, but that it is incoherent unless action and morality too are given up.[10]

Given these factors, a crucial aspect of Kantian moral agency hence consists in what O'Neill calls the "bare structure of hope": "[W]e must postulate, assume, hope for the possibility of inserting the moral intention into the world."[11]

Kant articulates the theme of necessary hope most explicitly in the essay "What Is Orientation in Thinking?," arguing that human agents have a need "to give objective reality" to the highest good. Only in affirming the objective reality of this moral end can we "prevent it, along with morality, from being taken merely as a mere ideal, as it would be if that whose idea inseparably accompanies morality should not exist anywhere" (WOT 139). Kant's point is that we must be able to affirm that the moral aims we undertake could come to be objective realities in the world. Any aim that does not meet this criterion becomes reduced to the status of a "mere ideal." If such a fate were to befall one of the moral ideals that reason itself presents as an intrinsic part of our moral obligations, rational consistency would lead to the absolute rejection of moral obligation. To offset this calamity, we must regard matters in a way that preserves the objective reality of moral ideals – which is to say, we must have rational hope.

Kant describes rational hope as a state in which an agent is *oriented in practical thought*. Drawing on the metaphor of navigation, he notes that we are able to use the stars in making objective judgements about our location by virtue of the fact that we make an inner subjective differentiation between right and left. Similarly, we join this inner subjective feeling with external reference points in order to orient ourselves while navigating through a familiar room or neighbourhood in the dark. Kant extends the trope to explain and justify our reliance on subjective maxims of moral belief as a necessary precondition of making objective moral principles into guides for practical judgement. The metaphor of orientation in thinking applies only to a situation in which "it is not arbitrary whether or not one will judge determinately, where there is some actual *need* – and moreover one attaching to reason in itself – which makes it necessary to judge, and yet we are limited by a lack of knowledge in respect of factors which are necessary for the judgment" (WOT 136). Such needs inherently belong to moral reflection, the only sphere of rationality that imposes unconditional obligations of judgement.

In "What Is Orientation in Thinking?," Kant applies the notion of orientation to a single aspect of moral consciousness: namely, the need for human practical rationality to postulate God's existence. Only by believing in an omnipotent, just and benevolent deity can we conceive of the realization of the highest good (i.e., a world in which happiness is proportioned to virtue). Since we are morally obligated to promote the highest good, we must be able to find this idea plausible or else consign morality in toto to incoherence and irrelevance. In affirming God's existence, we adopt a belief that differs from knowledge in lacking objective sufficiency, but one that nonetheless is found by us to be perfectly certain and subjectively sufficient. Its certainty comes from the awareness (established in the first *Critique*) that since nothing could ever disprove the existence of God, our rationally necessary belief will always be consistent with objective fact and hence unalterable.

Kant also stresses the importance of adding a supplement of rational belief to the immediately given rational fact of moral obligation. An agent who pridefully refuses to adopt rational belief on the grounds of its objective insufficiency risks the utter collapse of her practical rationality:

> Now the maxim of reason's independence of its *own need* (of doing without rational faith) is *unbelief*. This is . . . a precarious state of the human mind, which first takes from moral laws all their force as incentives to the heart, and over time all their authority, and occasions the way of thinking one calls *libertinism*, i.e. the principle of recognizing no duty at all. (WOT 146)

Kant's concern with libertinism tacitly implies that even morally committed agents could lose their orientation in thinking. While human reason rightly prizes its capacity for autonomous thought, it runs the risk of misusing this freedom through "a presumptuous trust in the independence of its faculties from all limitations, leading to a persuasion of the sole authority of speculative reason which assumes nothing except what it can justify by *objective* grounds and dogmatic conviction; everything else it boldly repudiates" (WOT 146). Our need to draw on the postulate of rational belief amounts to a chastening admission that we are *finite* rational beings who must use our rational faculties in awareness of the constraints that finitude imposes on our thought. Among these constraints is the fact that as we are embodied and needy beings, our desire for happiness inexorably gives rise to the moral idea of the highest good. We *must* believe that virtue ought to be (and eventually will be) linked to proportionate happiness; to suppose that we can do without this ideal is to misunderstand our own nature. Kant holds that if we refuse to affirm the postulate of rational belief giving this ideal its reality, we undermine the entire motivational and cognitive scheme of morality itself. Disoriented in thought, we will have entirely lost our bearings as autonomous agents in the world.

The argument of "What Is Orientation in Thinking?" might initially seem to be fatally flawed in virtue of its reliance on an implausible anthropological premise. This premise, in Schneewind's words, is that morality "make[s] sense for free and intelligent but needy and dependent creatures" only insofar as we consider the exercise of freedom in morality to be coordinated with the fulfillment of our needs.[12] We must believe in God's existence and providential ordering of the world because "our will to make personal sacrifices in order to act justly would be hampered if we could not think our desires would ultimately be satisfied."[13] Contemporary readers, however, will likely concur with Onora O'Neill's denial "that we *must* take it that a *complete* coordination of happiness and virtue in each of us is in the cards."[14] To reject this premise is also to dismiss Kant's claim that reason's striving for totality necessarily posits the idea of a highest good consisting in the complete coordination of happiness and virtue. On a modified view of practical rationality, it does not turn out to be a logical or psychological precondition that we affirm the possibility of complete success in order to sustain moral effort. Such grounds lead O'Neill to pose a revisionist question: "[w]hy should action not posit or hope for the possibility of moral progress, but make no assumptions about the possibility of achieving natural and moral perfection?"[15] It seems plausible that human beings can – some of us and some of the time, anyhow – be committed to realizing moral ideals even when doing so bears no conceivable causal relationship to future happiness. A sense of the worth of human beings, or a sense of one's own identity as a rational agent, might suffice to motivate moral agency even at the sacrifice of other sources of satisfaction.[16]

Insofar as this revision of Kant's anthropology is compelling, no grounds remain for endorsing his argument that theistic belief is a necessary dimension of all agents' practical orientation. To reject the foundational anthropological premise of "What Is Orientation in Thinking?" is thus to empty out all of the substantive content from the notion of practical orientation as described in the essay. If this were all Kant had to say about the concept, it would be rendered a superfluous part of his doctrine; human agents would have no need for any subjective 'supplement' to the objectively valid imperatives and incentives of pure reason. The danger of libertine atheism having been rendered harmless, the only impediment to moral agency would be the workings of self-interest.

However, matters look quite different in light of other writings in which Kant suggests further substantive dimensions to the notion of practical orientation. An examination of these writings reveals a strand of his thought that is both underappreciated in its own right and of considerable relevance for contemporary thinking about challenges of moral and political agency.

3. Further Problems of Disorientation

Even where Kant does not explicitly invoke the concept of orientation, the importance of basing thought on rationally sound principles of judgement is a ubiquitous theme in his later writings.[17] Many of his texts manifest a concern with ways in which practical rationality can go astray, or become disoriented, in the face of the complexity of actual human thought. The potential for disorientation arises at moments of reflection in which agents can become overwhelmed by the gulf between the morally corrupt world we know through experience and the morally perfected world we are obligated to pursue. At many times we face enormous cognitive challenges in trying to understand how one world can become, or have demands made on it by, the other; and at such junctures we stand in danger of finding the whole framework conceptually incoherent. Given our all-too-human immersion in the empirical world, it can seem to us that morality's demands cannot be realizable in the world as we know it, and hence that moral obligations themselves are inapplicable to us. To follow out this train of thought is to fall into a radical disorientation of practical reasoning. In highlighting contexts in which such a danger could arise, Kant implicitly appeals to the premise that sound moral reflection presupposes the existence of a coherent conceptual framework of knowledge and belief. From this perspective, the condition of practical orientation is revealed to be contingent and fragile. It hence becomes crucial for him to identify which aspects of practical reflection render agents susceptible to disorientation, and to indicate what can be done to offset the danger. I shall illustrate this dimension of Kant's thought by highlighting passages from three texts in which Kant raises the spectre of potential disorientation. These passages occur in Part II of the *Groundwork of the Metaphysics of Morals*; in the discussion of scriptural interpretation from *Religion Within the Limits of Reason Alone*; and in the essay "An Old Question Raised Again." Each passage manifests Kant's concern that practical thought can become disoriented in the face of the gulf between moral ideals and the observed realities of the human world. In each case, he responds by highlighting a cognitive 'supplement' that consists in an interpretive strategy that reaffirms a cognitive premise implicitly in doubt. These supplements enable agents to sustain their adherence to moral ideals and moral obligations amid the challenges of daily practice. The problem Kant tackles in these passages is essentially the same one that produces his argument for rational faith in "What Is Orientation in Thinking?" What differs are the dimensions of the problem Kant perceives and the kinds of solutions he offers.

The Role of Examples

In Part II of the *Groundwork* Kant explains why it is so important that agents grasp the purely a priori grounding of morality. As he notes, any "cool observer" of society will "become doubtful at certain moments (especially with increasing years, when experience has made one's judgement partly more shrewd and partly more acute in observation) whether any true virtue is to be found in the world" (G 407). Worldly experience often fuels a cynical suspicion that all appearances of virtue mask vice, and that true inner virtue is nonexistent among corrupt human beings. In such moments of cynical doubt, Kant insists, we must recall a crucial point: "[A]ctions of which the world has perhaps so far given no example, and whose very practicability might be very much doubted by one who bases everything on experience, are still inflexibly commanded by reason" (G 408). Here Kant affirms that morality is a purely a priori matter that cannot be theoretically derived from or located in particular instances of human action. It is, he asserts, "absolutely impossible by means of experience to make out with complete certainty a single case in which the maxim of an action otherwise in conformity with duty rested simply on moral grounds" (G 407). While an example of outwardly virtuous conduct suggests that its motivation *may* have been moral, no example can *prove* the reality of moral motivation in human willing. Consequently, it is of paramount importance to remember that examples are irrelevant to the possibility of human virtue and the reality of moral obligation.

It is no small matter for Kant to concede that cool observation of human affairs is liable to instill doubts about the reality of human virtue. Were such doubts to prevail, they would render the fulfillment of moral obligation logically impossible; morality itself would then appear to have no legitimate claim. What worries Kant more generally is an implicit sense that certain situations arise in which it seems to us that a crucial premise of morality lacks adequate justification, and in which practical orientation can be maintained only if some cognitive underpinning is found for the premise in question. In "What Is Orientation in Thinking?," where the premise at issue is the moral ideal of the highest good, cognitive reinforcement comes from the subjective affirmation of God's existence. In the preceding passage from the *Groundwork*, where the premise at issue is the possibility of moral willing, Kant give austere advice to a doubt-stricken observer of dismal worldly realities: when experience gives rise to doubt, turn away from observations and reflect on the abstractions of a priori reason.

In light of this austere and doctrinally orthodox directive for assuaging doubt, it is striking that one page later in the *Groundwork* Kant pronounces rather differently on the relevance of examples to moral agency: "[E]xamples serve only for encouragement, that is, *they put beyond doubt the practicability of what the law commands* [*sie setzen die Thunlichkeit dessen, was das Gesetz gebietet, außer Zwietel*] and make intuitive what the practical rule expresses more generally" (G 409; my emphasis). Here Kant asserts that observed instances of virtuous action can and should serve to settle doubts about the practicability of moral willing, and thereby to confirm the relevance of moral law to human agents. This claim obviously stands in tension with the doctrine that examples of outward virtue cannot demonstrate the possibility of moral willing. In asserting now that examples avert doubt by establishing the "practicability" of moral imperatives, Kant cannot mean that they show the mere possibility of acting in outward accordance with morality; after all, the most radical doubt questions not the degree of virtue in society but rather suspects that behind *all* apparent virtue lurks the motive of self-love. In the face of this latter doubt, any appeal to examples would seem utterly beside the point. What can Kant mean then in assigning the role to examples that he does?

Progress in answering this question can be made by focusing more closely on the need that Kant takes examples to satisfy. Notwithstanding his 'official' doctrine of a priori moral knowledge, he takes it to be obviously true that experience does give rise to doubts about the practicability of moral willing. (Otherwise, of course, we would not stand in need of reassurance on this score.) That experience inclines us to doubt our moral capacities is not a wholly surprising supposition for Kant to make, given his presumption (in the *Groundwork* and elsewhere) that we all recognize our failures and chalk these up to the depths of self-love. He expects that observation as well as introspection will lead us to doubt sometimes whether any other motive ever really moves us. According to his 'official' doctrine, such doubts are always already settled by the a priori assurance of 'ought implies can': since we know that we are obligated to will morally, we know we can do so. Yet Kant tacitly recognizes that a priori abstractions do not, in fact, suffice to eliminate experientially founded doubt about the possibility of human virtue. When doubt arises, it needs to be allayed by some observationally founded assurance that human beings do actually act out of moral motives. Kant hence admits that examples are indeed effective in showing that moral willing is a real possibility and a real obligation for a flawed species such as ours. At moments of impending disorientation, examples of virtue play an indispensable supplementary role in allowing agents to regain their bearings in practical thought.[18]

The suggestion that examples of virtue play a crucial role in averting practical disorientation might seem to impugn the rational integrity of moral agency. Within the rigorous structure of practical reason, how could Kant take it to be rational for an agent to find that an observed action confirms the reality of human moral willing? Presumably, he would not commend the usefulness of examples if their effectiveness came at the cost of deceiving or subverting reflective judgement. So what confers rational legitimacy on the apparently dubious process of empirical inference that takes place in finding the reality of moral willing to be demonstrated by an example? An understanding of why Kant considers it rationally legitimate to offset doubt with examples can be gleaned from some passages in the *Religion Within the Boundaries of Mere Reason.* As he grapples in this text also with potential threats of disorientation, Kant expands on the *Groundwork*'s suggestion that distinctive features of human practical rationality give rise to a need for experiential reinforcements of a priori moral doctrine. The *Religion*'s innovative conceptual move consists in using the notion of authentic interpretation to explain how these reinforcements can be secured without violating rational integrity.

Human Nature and Textual Interpretation

In Book Three of the *Religion,* Kant considers the possibility of reconciling the existence of diverse historically founded religions with the purely rational moral faith that is the truth of religion per se. Only a purely rational religion can command the universal belief requisite to a cosmopolitan ethical community, he argues, since every historically revealed religion, "based merely on facts, can extend its influence no further than the tidings relevant to a judgment on its credibility can reach" (R 103). Yet even as he asserts the supremacy of rational faith, Kant concedes that "*due to a peculiar weakness of human nature,* pure faith can never be relied on as much as it deserves, that is, [enough] to found a Church on it alone"

(R 103; my emphasis). The "peculiar weakness of human nature" he refers to is a requirement of human moral orientation: in virtue of our reliance on experience as a touchstone of rational reflection, human beings become disoriented in thought in the absence of empirically observed reference points that serve to corroborate and reinforce the edifice of pure reason. This idea is reiterated in Kant's remark that "because of the natural need of all human beings to demand for even the highest concepts and grounds of reason something that *the senses can hold on to,* some confirmation from experience or the like, . . . some historical ecclesiastical faith or other, usually already at hand, must be used" (R 109). Although adherence to these particular religions detracts from the universality of rational belief, human nature's need for experiential supports produces our dependence on the sensibly tangible texts and authorities of historically revealed religions.

Together these two passages constitute Kant's most explicit acknowledgement of the difficulty human agents face in sustaining their practical orientation through pure reason alone. Tacitly, at least, he sees human rationality as characterized by a thoroughgoing reliance on the empirical sphere as well as the a priori. While a priori concepts and principles provide the normative foundation for practical reasoning, human nature is such that the authority and coherence of these principles are endangered unless they receive some element of experientially derived corroboration. Securing a sensibly tenable supplement to pure reason is crucial for preventing disorientation in practical thought.

It might seem that the interpretive maneuvers enabling agents to find reassurance in empirical signs are highly dubious in terms of their rational integrity. Kant shows his own awareness of this problem in a discussion of religious hermeneutics, where he explains how interpretation can legitimately secure experiential supplements for moral orientation. Having just argued that the revealed faith of Christianity is required to inculcate an ethos of universal rational community, he states that such revealed religion must be shown to be consistent with "the universal practical rules of a pure religion of reason" (R 110). Kant admits that it is a delicate enterprise to render the empirical data of revelation consistent with a priori rational principle. Often it may happen that when religious scripture is given a rational interpretation,

[t]his interpretation may often appear to us as forced, in view of the text (of the revelation), and be often forced in fact; yet, if the text can at all bear it, it must be preferred to a literal interpretation that either contains absolutely nothing for morality, or even works counter to its incentives. (R 110)

Here Kant carefully frames matters so as to convey that no abuse of rationality is involved in the a priori (or 'authentic')[19] interpretation of Scripture. He endorses a strikingly low standard of exegetical plausibility: the morally salutary interpretation need only be a rationally *possible* one (even if not the most plausible) in order to be legitimate (R 111). As long as the slightest bit of casuistic leeway exists, we are not guilty of foisting a false reading on Scripture.[20] What holds here for the propagation of rational faith also holds more generally for the operations through which examples and the particulars of revealed religion are used for orienting practical thought. The success of these efforts depends on an interpretation – and often an admittedly forced one – of what is given in experience. If the world is a text (as the trope of an earlier age had it), we must affirm a construal of it that satisfies the practical needs of human rationality. As seen earlier, in the *Groundwork* Kant holds that doubts about the possibility of moral motivation require us to seek encouragement through strategic interpretation of examples, inferring the presence of genuine virtue where such an inference is consistent with empirical fact. Similarly, in the *Religion* he holds that in order for the revealed faith of Christianity to be an effective vehicle for the propagation of universal rational faith, its Scriptures may be given interpretations that will serve this purpose. Although our peculiarly human craving for experiential reference points is a weakness, it is not one that can be overcome. Accommodating this dimension of human rationality mandates the interpretation of experience in ways that support the cognitive framework of moral agency.

The sections of the *Religion* just discussed amount to the posing and solution of a problem seen previously in the *Groundwork*'s treatment of examples. The problem is that notwithstanding our status as rational beings capable of intuiting a priori principle, we are also human beings whose reflective judgements look to the realm of experience for corroboration of – or at least assurance of compatibility with – the principles of pure practical reason. When we cannot find such experiential touchstones, our affirmation of principle becomes attenuated or even wholly impossible. The solution, then, is to embrace a notion of authentic, rationally legitimate interpretation that enables us to discover in experience the kinds of meanings that sustain a coherent practical outlook. In the *Religion*, Kant posits that these meanings are to be found in authentic interpretations of religious texts and in the tangible particulars of historically revealed religious traditions. As the next section of the essay shows, some of Kant's later writings on history and politics suggest that similar problems in these spheres give rise to parallel solutions.

Historical Example and Political Orientation

The potential for another kind of practical disorientation motivates Kant's late essay "An Old Question Raised Again: Is the Human Race Constantly Progressing?" Starting with its opening query, "What do we *want* to know in this matter?" (OQ 79), the essay explores the notion that requirements of moral agency produce a rational need to affirm a progressive moral history of humanity. We cannot be indifferent to the question of progress, Kant argues, because the continuation of our own moral agency depends on our being able to understand our moral efforts as fitting meaningfully into a teleological narrative. Two premises about human rationality inform these claims. First, there is the fact of our substantive moral obligations: each agent is obligated to manifest respect for humanity by striving to realize a morally perfected world. Second, according to Kant's theory of rationality, an agent can adopt a particular practical aim only insofar as she can see that her striving could plausibly realize that aim. If an end were to seem impossible to realize, it could not rationally be adopted as an object of willing (nor, a fortiori, could it be morally obligatory to adopt it). Together, these two premises give rise to a question of acute interest to all agents: can we know that the moral progress we hold ourselves obligated to promote is indeed a rationally legitimate object of our practical efforts? Only if moral progress is possible can we take its promotion to be a genuine obligation. Were we to see human history as a story of decline or stasis, we would conclude that the moral obligation we thought we had dissolves into incoherence. The aim of "An Old Question Raised Again" is to supply rational grounds for affirming that human history is indeed a narrative of moral progress to which individuals' efforts can contribute.

Since experientially observed laws of nature cannot supply a predictive history of humanity's moral development, Kant argues that it must be possible to find one by appealing to the revelation of pure reason. If a coherent a priori narrative of humanity's future can be found, we can take this account to have predictive value insofar as "the diviner himself *makes* and contrives the events which he announces in advance" (OQ 80). Kant posits that there are three possible wholly a priori representations of human history, two of which are straightforwardly incoherent. The 'terroristic' hypothesis that humanity continually degenerates in its moral stature cannot be correct, since mounting evils would eventually lead the species "to destroy itself" (OQ 81). The progressive or 'eudaimonistic' hypothesis that humanity is constantly perfecting itself cannot be true either, since flawed human beings cannot rid themselves of evil (OQ 82). The third option is the 'abderitic' hypothesis that the human species undergoes cyclical advances and declines in its moral condition, producing stasis in the long run. There is no logical incoherence to be found in the notion that the mixed good and evil in the human species produces an eternal forward-and-backward motion; we could consistently prophesy this narrative in the expectation that through our own agency we would bring it about. As Kant notes, many people do find this narrative plausible.

Yet notwithstanding the logical coherence of the abderitic hypothesis, Kant declares it untenable from a practical point of view:

> It is a vain affair to have good so alternate with evil that the whole traffic of our species with itself on this globe would have to be considered as a mere farcical comedy, for this can endow our species with no greater value in the eyes of reason than that which other animal species possess, species which carry on this game with fewer costs and without expenditure of thought. (OQ 82)

Kant's claim here is that positing stasis in the human moral condition produces a condition of existential meaninglessness, in which all of the unique ills and burdens of human rationality lose their teleological justification. A related claim appears in his earlier essay "Conjectural Beginning of Human History," which asserts that human rationality is to be valued not for the happiness it brings us (for animals live more content lives governed by instinct), but because it allows us to make ourselves into autonomous moral beings. Only in virtue of this capacity for autonomy does humanity have value as an end in itself (CB109–15). The problem with the farcical narrative of abderitism is that it removes all purpose from human history and thereby strips humanity of its unique dignity as an end of nature. On such a view, spectators would reject the notion of having moral obligations toward humanity as such. Moreover, if we regarded the spectacle of history as meaningless stasis, we would conclude that no efforts we could undertake would produce genuine moral progress, and hence that we cannot after all be obligated to promote moral ends. Were the substantive ideals of morality to be dissolved in this way, the obligatory status of morality itself would be undermined. In the essay "Theory and Practice" Kant reiterates the danger of endorsing the abderitic hypothesis, asserting that anything other than a morally progressive view of humanity inevitably leads us to feel hatred or contempt for our species. Under these circumstances, even if we manage to refrain from active malevolence toward others, we will want "to have as little as possible to do with" them (TP 307). The interpretation we give human history as its spectators determines the possible form of our intervention in it as moral agents:

[I]t is a sight most unworthy... even of the most common but well-disposed human being to see the human race from period to period taking steps upward toward virtue and soon after falling back just as deeply into vice and misery. To watch this tragedy for a while might be moving and instructive, but the curtain must eventually fall. For in the long run it turns into a farce; and even if the actors do not tire of it, because they are fools, the spectator does, when one or another act gives him sufficient grounds for gathering that the never-ending piece is forever the same.[21] (TP 308)

Kant insists that we cannot, in all rational consistency, affirm the abderitic interpretation while remaining committed moral agents. The danger inherent in affirming abderitism is not allayed by the perfectly valid speculative thought that things might take a decisive turn for evil or good in the future. Even allowing such uncertainty, any spectator who views past history as *sub specie* farce will already have descended into ennui, apathy and contempt for humanity.

These recurrent arguments underline Kant's conviction that moral agency can be sustained only in conjunction with an agent's affirmation that progress is a reality in the human species. There is a clear need for practical reason to be able to affirm that this is so. Conversely, the fact that Kant sees the necessity for philosophical exploration of this topic indicates that he sees a real risk of practical disorientation in a failure to understand the importance of historical narrative and to respond appropriately. Yet in light of the moral untenability of the abderitic hypothesis and the incoherence of the other two modes of a priori prophecy, there still remains the problem of how the affirmation of humanity's moral progress – and thereby the stability of moral orientation – is to be secured. At this conceptual juncture, the argument of "An Old Question Raised Again" departs in two respects from wholly a priori modes of prophetic history. Firstly, Kant's declaration that an alternative standpoint on the question of moral progress must be found signals his abandonment of the question of moral progress in the *inner* perfection of individuals' wills, and his new turn to the question of moral progress in the *outer* perfection of political institutions. Correspondingly, he also abandons the quest for a purely rational basis of prophecy. The next section heading of his essay abruptly declares that "the prophetic history of the human race must be connected to some experience" (OQ 84); the experience then invoked is the famous example of spectators' sympathy with the French Revolution. Before turning to that issue, though, it is worth considering why the argument of "An Old Question Raised Again" takes the turn it does here. Kant might have been expected to proceed in this essay, as he does in "What Is Orientation in Thinking?", by justifying the subjective affirmation of moral progress as an a priori postulate that legitimately satisfies a need of pure practical reason. Having argued in this manner for the postulate of God's existence, it would be in keeping with the architectonic of critical reason for him to make a parallel transcendental argument justifying belief in historical progress by appeal to the conditions of the possibility of moral agency. Given the fact that many observers do find both coherence and plausibility in the abderitic view, it might seem that we could endorse the abderitic hypothesis qua disinterested observers of human history while affirming the progressivist hypothesis qua practical agents. This solution would allow for the a priori rational legitimacy of affirming the reality of progress while staying removed from the ambiguities of empirical detail. So what conceptual necessity produces Kant's abrupt declaration that a prophetic history of humanity's moral progress *must* have a starting point in experience?

The answer is bound up with the anthropological premise underwriting Kant's emphasis on the importance of moral examples and historically revealed religion: namely, the premise that in morality, as in other aspects of practical reflection, human beings are so deeply dependent on the 'sensibly tenable' that they cannot rely on pure reason alone as the touchstone of moral agency. Because he takes this to be so, Kant concludes that the plausibility of the abderitic hypothesis renders human agents susceptible to practical disorientation. Even from a quasi-detached speculative perspective, endorsement of the abderitic hypothesis disorients moral agency. Insofar as we find ourselves prone to see human history abderitically as meaningless farce, we must find a way to restore confidence in the morally progressive capacities of the human species. The thought Kant takes up here is that orientation is possible *only by turning to a different facet of experience.* His turn to experiential evidence in "An Old Question Raised Again" occurs because he perceives that this strategy is the only one that provides rational considerations capable of dispelling the abderitic reactions of cynicism, disgust and ennui. The shift in Kant's argument marks the place at which he fully recognizes human agents' experiential susceptibility to disorientation, and their dependence on experience for confirmation of morality's a priori truths.

The task we face is to find experiential evidence capable of solidifying our conviction in moral progress. Hence Kant proceeds to supply a suitable interpretation: what confirms the reality of humanity's moral progress is the indirect empirical evidence found in the sympathy expressed by onlookers of the French Revolution. The spectators' reaction of moral solidarity with the cause of justice, he asserts, demonstrates the existence of a moral 'tendency' in humanity that will ultimately produce a condition of peaceful constitutional republicanism.

[S]uch a phenomenon in human history *will not be forgotten*, because it has revealed in a tendency and faculty in human nature for improvement such that no politician, affecting wisdom, might have conjured out of the course of things hitherto existing, and one which nature and freedom alone, united in the human race in conformity with inner principles of right, could have promised. But so far as time is concerned, it can promise this only indefinitely and as a contingent occurrence. (OQ 88)

Kant's logic here is difficult to parse, but Larry Krasnoff seems right to emphasize that the relevant fact at stake is not the specific *content* of the judgement (i.e., that this particular revolution is justified) but the moral *form* of the spectators' approval, which embodies a public political demand for justice.[22] Kant advocates the morally evidentiary status of the spectators' reaction to the French Revolution in such a way that makes our recognition of its significance compatible with recognizing the horrors, ambiguities and disappointments of the event. What is supposed to reaffirm our conviction in the progress of humanity's political institutions is that the spectators' sympathies embody a moral enthusiasm of such an intensity that it must, over time, produce substantively just reforms in society.

Kant's argument itself relies heavily on a morally salutary (or what the *Religion* calls "authentic") interpretation of the facts involved in his example. Only if crucial interpretive assumptions are accepted can the spectators' expressed sympathy with the French Revolution carry the crucial evidential weight assigned to it. We must assume that the spectators' feelings actually embody a judgement of moral right rather than self-interest, and we must posit that their public expressions of sympathy manifest a tendency in human nature that really guarantees a future of substantive social progress. The very articulation of these premises shows how disputable they are. A dispassionate interpreter of the example might incline toward a cynical reading, or might plead agnosticism in the face of diverse plausible accounts of the spectators' sympathy. But Kant's argument presupposes that agents can never be dispassionate observers or agnostic interpreters of human history. We always already affirm the principles and ideals of a priori reason; we are moved by the moral feeling of respect; and we value ourselves and others as persons who are capable of willing humanity's moral perfection. These factors give us a rational interest in finding examples capable of sustaining our conviction in the reality of moral progress. For the most part, the interpretive activity that satisfies this need may occur tacitly as we perceive worldly realities in a manner that coheres with our larger practical understanding. But at times, our characteristically human doubts about moral questions require that we *deliberately* draw on interpretive strategies capable of giving experientially derived examples their salutary orienting effect. Whether we adopt these interpretive activities tacitly or deliberately, their rational integrity comes from the fact that the range of acceptable interpretations is limited to those that are compatible with objectively known facts. Our commitment to rationality means that we may not orient practical thought by making a travesty of theoretical reason. Accordingly, Kant can justifiably claim that the proposition of humanity's moral progress "is a proposition valid for the most rigorous theory, in spite of all skeptics, and not just a well-meaning and a commendable proposition in a practical respect" (OQ 88). Although the teleological view of history must be compatible with theoretical rationality, it is itself not a theoretical claim but rather a practical claim about the necessary subjective conditions of human moral agency.[23] While this much is recognized by careful readers of Kant, it is generally assumed that the necessity at issue in "An Old Question Raised Again" is merely analytic, describing what is always already the case. By contrast, the reading of Kant's concerns I have advanced also identifies a *prescriptive* dimension to his argument for the necessity of teleological thinking. Given that practical disorientation follows from endorsing the abderitic thesis, and given our tendency to find this thesis highly plausible, we *deliberately* may have to affirm a progressive interpretation of experience.

This possibility is more prominent in "An Old Question Raised Again" than in Kant's earlier writings on history and politics. When Kant previously trod much the same conceptual ground in "Theory and Practice," he did not then suggest that practical orientation requires interpretations of experience. To the contrary, that essay asserts that unprovable doubts about empirical history cannot have any effect on an agent's commitment to promoting progress:

[H]owever uncertain I may always be and remain as to whether something better is to be hoped for the human race, this cannot infringe upon the maxim, and hence upon its presupposition, necessary for practical purposes, that it is practicable. (TP 309)

After underlining the innocuousness of speculative doubts, Kant further declares that "[e]mpirical arguments against the success of these resolutions, which are taken on hope, accomplish nothing here" (TP 309). Yet no sooner has Kant declared the irrelevance of empirical evidence than he smuggles the empirical back in again with an offhand remark: "Besides, a good deal of evidence can be put forward to show that in our age, as compared with all previous ages, the human race as a whole has actually made considerable moral progress (short-term checks can prove nothing to the contrary)" (TP 310). Notwithstanding the 'official' irrelevance of historical examples to the issue of progress, Kant goes out of his way to note their availability.

By contrast, when these issues reappear in "An Old Question Raised Again," he is more forthright about the necessary role of experience in sustaining moral efforts. Now he takes more seriously the threat of disorientation produced by the gulf between our moral ideals and our experience of the world. Rejecting his own earlier arguments in "Conjectural Beginning of Human History" and "Idea for a Universal History," Kant comes to hold that we cannot posit natural mechanism as the engine of human moral progress.[24] Nor can we find any coherent way of positing a priori that a corrupt human species could ever perfect its own inner moral disposition. Given the human propensity to see history as a farcical oscillation of progress and regress, we stand in danger of concluding that we cannot be obligated to realize the rational ideal of a just and peaceful world. Averting such a prospect requires the adoption of interpretive strategies whereby we look to experience for the reassurance in humanity's moral progress that will keep the cognitive framework of practical reason intact.

This tacit doctrine is the culmination of Kant's decades-long reflections on the complex subjective conditions of human moral agency. To be sure, it stands in some tension with his more austere 'official' claims about the sufficiency of a priori practical reason to regulate moral agency. On his official account, there would be no problems of disorientation giving rise to a need for empirical examples or particulars. Yet because Kant is concerned not just with the architectonic structure of rationality per se but also with the distinctive features of *human* rationality, he is committed to wrestling with the all-too-human threats of disorientation he perceives to exist in agents' lived experience. Disorientation in thinking is an ineradicable possibility within human moral subjectivity, and it requires agents to embrace salutary interpretations of experience that cohere with and corroborate the ideals of pure practical reason.

Taking Kant Seriously

If the preceding exegesis is correct, a substantial dimension of Kant's thought has remained unnoticed and untested amid the recent flourishing of Kant scholarship. The problem is not that his arguments about hope or belief in progress are themselves ignored; recent years have seen numerous discussions of Kant's views emphasizing his account of this-worldly (rather than religious) hope.[25] Commentators certainly do find philosophical merit in his notion that hope or belief in progress is necessary for moral and political agency.[26] Yet the philosophical value they find is in the *descriptive* analysis of moral agency as intrinsically embodying an element of this-worldly hope or belief. Such accounts construe moral hope or belief as though it were affirmed a priori along with other cognitive presuppositions of practical rationality.[27] To cite one example of this approach, Onora O'Neill describes Kant as offering the argument "that we must postulate, assume, hope for the possibility that our moral commitments are not futile: we must hope for the possibility of inserting the moral intention into the world."[28] O'Neill's rationalist construal of a Kantian "bare structure of hope" seeks to establish that the particular accoutrements of revealed religion – together with everything else experiential or "sensibly tenable" – are nonessential to moral agency. Such an account relegates to insignificance those aspects of Kant's arguments suggesting otherwise, passages such as the *Religion*'s allusion to a "human need" for the sensibly tenable. Moreover, it suggests that Kant is mistaken to take the argument of "An Old Question Raised Again" in the direction he does: rather than positing that belief in historical progress must be underwritten by some sort of experience, Kant ought to have stayed on the plane of the pure a priori and declared that belief in progress is adopted as a postulate of practical reason.

As I have argued, however, Kant himself takes his argument in a different direction. In the end, he suggests that human agency needs a grounding in the robustly empirical as well as the a priori. Are there reasons to give this view serious philosophical consideration? And if so, what does it offer a contemporary philosophical understanding of moral agency? With respect to the latter question, several points follow from the account of Kant's concerns I have offered. Firstly, it turns out that the precisely demarcated spheres of reason in Kant's official architectonic doctrine fail to provide an accurate description of human practical rationality. This official doctrine holds that human practical rationality's failure to produce moral willing comes about simply because our embodied nature gives rise to desires that sidetrack rational choice away from the dictates of pure practical reason. What Kant's concern with practical disorientation suggests is that humans agents face an *additional* problem in attempting to be moral: namely, the problem of understanding how the ideals we embrace could come to be realized in the world as we know it. Where incoherence and practical disorientation loom on the horizon, we must adjust either our ideals or our view of the world; and if it is not to be the former, then for the sake of morality itself we must deliberately affirm rationally permissible interpretations of the world that offer a better fit with our ideals. On this view, moral orientation is arrived at in a way akin to Rawlsian reflective equilibrium. By moving between affirmed ideals and interpretive judgements of the world, we find an outlook from within which moral agency is rationally coherent.

What also follows from taking up the Kantian problematic of practical disorientation is that a new dimension of moral agency comes to light. As agents obligated to realize ideals of peace and justice, it becomes part of our responsibilities to view the world in a way permitting us to affirm that this world is one in which ideals can be realized. We must avert the possibility of coming to the despairing conclusion that our ideals are impossible to translate into practice and hence, in the name of 'realism', must be abandoned. In the texts surveyed earlier, Kant suggests only that a morally informed interpretive understanding of the world is something that agents must carry out *individually* to ensure the integrity of their own moral agency. Elsewhere in his writings, however, he hints that there also might be broader *societal* responsibilities to ensure that social interactions conform to the standards of decorum and the virtuous appearances that support morally salutary interpretations of humanity, in order to help all persons cultivate better moral dispositions of willing.[29]

The notion of responsibilities of public interpretation is an idea that might be richly developed in the present age, given the plethora of mass communication and the increasing globalization of certain shared public discourses such as Kant-inflected liberalism. In the global climate of public opinion, it is easy for agents to succumb to practical disorientation with respect to the scope of moral ideals such as human rights and the rule of law. The identification of intrinsically legitimate ideals is only one dimension of what it means to adopt a morally engaged attitude towards the world. The question of where and how vigorously agents see fit to pursue these ideals is a distinct and equally important aspect of moral agency. Unless agents see that these ideals can be and are actually manifested in this world, a commitment to realizing them pales into insignificance by contrast with the cynicism-inducing realities of current practice. When Kant's concerns with moral disorientation touch on the context of this-worldly historical hope – as they do in "An Old Question Raised Again" – it is unclear whether he supposes the morally salutary use of historical example to be strictly an interpretation that individuals carry out privately and on their own behalf. In any case, though, it would make sense for Kant to affirm that for the sake of fostering belief in progress and thereby fostering political engagement, we should affirm publicly shared interpretations of examples such as the spectators' sympathy with the French Revolution. Just this inculcation of a publicly shared interpretation is presumably what Kant hopes to effect in offering his essay to the reading public.

The specific role that interpretations of experience play in sustaining moral agency may be conceptualized in different ways. In "An Old Question Raised Again," the interpretation of experience is mandated by the necessity of grounding belief in humanity's moral progress through history. Other approaches are also possible, of course. For instance, in *Between Vengeance and Forgiveness*, Martha Minow reflects on the question of what justification can be given for war crimes in light of serious questions about the partiality, limited scope and dubious deterrent value of the justice they can deliver.[30] In appropriate circumstances, she concludes, it is worthwhile to undertake trials despite these drawbacks. Given the right public presentation, war-crimes prosecutions can foster an anticynical inspiration and engagement that is valuable in its own right. What needs to be impressed on public consciousness is not any grand belief that holding trials will eventually eliminate atrocity altogether; rather, Minow urges that public awareness of trials is (in certain conditions) part of a long-term effort to inculcate norms of human rights and the rule of law. Even where trials are not the best way of responding to atrocity, efforts to inculcate these norms more indirectly are still eminently worthwhile. The hope that needs sustaining is that over time, the right kind of advocacy will create an effective public demand for, and adherence to, liberal democratic norms.

In the end, we do not need to endorse Kant's own view of the necessary scope of hope in order to take seriously his idea that hope must be present in moral agency. If it is worthwhile to take Kant seriously enough to part ways with him on this issue, it is also worthwhile to extend engagement with his thought further, by taking seriously his concern with human agents' need for experiential groundings of hope. In conjunction with contemporary analyses, Kant's conceptualization of the problem of practical disorientation may allow philosophers to identify more lucidly the full range of challenges facing politically engaged moral agents.

Notes

With this essay I want to pay tribute to Jerry Schneewind not just as a preeminent scholar of the history of moral philosophy, but also as a teacher and mentor. Inasmuch as he has encouraged me to approach this history with an eye to its unfamiliar regions and their relevance for constructive philosophical reflection, I hope that some fruits of his encouragement can be discerned here.

The English translations of the Kant texts cited are listed here, preceded by the abbreviations used in the text. All references are to the page numbers of the standard Akademie Ausgabe edition of Kant's works (De Gruyter, 1902–).

CB "Conjectures on the Beginning of Human History," in Hans Reiss, ed., *Kant: Political* Writings, 2nd ed. (Cambridge University Press, 1991).

CF "The Conflict of the Faculties," in *Religion and Rational Theology*, ed. Allen W. Wood and George Di Giovanni (Cambridge University Press, 1996).

EAT "The End of All Things," in *Religion within the Boundaries of Mere Reason and Other Writings*, ed. Allen W. Wood and George Di Giovanni (Cambridge University Press, 1998).

G "Groundwork of the Metaphysics of Morals," in *Practical Philosophy*, ed. Mary J. Gregor (Cambridge University Press, 1996).

LE Lectures on Ethics, ed. Peter Heath and J. B. Schneewind (Cambridge University Press, 1997).

OQ "An Old Question Raised Again: Is the Human Race Constantly Progressing?" (Part II of *The Conflict of the Faculties*), in *Religion and Rational Theology*, ed. Allen W. Wood and George Di Giovanni (Cambridge University Press, 1996).

R "Religion within the Boundaries of Mere Reason," in *Religion within the Boundaries of Mere Reason and Other Writings*, ed. Allen W. Wood and George Di Giovanni (Cambridge University Press, 1998).

TP "On the Common Saying: That May Be True in Theory, But It Is of No Use in Practice," in Kant, *Practical Philosophy*, ed. Mary J. Gregor (Cambridge University Press, 1996).

WOT "What Does It Mean to Orient Oneself in Thinking?" in *Religion within the Boundaries of Mere Reason and Other Writings*, ed. Allen W. Wood and George Di Giovanni (Cambridge University Press, 1998).

1. J. B. Schneewind, *The Invention of Autonomy* (Cambridge University Press, 1998), p. 5.
2. Ibid., p. 5.
3. Ibid., p. 553.
4. Ibid., p. 554.

5. Ibid., pp. 518–19, 554.
6. Ibid., p. 4.
7. Mary Midgley, "Towards an Ethic of Global Responsibility," in *Human Rights in Global Politics*, ed. Tim Dunne and Nicholas J. Wheeler (Cambridge University Press, 1999), pp. 169–70.
8. For a summary and discussion of these doctrines, see Robert Louden, "Go-Carts of Judgement: Exemplars in Kantian Moral Education," *Archiv für Geschichte der Philosophie* 74:3 (1992), pp. 303–22.
9. Recent works focusing on this dimension of Kant's thought include Robert B. Louden, *Kant's Impure Ethics* (Oxford University Press, 1999); G. Felicitas Munzel, *Kant's Conception of Moral Character* (University of Chicago Press, 1999); Allen W. Wood, *Kant's Ethical Thought* (Cambridge University Press, 1999), Part II.
10. Onora O'Neill, "Kant on Reason and Religion," in *The Tanner Lectures on Human Values* 18, ed. Grethe B. Peterson (University of Utah Press, 1997), p. 284.
11. Ibid., p. 304.
12. Schneewind, *The Invention of Autonomy*, p. 511.
13. Ibid., p. 527.
14. O'Neill, "Kant on Reason and Religion," p. 286. O'Neill applies the same point to Kant's claims for the necessity of believing in the immortality of the soul.
15. Ibid., p. 286.
16. This line of argument is developed in Christine Korsgaard, *The Sources of Normativity* (Cambridge University Press, 1996).
17. This point is discussed in more detail in Munzel, *Kant's Conception of Moral Character*, pp. 192–202. Munzel describes Kant's general notion of subjective orientation as "signposts along the road of life that point the human subject toward ultimate human purpose" in effecting "the translation of the morally good form of thought into the morally good form of life" (p. 202).
18. This advice is paralleled by the advice Kant gives in the *Lectures on Ethics* to agents who are beset by doubts about the possibility of their *own* moral willing: in such moments, he says, we must recall some previous time at which we acted in a way that could only have been produced by genuinely moral motivation (LE 351). I discuss this topic more fully in Chapter 2 of my Ph.D. dissertation, *Precarious Positions: Aspects of Kantian Moral Agency* (Johns Hopkins University, 1997).
19. See R 114/121. For discussions of Kant's notion of authentic interpretation, see Rudolph A. Makkreel, *Imagination and Interpretation in Kant* (University of Chicago Press, 1990), Ch. 7; and Onora O'Neill, "Within the Limits of Reason," in *Reclaiming the History of Ethics*, ed. Andrews Reath, Barbara Herman and Christine Korsgaard (Cambridge University Press, 1997), pp. 179–81.
20. In *The Conflict of the Faculties* Kant similarly asserts that the object of scriptural interpretation is not what an author is likely to have intended but "what teaching reason can ascribe (a priori), for the sake of morality"; and this popular presentation of the Gospels, he says, "takes place honestly and openly without deception" (CF 67).

21. Kant also compares moral reflection on humanity to theatrical spectatorship in "The End of All Things: "The ground of the first point [that humans expect an end of the world] appears to lie in the fact that reason says to them that the duration of the world has worth only insofar as the rational beings in it conform to the final end of their existence; if, however, this is not supposed to be achieved, then creation itself appears purposeless to them, like a play having no resolution and affording no cognition of any rational aim" (EAT 331). For seventeenth- and eighteenth-century uses of the trope of theatrical spectatorship to explore moral subjectivity, see Luc Boltanski, *Distant Suffering: Morality, Media and Politics* (Cambridge University Press, 1999), pp. 24–7.
22. See Larry Krasnoff, "The Fact of Politics: History and Teleology in Kant," *European Journal of Philosophy* 2:1 (1994), p. 31.
23. Cf. ibid., p. 22.
24. On the logic behind Kant's repudiation of his earlier doctrine that natural mechanisms effect moral progress, see Krasnoff, "The Fact of Politics," pp. 26–9. Also see Axel Honneth, "Is Universalism a Moral Trap?", in *Perpetual Peace*, ed. James Bohman and Matthias Lutz-Bachmann (MIT Press, 1997), pp. 161–2.
25. See the discussion of this trend in Robert Merrihew Adams's "Introduction" to Kant, *Religion within the Boundaries of Mere Reason*, ed. Allen Wood and George di Giovanni (Cambridge University Press, 1998), pp. xxv–xxvii.
26. In addition to the works by Korsgaard, Krasnoff and O'Neill cited previously, see Susan Neiman, *The Unity of Reason* (Oxford University Press, 1994), pp. 177–81; Martha Nussbaum, "Kant and Cosmopolitanism," in *Perpetual Peace*, ed. Bohman and Lutz-Bachmann, pp. 50–1.
27. That these two assumptions of analytic necessity and a priori justification are separable is shown in the discussions by Neiman and Munzel (cited earlier). Both discussions present Kant's doctrine of hope as a purely a priori postulate of practical rationality; but both also hint at the notion that hope or rational faith is something we are obligated to adopt for the sake of morality itself (Neiman) or as part of cultivating a morally good character (Munzel), rather than taking it as simply an analytically necessary condition of moral agency. Neither author, however, elaborates on *what is involved* in affirming that moral ideals are realizable through our own agency.
28. O'Neill, "Kant on Reason and Religion," p. 304.
29. See Chapter 3 of Brender, *Precarious Positions*.
30. Martha Minow, *Between Vengeance and Forgiveness: Facing History after Genocide and Mass Violence* (Beacon Press, 1998).

8

Autonomy, Plurality and Public Reason

Onora O'Neill

"Kant," writes Jerry Schneewind in the first sentence of *The Invention of Autonomy*,[1] "invented the conception of morality as autonomy" (IA 3). He sees this invention most fundamentally as a conception of morality as self-governance, which can replace more traditional moralities of obedience and avoid their persistent difficulties.

There are, Schneewind notes, "various conceptions of self-governance" (IA 5). The specifically Kantian inflection of self-governance equates it with autonomy, that is, with the thought that "we ourselves legislate the moral law" (IA 6) or that "It is only because of the legislative action of our own will that we are under moral law" (IA 483). Autonomy or self-legislation is the fullest conception of self-governance. Earlier writers moved in the direction of a morality of self-governance but did not articulate the idea fully; they still saw God and obedience to God's law as indispensable to morality. Voluntarists had seen morality as God's creation, the arbitrary fiat of His will; intellectualists had seen it as reflecting eternal truths that were mirrored both in the Divine and (more confusedly) in human intellects. Kant decisively rejects both voluntarism (IA 495ff.) and intellectualism and proposes a conception of morality as autonomy.

In *The Invention of Autonomy* Schneewind neither summarises Kant's position nor offers an extended exegesis (IA 483), assuming that readers are familiar with the position. I believe that readers may be familiar with it but that they are often also deeply puzzled by Kant's conception of autonomy, and its relationship to morality and to reason. So I shall offer

I am grateful to Robert Hanna and to seminar audiences in Baltimore, Toronto, Berlin and Edinburgh for help in writing this essay and other related papers.

a reading of Kant's conception of autonomy, distinguish it from some other ideas that go by the name of autonomy, and propose some reasons for thinking that autonomy *in Kant's sense of the term* is indeed both a conception of practical reason and fundamental to morality. The line of thought I shall pursue is, I hope, both compatible with and a sympathetic extension of claims that Schneewind makes about Kant's position.

1. Autonomy as Individual Independence

Two familiar observations about conceptions of autonomy can serve as landmarks for charting the vast changes that have taken place in under-standings of the term. In antiquity autonomy was a political or consti-tutional idea, a characteristic of cities that made their own laws, rather than receiving them from mother cities, as colonies do.[2] By contrast, at least for the past fifty years, autonomy has commonly been construed as a feature of individuals who make or shape or, as we sometimes say (with due deference to the political origins of the term), govern their own lives. During this period autonomy has been seen mainly as a matter of individual independence of various sorts, a relational characteristic (independence is independence *from* something) that individuals can have in some but not other contexts and to varying degrees.[3]

Unsurprisingly, this transformation in understandings of autonomy has led to varying views of its value and its importance. The autonomy of cities – or more generally of polities – is widely admired and aspired to be-cause it amounts to escape from tyranny or colonial status; the autonomy of individuals is sometimes admired and sometimes seen as suspect. Some commentators think that the autonomy of individuals threatens ethical standards rather than supporting them. Although some terms with affin-ity to autonomy, such as 'self-control', 'self-realisation', 'self-governance' and 'self-legislation', each suggest that there is at least something pos-itive to be said about individual autonomy, the truth may be less com-fortable. May not individual autonomy also be manifest in action that is self-centred, self-interested, self-indulgent or even selfish? If so, au-tonomous action may undercut rather than manifest morality. One of the core contentions of antiliberal and anti-Kantian work in ethics in the past two decades[4] has been that ethical positions that emphasise individ-ual autonomy point to a conception of life that short-changes solidarity, beneficence and community; that endorses self-centred, even possessive, individualism; that overvalues independence and wrongly devalues forms of valued dependence that are ubiquitous in human life.

Commonly enough individualistic conceptions of autonomy are read back onto Kant, since he is generally viewed as the greatest proponent of an ethics of autonomy. Many of the critical claims about its relevance and its contribution to morality are then also directed at Kant. He is then easily seen as a proponent of an individualistic ethics, in which human affection and solidarity are marginalised or even viewed as hostile to morality; in which human life is seen as disembodied and lacking in social context; and in which the unavoidable antagonisms between individuals who are autonomous in the contemporary, individualistic sense are not seen as moral failure.

The conception of individual autonomy that forms the target of these criticisms is indeed unappealing in some ways and implausible in others, but I believe that it is now quite well established that this individualistic conception of autonomy has its place in our own times and differs from Kant's conception of autonomy.[5] So rather than exploring the ethical critique of individualistic conceptions of autonomy, I shall look critically at a conception of autonomy that is a plausible reading of the conception that Kant invented, and show how and why it is more interesting and more powerful than its better-known twentieth-century namesakes. This Kantian conception of autonomy raises a distinctive range of hard and important questions.

2. The Kantian Conception of Autonomy

The most elementary of the difficulties with Kantian autonomy is that it is hard to see how there can be a coherent conception of autonomy that is neither political nor individualistic. Kant's conception of autonomy as characterising "a will that enacts universal law" seems to head towards an immediate contradiction. How can we even make sense of a Formula of Autonomy that appeals to "the idea *of the will of every rational being as a will giving universal laws?*"[6]

Long familiarity with Kant's idiom can make it hard to see just how odd this formulation is. It is revealing to ask some literal-minded questions: How can we imagine each of a plurality of rational agents making universal law for all? Would not the principles that some 'legislate' conflict with those that others legislate? If so, how could these principles count as (moral) laws? Far from being principles by which all could live, would they not be principles by which none could live? How can a plurality of wills not antecedently coordinated by some preestablished harmony either be or become universal legislators? (And if they were precoordinated, would universal legislation be either possible or necessary?) In short, does it make any sense to speak of each of a plurality of individuals who share a world as a universal legislator? We can make sense of a single individual – for example, the Divine author of the moral law – legislating for all, or of a single political agent or institution legislating the civil law for all citizens of some polity. But can we make sense of a plurality of legislators who all make law for all in a common domain? Isn't the metaphor of legislation tied firmly to the picture of an individual legislator or legislative body with an integrated decision-making procedure, which can produce a single set of laws to regulate the lives of a plurality of subjects within some domain? Perhaps the idea of a moral law is as dependent on a theological context as the idea of a civil law is dependent on a political context.

These difficulties can be resolved only if the principles selected by agents who legislate for all meet two stringent conditions. First, they must select principles that any, hence all, could select; otherwise, at least some agents could not be universal legislators. Second, they must select principles that all, hence any, could adopt as a basis for leading their lives; otherwise, at least some agents would be exempt from whatever principles are selected, which consequently could not be universal laws.

Self-legislation is then a very specific understanding of the general idea of self-governance. Legislation or law-giving yields laws, and laws have a formal structure: they are formulated as principles for all within a certain domain. The idea of universal self-legislation contains a *double* reference to universality: it is the idea of *legislation by all agents for all agents*. From this we can see immediately that Kantian autonomy has its context not in the lives of individual agents, but in the lives of a plurality of agents. Its context is one in which the same plurality of beings are to be agents and subjects, law givers and law respecters.

Once the constraints that are latent within the notion of universal self-legislation are emphasised, we can see that Kant's *Formula of Autonomy* is analogous to an equation that, while quite abstract, can be solved only for specific combinations of values of its variables. Kant labels the fundamental principles of morality 'Formulae'[7]: they do not state the content of morality, but rather set out procedure(s) for identifying this content. His approach is analogous to Rousseau's, who characterises the social contract as the solution to a formula, which specifies certain requirements:

"To find a form of association that will defend and protect the person and goods of each associate with the full common force, and by means of which each, uniting with all, nevertheless obeys only himself and remains as free as before." This is the fundamental problem to which the social contract provides the solution.[8]

This understanding of the Formula of Autonomy provides an answer to the thought that the very idea of universal self-legislation must be incoherent. The key to a coherent reading of the Formula of Autonomy is to recognise that in requiring universal legislation (by all, for all), it sets a constraint on the content of such legislation. Universal legislators can 'legislate' only those principles that could be selected by all and prescriptive for all.

This combination of the perspectives of agent and subject, and specifically of a plurality of agents who are subjects, ensures that the Formula of Autonomy is neither incoherent nor vacuous. It also explains the very close connection in the text of the *Groundwork* between the Formula of Autonomy and the Formula of the Kingdom of Ends, in which the duality of perspectives is made explicit. Kant defines a kingdom as "a systematic union of various rational beings through common laws" (G 4:433), and thinks of a Kingdom of Ends as one in which each agent is both legislator and subject to law: the formula also makes fully explicit the double universality that is the key to Kant's conception of autonomy.[9]

3. The Grounds of Kantian Autonomy

However, Kant does more than claim that the idea of universal self-legislation, or autonomy, is coherent. He claims also that it is constitutive of morality: "the above principle of autonomy is the sole principle of morals" (G 4:440). As we have seen, he does not mean that alternative formulations of the supreme principle of morality are impossible: on the contrary, he offers a number of formulations of the Categorical Imperative and claims (controversially) that they are equivalent. What he means is that any nonequivalent principles of morality will be subordinate to the Formula of Autonomy (or, equivalently, to one of the other formulations of the Categorical Imperative).

Allen Wood states the difficulty of construing autonomy as the ground of moral obligation perspicuously in *Kant's Ethical Thought*:

Autonomy of the will as the ground of moral obligation is arguably Kant's most original ethical discovery (or invention). But it is also easy to regard Kant's conception of autonomy as either incoherent or fraudulent. To make my own will the author of my obligations seems to leave both their content and their bindingness at my discretion, which contradicts the idea that I am *obligated* by them. If we reply to this objection by emphasising the *rationality* of these laws as what binds me, then we seem to be transferring the source of obligation from my will to the canons of rationality. The notion of *self*-legislation becomes a deception or at best a euphemism.[10]

The first horn of the dilemma takes us back to an individualistic reading of the idea of autonomy: "To make my own will the author of my obligations seems to leave both their content and their bindingness at my discretion." To construe autonomy in this way is to adopt a form of voluntarism without God: there is no reason to think that an account of autonomy of this individualistic sort could be the basis of morality. Schneewind points out that the voluntarist theologies of Scotus, Luther and Calvin, in which divine willing rather than reason provides the grounds for ethical principles, deprive God's will of ethical value: "Omnipotence is secured, at the cost of making God's commands concerning the moral relations of human beings to one another an outcome of his arbitrary will" (IA 25). Despite its popularity in some quarters, the attempt to locate ethical value in an individualistic conception of autonomy ends up pointing not to morality but to mere, sheer, arbitrary willing: it deprives human willing of ethical value.

The second horn of Wood's dilemma may seem equally unpromising: "by emphasising the *rationality* of these laws as what binds me, we seem to be transferring the source of obligation from my will to the canons of rationality. The notion of *self*-legislation becomes a deception or at best a euphemism." If Kant derives the significance of universal legislation "from the canons of rationality," will he not have retreated to some form of intellectualism, and in doing so identify the principles of ethics, or the moral law, with the antecedently given dictates of right reason? (See IA Ch. 2.) And will not a retreat to intellectualism of any form undermine the view that morality is a matter of self-governance or autonomy, and concede that, in the end, morality is a matter of subordination or obedience to standards set by something or someone else?

Kant clearly does not think that an ethics based on autonomy is unreasoned. On the contrary, he insists firmly that autonomy, far from being a principle that conforms to or derives from antecedently given standards of reason, itself provides the supreme principle of practical reason. If this claim is correct, then identifying morality with autonomy will not mark any return to a conception of morality as obedience to an antecedently known standard of the good, or to antecedently given standards of reason.

Everything then hinges on showing that by making the principle of autonomy a fundamental principle of our willing, we do not subordinate our wills to antecedently established, 'eternal' standards of reason, but rather invent or construct standards for reasoned thinking and acting, standards that have the sort of generally recognised authority that we would look to find in anything that could count as a requirement of reason.

4. Autonomy as Practical Reason

Two features frame all of Kant's discussions of reason. The first is his insistence that there is no independently given "canon of reason" that sets the standard for human reason. The second is his thought that since we have not been given standards for reasoning we must construct them, and that this is a shared task, to be undertaken by a plurality of free agents.

The predicament of lacking a canon of reason is referred to repeatedly in the Prefaces of the *Critique of Pure Reason*, where Kant points out that what we habitually take for human reason may simply mislead us. In the Doctrine of Method of the same work he likens our predicament as would-be reasoners without built-in standards of reason to that of the plurality of builders of the Tower of Babel, who had materials in plenty but could not proceed because they lacked a common plan. If we can construct no standards of reason, disasters threaten.

Frequently Kant images the lack of imposed standards of reason with political metaphors. "Reason," he notoriously insists, "has no dictatorial authority" (CPR A738/B767). No canons of rationality are given, and no external authority tells us how to structure our thinking and acting. We are free to judge and to will in various ways.

The puzzle then is to grasp why some ways of judging or willing should be thought to have the sort of general authority that we may speak of as that of reason and others do not. How can Kant draw *any* distinction between reasoned and unreasoned ways of thinking and willing? If we do not "transfer the source of obligation from my will to the canons of rationality," can there be any grounds for thinking that autonomous willing is reasoned? Can we have standards of reason without submitting to cognitive or moral despotism, and ultimately to a morality of obedience rather than autonomy?

Kant's response to this line of inquiry is simple but dramatic. He claims that the demands of reason in theory and practice, in thinking and in willing, run parallel. Both are constituted or constructed by the specific yet minimal structure that must be imposed on thought and action if any plurality of free agents is to be able to follow one another's thinking or acting. Kant claims that only when free agents discipline their thinking and acting in ways that others can follow do their thought and practice exemplify the fundamental, if meagre, requirements of reason. We do not offer reasons if we offer something that we think cannot be followed by its intended audiences. Autonomy in thinking is no more – but also no less – than the attempt to conduct thinking (speaking, writing) on principles on which (we take it) all others whom we address could also conduct their thinking (speaking, writing). Autonomy in action is no more – and also no less – than the attempt to conduct ourselves on the basis of principles on which (we take it) all others could conduct their lives. Reason is then in the first place no more than a matter of striving for autonomy in the spheres of thinking and action.

The difficult aspect of these claims is to show why just *this* way of disciplining thought and action should count as exemplifying the basic strategy of reason. Perhaps the most useful texts for understanding the way in which Kant hopes to ground reason in autonomy rather than autonomy in reason are two popular but deep essays of the mid-1780s, "What Does It Mean to Orient Oneself in Thinking?" and "What Is Enlightenment?"[11]

In each essay Kant argues that reasoning that defers to any civil or ecclesiastical (or, we may add, ideological) authority is defective. Reasoning must be free. However, if the free use of reason is not disciplined – if it is lawless – then it fails because it cannot be followed by others. Consequently the only thought or action that can count as reasoned is that which we structure by imposing "the form of law" – of universality. Reasoned thinking and action must both be lawlike (not 'lawful', a common mistranslation which hints at some further unexplained source of reason or legitimation).

At first sight we might think that even this weak requirement for lawlikeness must be derived from some external authority of exactly the sort that Kant thinks we lack. Why, one may ask, cannot free beings simply dispense with *all* standards or constraints, including those that purport to be standards or constraints of reason, conducting their thinking and acting however they may wish? Indeed, would not any constraint on their thinking and willing defer to some other authority – so returning us to a morality of obedience? Can thinking and willing that are wholly free allow for any claims of authority, even for the authority of reason?

In "What Does It Mean to Orient Oneself in Thinking?" Kant makes it clear that he rejects this postmodernist fantasy about the thinking of free agents. He repeatedly characterises thought that is not disciplined in *any* way as a lawless use of our cognitive capacities that would lead not to freedom of thought but to incoherence, and thought that is disciplined by an external authority as deferential obedience. He writes:

[F]reedom in thinking signifies the subjection of reason to no laws except those which it gives itself; and its opposite is a lawless use of reason . . . if reason does not wish to subject itself to the laws it gives itself, it has to fall under the yoke of laws given by another; for without any law, nothing, not even nonsense can play its game for long. Thus the unavoidable consequence of declared lawlessness in thinking (of a liberation from all the limitations of reason) is that freedom to think will ultimately be forfeited ... [or] trifled away. (WO, 8:303–4)

Reasoned thought must have at least some discipline, which permits others to follow it. Indeed, on Kant's view, the discipline of lawlikeness provides the *only* fundamental standard of reason that we can attain:

To make use of one's reason means no more than to ask oneself, whenever one is supposed to assume something, whether one could find it feasible to make the ground or the rule on which one assumes it into a universal principle for the use of reason. (WO, 8: 146n)

Reasoned thinking (speaking, writing) must be autonomous in the strict Kantian sense of freely following or adopting some law or principle rather than deferring to some supposed authority who ordains or prescribes the law. It must therefore incorporate a structure by which others can follow the thinking (speaking, writing). This is the basic strategy of any exercise of reason:

[T]he power to judge autonomously – that is, freely (according to principles of thought in general) – is called reason. (CF, 7:27)

It is the only option if thinking is neither to defer to "despotic" constraint nor languish in "anarchic" incoherence.

"Self-legislation" is not then a mysterious phrase for describing a merely arbitrary ways in which a free individual might or might not think, but a characteristic of thinking that free individuals achieve by imposing the discipline of lawlikeness, so making their thoughts or their proposals for action followable by or accessible to others, hence in principle intelligible to them and open to their criticism, agreement or rebuttal.

Parallel considerations about reason and autonomy are presented in "What Is Enlightenment?", but in this essay Kant's attention is as much on willing and acting as on thinking (speaking, writing, communicating). Here he explicitly parts company with intellectualist conceptions of the Enlightenment and of reason. Enlightenment, he claims, is not merely a matter of questioning the guidance of received authorities, of experts such as priests or state officials: those who appeal to reason's authority without offering an account of that authority take a too limited view of enlightenment. Full enlightenment is autonomy in the conduct of thought and life, rather than deference to any authorities. It is a process of freely imposed self-discipline in the use of one's capacities, in which limited and incomplete forms of reason – Kant calls them "private" uses of reason – are progressively replaced by what Kant calls "public" uses of reason, which do not presuppose the authority of any arbitrary institution, person or tenet, or terms of discourse.

Private uses of reason are designed to be followed only by some restricted audience: they presuppose at least some arbitrary assumptions, which define and are shared by that restricted audience. The principles of private reasoning cannot therefore be universally legislated. Insofar as we rely on partial, private uses of our reasoning capacities, we conform to or obey some given authority, for which we can give no reason, so can offer only reasons that are conditional on that authority. For example, insofar as we simply rely on or accept the demands of officials or priests, of received views or local ideologies, we merely assume their authority, and our thinking and acting cannot be fully reasoned. In some contexts of life, reliance on such arguments from authority may be enough, but in others it will be question-begging. Only thinking and willing that do not presuppose any such arbitrary authorities are fit to reach all others; only such reasoning is fully public and fully lawlike. Fully public reasoning is designed to reach "the world at large"; its structure or strategy is that of autonomy in thought and action:

> The touchstone of whatever can be decided on as a law for a people lies in the question: whether a people could impose such a law on itself. (*WE* 8:39)

On Kant's account, nothing forces free agents to make lawlike use of their freedom: we are not forced to be autonomous in thought or in action. But if we are autonomous, our choices will indeed be self-legislated. The emphasis on the term 'self' makes this sound familiar enough, and suggests that individual autonomy might be all that is at stake. But Kant's emphasis is equally on the term 'legislated,' and this is much more demanding. Often enough people are tempted not to strive for autonomy: as Kant wryly observes in "What Is Enlightenment?", it is so comfortable to "have a book that understands for me, a spiritual adviser who has a conscience for me, a doctor who decides on a regimen for me and so forth."[12] It is all too tempting to lead a life that is shot through both with arbitrariness and with subservience and deference in thought and action, rather than to think and act autonomously. But such ways of thinking come at a high price. We have profound, practical and pressing needs to understand others' beliefs and to communicate our own, to give others reason to act and to receive reasons from them. Insofar as we fail to discipline our thinking and acting by giving it a form that (we take it) others can follow in thought or in action, we will fail to engage with others in ways that permit any exchange of reasons. Reason's authority grows out of the mere fact that its standards – *lawlikeness without a law* – provide the only means for a plurality of free beings to avoid thought that dissipates in anarchic fragmentation or subservience to groundless categories and standards and the edicts of bogus 'authorities.'

These considerations explain how Kant can draw on an account of reason without reverting to any form of intellectualism. If we ask what we would expect reason – if we can find or construct any such thing – to provide, we are likely to reply that we would expect it to provide some authoritative standard(s) that are accessible, by which we could then organise and structure our thinking and our doing in ways that others could follow. For without such standards, we could not even be in the business of giving and receiving, exchanging and refusing reasons. But if we are not given such standards from on high, we must either do without them or construct them, relying on no more that the fact that anything that will count as reasoning must be usable by a plurality of free beings who lack imposed forms of coordination. The enterprise of reason cannot get going without some commitment to finding ways of thinking and willing that others with whom we seek to live or interact can follow.

In matters of explanation and knowledge, we do not give others reasons unless we produce thoughts that (we take it) they can follow in thought and so find intelligible: communication, agreement and disagreement will all be disrupted between those who cannot follow one another's line of thought. Equally, in matters of action we do not give others reasons for action unless the principles and proposals that we set before them are ones that they could in principle follow: others may refuse to adopt some principle and proposal that is set out for them, but if the principle or proposal is one that they could not adopt, they will not have been offered anything that could count as a reason for action for them.

5. Reason, Autonomy, Morality

In Kant's philosophy we find a consistent attempt not only to show how thought and action may proceed without external guidance, hence without deference or obedience, but also how thought and action can nevertheless incorporate authoritative standards for communication and criticism. His account of public reason is anchored in the thought that nothing will count as a reason unless its audience can in principle follow it, and that we are not 'given' any antecedent principle of reason. The requirement for reasoning is therefore to structure thinking and doing in ways that are lawlike rather than arbitrary, so followable by others. Those who structure their thinking and willing in this way exhibit the requirements of reason because and insofar as their thinking and willing is autonomous in Kant's sense.

The constraints of Kantian autonomy in thinking are vastly complex. Even if we are sure that others can follow some stretches of our thinking, most of us are also uncomfortably aware of the many limits of our thinking, and of places where others might think that we wander into incoherence and self-contradiction. But the constraints of autonomy in action are, in Kant's view, considerably clearer. For here we can at least identify certain principles that we shall have to reject if we are to be autonomous: there are many tempting ways of willing and acting that on reflection turn out not to be ones that we can legislate universally, both for narrower and for more extended views of the domain across which universality is to hold. The mere fact that human agents impinge on one another picks out certain principles of action as ones that we could not will for all. Kant is therefore able to set out the connection between morality and autonomy quite explicitly:

Morality is thus the relation of actions to the autonomy of the will, that is, to a possible giving of universal law through its maxims. An action that can coexist with the autonomy of the will is *permitted*; one that does not accord is *forbidden*. A will whose maxims necessarily harmonise with laws of autonomy is a *holy*, absolutely good will. The dependence upon the principle of autonomy of a will that is not absolutely good (moral necessitation) is *obligation*. This accordingly cannot be attributed to a holy being. The objective necessitation of action from obligation is called *duty*. (G 4:439)

The close links between reason, autonomy and morality in Kant's thought can now, I think, be set out quite simply. Autonomy, Kantianly conceived, is the practice of disciplining thought and action in ways that make them followable by others – and if we are fully autonomous, by *all* others. The lawlike structure and strategy that autonomous agents incorporate in their thinking and willing, considered in the abstract, are the basic structures and strategies of reason, to which all other reasoned principles are subordinate. The more determinate implications of autonomous willing and action define the range of permissible action, and the limits of autonomous willing determine the principles of action that there is reason to reject, and thereby fix the basic shape of principles of obligation among a plurality.

Notes

1. J. B. Schneewind, *The Invention of Autonomy: A History of Modern Moral Philosophy* (Cambridge University Press, 1998). References to the text are given parenthetically with the abbreviation IA and a page number.

2. R. Pohlmann, "Autonomie," in Joachim Ritter, ed., *Historisches Wörterbuch der Philosophie* (Wissenschaftliche Buchgesellschaft, 1971), Vol. I, 701–19.

3. For an indication of the range of notions that have been identified with autonomy in recent work see Gerald Dworkin, *The Theory and Practice of Autonomy* (Cambridge University Press, 1988); for some of the difficulties that arise when an account of autonomy is combined with an empiricist theory of action see Onora O'Neill, "Agency and Autonomy," in *Bounds of Justice* (Cambridge University Press, 2000), 29–49; for the distance between contemporary views of autonomy and Kant's conception see Onora O'Neill, *Autonomy and Trust in Bioethics* (Cambridge University Press, 2002).

4. Many of these endlessly repeated criticisms originated in the 1970s and early 1980s. For early versions see Iris Murdoch, *The Sovereignty of the Good* (Routledge and Kegan Paul, 1970); Michael Sandel, *Liberalism and the Limits of Justice* (Cambridge University Press, 1982); Lawrence Blum, *Friendship, Altruism and Morality* (Routledge and Kegan Paul, 1980); Carol Gilligan, *In a Different Voice: Psychological Theory and Women's Dependence* (Harvard University Press, 1982; 2nd ed. 1993).

5. See Thomas E. Hill, Jr., "The Kantian Conception of Autonomy," in his *Dignity and Practical Reason in Kant's Moral Theory* (Cornell University Press, 1992), 76–96, especially the section titled "What Kantian Autonomy Is Not," 77–82, and "The Importance of Autonomy" in his *Autonomy and Self-Respect* (Cambridge University Press, 1991), 43–51; Barbara Herman, *The Practice of Moral Judgment* (Harvard University Press, 1993); Marcia Baron, *Kantian Ethics Almost without Apology* (Cornell University Press, 1995); Jane Kneller and Sidney Axinn, eds., *Autonomy and Community: Readings in Contemporary Kantian Social Philosophy* (State University of New York Press, 1998); Allen Wood, *Kant's Ethical Theory* (Cambridge University Press, 1999), Ch. 5; O'Neill, "Agency and Autonomy."

6. This is the first version of the Formula of Autonomy in the *Groundwork*; see Immanuel Kant, *Groundwork of the Metaphysic of Morals*, tr. Mary J. Gregor, in Immanuel Kant, *Practical Philosophy* (Cambridge University Press, 1996), 4:431. See Allen Wood, *Kant's Ethical Thought* (Cambridge University Press, 1999), 163–4, for a list of versions of the Formula of Autonomy.

7. In the Preface to the second Critique he remarks that "whoever knows what a Formula means to a mathematician which determines quite precisely what is to be done to solve a problem and does not let him miss it, will not take a formula that does this with respect to duty in general as something that is insignificant and can be dispensed with." (*Critique of Practical Reason*, in Immanuel Kant, *Practical Philosophy*, 5:9 note.)

8. Jean-Jacques Rousseau, *Social Contract*, Part I, Ch. 6, 49–50, in *The Social Contract and Other Writings*, tr. and ed. Victor Gourevitch (Cambridge University Press, 1997). See also Wood's comment that "the principle of autonomy is the only possible solution to the riddle of obligation," *Kant's Ethical Thought*, 159.

9. In drawing attention to the close connection between the Formula of Autonomy and the Formula of the Kingdom of Ends, I do not mean to suggest that other formulations of the Categorical Imperative are not equivalent. Although the Formula of Autonomy and the Formula of the Kingdom of Ends are variously criticised for omitting crucial aspects of Kant's moral thought, I believe that neither can be adequately interpreted without reference to the combination of agent and recipient perspectives and that, taken charitably, Kant's claims about the equivalence of the formulae are correct. See Onora O'Neill, "Universal Laws and Ends in Themselves," in *Constructions of Reason* (Cambridge University Press, 1989), 126–44.

10. Wood, *Kant's Ethical Thought*, 156.

11. "What Does It Mean to Orient Oneself in Thinking?" [WO], tr. Allen W. Wood, in Immanuel Kant, *Religion and Rational Theology* (Cambridge University Press, 1996), 8:133–46; "What Is Enlightenment?" [WE], tr. Mary J. Gregor, in Immanuel Kant, *Practical Philosophy* (Cambridge University Press, 1996), 8:35–42. A third, considerably later text also relevant to these themes is *The Conflict of the Faculties* [CF], tr. Mary J. Gregor and Robert Anchor, also in Immanuel Kant, *Religion and Rational Theology*, 7:5–116.

12. WE 8:35.

9

Trapped between Kant and Dewey

The Current Situation of Moral Philosophy

Richard Rorty

In recent decades, anglophone philosophy professors have had a harder and harder time explaining to their fellow academics, and to society at large, what they do to earn their keep. The more specialized and professionalized the study of philosophy becomes, the less respect it is paid by the rest of the academy or by the public. By now it runs some risk of being ignored altogether, regarded in the same way that classical philology is, as a quaint, albeit rather charming, survival.

This problem is less acute, however, in the case of moral philosophy, which is the most visible and generally intelligible of the various philosophical specialties. But even moral philosophers are hard pressed to explain what they think they are doing. They need to claim an ability to see more deeply into matters of right and wrong than most people. But it is not clear what it is about their training that permits them to do so. People who have written their Ph.D. dissertations in this area of philosophy can hardly claim to have had more experience with difficult moral choices than most. But what exactly *can* they claim?

A familiar sort of answer to this line of questioning was given by Peter Singer twenty-five years ago in a much-discussed article in the *New York Times Magazine*. The article was called "Philosophers Are Back on the Job."[1] Singer thought of himself as bringing glad tidings. Philosophers, he explained, had once held that moral judgments were unarguable expressions of emotion, but now they had come back to their senses. They had joined the rest of the population in believing that there were good and bad arguments in favor of alternative moral choices.

Now that they had come to appreciate this fact, Singer continued, the public would be well advised to listen to moral philosophers' views on such vexed topics as abortion. For, he explained, "No conclusions about what we ought to do can validly be drawn from a description of what most people in our society think we ought to do."[2] On the contrary, "if we have a soundly based moral theory, we ought to be prepared to accept its implications even if they force us to change our moral views on major issues." Fortunately, he continued, philosophers are capable of providing such theories and thus correcting society's moral intuitions. As he put it, "the philosopher's training makes him more than ordinarily competent in assessing arguments and detecting fallacies. He has studied the nature of moral concepts, and the logic of moral argument."[3] Singer concluded his article by saying that "the entry of philosophers into areas of ethical concern from which they have hitherto excluded themselves is the most stimulating and potentially fruitful of all the recent developments in philosophy."[4]

When I read this article twenty-five years ago, I squirmed in embarrassment. Singer's view of the social role of philosophy professors struck me as calculated to make the public even more suspicious of us philosophers than it already was. For on his account, moral philosophers have "soundly based theories" that are grounded on something quite different from the moral intuitions of the public. They have a different, and better, source of moral knowledge than those intuitions can provide. This source, which philosophers traditionally refer to as "reason," has an authority that takes precedence over any alternative source.

On Singer's account, moral philosophers are somehow more in touch with this source, and therefore more rational, than the vulgar. It is not clear whether this is the cause or the effect of their superior grasp of what Singer calls "the nature of moral concepts of the logic of moral argument." However that may be, I think the notion of a moral theory based on something sounder than a set of moral intuitions as dubious as the idea that moral concepts have a special nature that the experts understand better than the vulgar, and as the idea that moral argument has a special logic that philosophical training enables one to appreciate.

To grasp a concept is just to know how to use a word. You grasp the concept of "isotope" if you know how to talk about physical chemistry, and the concept of "mannerism" when you know how to talk about the history of European painting. But concepts like "right," "ought" and "responsible" are not technical concepts, and it is not clear what special training could enable you to grasp the uses of these words better than do the laity.

When it comes to "the logic of moral arguments," I am again baffled. I cannot think of any sense of the word "logic" in which arguments about the right thing to do have a different *logic* than arguments about what profession to go into or what house to buy or whom to vote for. I cannot imagine how Singer would defend the claim that judges and social workers, for example, are less familiar with this "logic" than are trained moral philosophers, or the claim that philosophical training would help such people do their jobs better.

I do not mean to be philistine about this. I quite agree that widely read people are often better at making moral choices than people with little learning and, consequently, little imagination. Moral philosophers are, typically though not invariably, widely read and imaginative people. But I do not think that Singer, and others who agree with his evaluation of the social value of moral philosophy, give us much reason to believe that training in philosophy rather than in, for example, anthropology or the history of European literature or the criminal law will be especially helpful in giving one a superior ability to make moral decisions. I admire many of my colleagues who specialize in moral philosophy, and I read many of their books with pleasure and profit. But I should never dream of making the sorts of claims for them that Singer did.

I would like to suggest an alternative answer to the question of what most professors of moral philosophy have that others do not. They do not have more rigor or clarity or insight than the laity, but they do have a much greater willingness to take seriously the views of Immanuel Kant. More than any other author in the history of philosophy, Kant gave currency and respectability to notions like "the nature of moral concepts" and "the logic of moral argument." For he claimed that morality was like nothing else in the world – that it was utterly distinctive. He argued that there is a vast and unbridgeable difference between two realms – the realm of prudence and that of morality. If one agrees with him about this, as many moral philosophers still do, then one will be predisposed to think that one might make a professional specialty out of the study of moral concepts. But if one has not read Kant, or if one's response to reading *The Fundamental Principles of the Metaphysics of Morals* is either revulsion or a fit of the giggles, the idea that morality can be an object of professional study may well seem farfetched.

Again, if one takes Kant seriously, then Singer's idea that there is a separate source for moral principles, one that provides the principles that ground a "soundly based moral theory," will sound plausible. If you have not read Kant, or have failed to find his views attractive, you may think, as I do, that all a moral principle can possibly do is to abbreviate a range of moral intuitions. Principles are handy for summing up a range of moral reactions, but they do not have independent force that can correct such reactions. They draw all their force from our intuitions concerning the consequences of acting on them.

As I read the history of philosophy, Kant is a transitional figure – somebody who helped us get away from the idea that morality is a matter of divine command, but who unfortunately retained the idea that morality is a matter of unconditional obligations. I would accept Elizabeth Anscombe's suggestion that if you do not believe in God, you would do well to drop notions like "law" and "obligation" from the vocabulary you use when deciding what to do.

Like other great thinkers of the Enlightenment, Kant wanted to get rid of the idea that the priests were moral experts, and to establish the democratic doctrine that every human being, or at least every male human, had the inner resources necessary to make sound moral decisions. But he thought that these resources consisted in the possession of an unconditional principle – the categorical imperative – that would enable us to decide how to resolve moral dilemmas. He saw this imperative as the product of a special faculty that he called "pure practical reason," a faculty whose deliverances were entirely unaffected by historical experience. We can appeal from society's moral intuitions to that faculty, and it will tell us which intuitions to keep and which to throw out.

Nietzsche said that a bad smell of blood and the lash hangs over Kant's categorical imperative. My favorite contemporary moral philosopher, Annette Baier, detects the same stench. As Baier sees the matter, the Kantian notion of unconditional obligation is borrowed from an authoritarian, patriarchal, religious tradition that should have been abandoned rather than reconstructed. Had we followed Hume's advice, we should have stopped talking about unconditional obligations when we stopped being afraid of postmortem tortures. When we ceased to agree with Dostoevsky that if God did not exist, everything would be permitted, we should have put aside the morality–prudence distinction. We should not have substituted "Reason" for "God" as the name of a law-giver.

We are often told by contemporary moral philosophers that Kant made a breathtaking discovery, and gave us a vitally important new idea, that of moral autonomy. But I suspect that when Kant is given credit for this discovery, we are using the term ambiguously. Everybody thinks autonomy in the sense of freedom from outside impositions is a fine thing. Nobody likes either human or divine tyrants. But the specifically Kantian sense of autonomy – having one's moral decisions made by reason rather than by anything capable of being influenced by experience – is quite a different matter. Relatively few people agree with devotees of Kant such as Christine Korsgaard – perhaps the most eminent, and certainly the most uncompromising, of contemporary Kantian moral philosophers. She thinks that Kant was right to hold that there is a special kind of motivation called "moral" and that "moral motivation, if it exists, can only be autonomous."[5] Autonomy in the sense of obedience to reason's unconditional command is a very special, very technical, concept – one that has to be learned in the way that any other technical concept is learned, by working one's way into a specifically Kantian language game.

This language game is one that you have to know how to play in order to get a Ph.D. in moral philosophy. But a lot of people who spend their lives making hard moral decisions get along nicely in blithe ignorance of its existence. A great deal of contemporary anglophone moral philosophy takes for granted a discourse in which the idea of "specifically moral motivation" goes unquestioned, as does the idea that "morality" is the name of a still rather mysterious entity that requires intensive study. Reading Kant is a good way to get initiated into this discourse.

Reading my own philosophical hero, John Dewey, is a good way to find one's way out of this discourse. Dewey hoped that there would be fewer and fewer people who found Kant's way of talking about moral choice attractive. Dewey thought that it was a very bad idea to separate morality from prudence, and a particularly bad idea to think that moral imperatives have a different source than prudential advice. He viewed Kant as a figure whose view of human beings could never be reconciled with Darwin's naturalistic account of our origins. On a post-Darwinian view, Dewey argued, there can be no sharp break between empirical and nonempirical knowledge, any more than between empirical and nonempirical practical considerations, or between fact and value. All inquiry – in ethics as well as physics, in politics as well as logic – is a matter of reweaving our webs of beliefs and desires in such a way as to give ourselves more happiness and richer and freer lives. All our judgments are experimental and fallible. Unconditionality and absolutes are not things we should strive for.

As Dewey saw these matters, the Kantian split between the empirical and the nonempirical was a relic of the Platonic distinction between the material and the immaterial, and thus of the theologico-metaphysical distinction between the human and the divine. Dewey thought this "brood and nest of dualisms," as he called it, should be swept aside, taking Plato and Kant with it.

I think of contemporary moral philosophy as trapped between Kant and Dewey because most philosophers these days are naturalists who would like their views to be readily reconcilable with a Darwinian view of how we got here. But Darwinians cannot be at ease with the Kantian idea of a distinctively moral motivation, or of a faculty called "reason" that issues commands. For them, rationality can only be the search for intersubjective agreement about how to carry out cooperative projects. That view of rationality is hard to reconcile with the Kantian distinction between morality and prudence.

Learning how to play the language game in which the Kantian concept of autonomy has its original home requires taking Kant's baroque faculty psychology seriously. For to wield this concept one must first break up the person so as to distinguish the law-giving from the law-receiving psychical elements. Dewey devoted a lot of energy to helping us get rid of this distinction, and he was largely successful. The idea of a law-giving faculty called "reason," it seems to me, lingers on only among two sorts of people. The first are masochists who want to hold on to a sense of sin while still enjoying the comforts of a clean, well-lighted, fully mechanized, Newtonian universe. The second are professors of moral philosophy whose job descriptions presuppose a clear distinction between morality and prudence, and so are suspicious of Deweyian attempts to break that distinction down.

Dewey was, I think, on the right track when he wrote:

Kant's separation of reverence [for the commands of reason], as the one moral sentiment[,] from all others as pathological, is wholly arbitrary.... And it may even be questioned whether this feeling, as Kant treats it, is even the highest or ultimate form of moral sentiment – whether it is not transitional to love.[6]

In his thirties, when he was still a follower of T. H. Green, Dewey saw Hegel as having moved beyond Kant in the same way that the New Testament had moved beyond the Old – by replacing the law and the prophets with love. Both Hegel and Christ, as Dewey read them, had managed to move beyond the obsessive desire for ritual purity (or, as Kant called it, the need to cleanse morality of all traces of the merely empirical). Even after Dewey had ceased to think of himself as a Hegelian, he never faltered in his attempt to tear down the dualisms that moral philosophy had inherited from Kant.

My other favorite contemporary moral philosopher, J. B. Schneewind, manages to respect and admire Kant in a way that Baier and I do not. But he has tried to distance himself from the worst parts of Kant in various essays. One of these is an early article, published in 1968, called "Moral

Knowledge and Moral Principles." There he urges that we drop the idea
that moral philosophers have a duty to provide us with moral principles
that are completely context-free, in the sense of "capable of being applied
to any kind of situation."[7] He supports this point by saying:

From the fact that a given principle is supreme in resolving conflicts it does not
follow that it must be supreme in every context. To suppose that it does follow
would be like supposing that every decision and rule agreed upon by a happily
married couple depends upon the authority of the divorce court, since that court
has the final word in settling all their affairs if they cannot settle them by other
means. . . . Any principle established with the help of argument might simply be as
it were a moral ambulance, not for everyday use, having the right of precedence
only in emergencies and not in the ordinary run of events.[8]

In this essay, Schneewind did not explicitly endorse this "only in emergencies" view of moral principles, but much that he has said in later years
seems to accord with it. Thus in an essay criticizing Korsgaard's emphasis
on the unconditionality of moral principles Schneewind remarks:

In deliberations embedded in a complex context of shared assumptions and
agreements there may be no practical need to continue to seek for reasons until
we find one that meets Korsgaard's requirement [the requirement that justification be conclusive]. Justificational skepticism does not naturally arise in these
contexts. . . . Philosophical skepticisms would lead us to think that we can never
rightly rely on even possibly doubtful premises. But Korsgaard would have to justify this standard in order to use it to start us on the regress argument that leads
her to the principle no free agent could question.[9]

Schneewind goes on to say that in emergencies – situations in which we
have reasons for criticizing some of our hitherto unquestioned moral
commonplaces, or are facing radically new problems, or are dealing with
or affecting people whose morality and culture are unfamiliar to us –
the Kantian formulations (of the categorical imperative) are just what we
need.[10] It may indeed be useful, in those cases, to ask ourselves whether
we are using other human beings merely as means. But he notes that
the utilitarian principle may be helpful too. It may be useful, in such
cases, to ask ourselves which decision will increase human happiness –
will produce more pleasure and less pain. Schneewind says that

both sorts of principle possess the unlimited generality that makes them suitable
for help us reach reasoned agreement in the special kinds of deliberative situation
where our "thicker" or more specific reasons no longer do the job.[11]

Although Schneewind says that he thinks Kant's ambulance service better than Mill's, he does not seem to care much about the Kant–Mill

difference. Like Annette Baier, Schneewind has evinced exasperation with the fascination that this difference exerts on contemporary moral philosophers – the obsession with the opposition between consequentialism and nonconsequentialism that still dominates Ethics 101. When reading later chapters of Schneewind's recent history of moral philosophy, *The Invention of Autonomy*,[12] one gets the sense that Schneewind's favorite eighteenth-century moral philosopher is not Kant but rather Diderot, of whom he writes: "Seek happiness with justice in this life; if this is a moral principle, it is the one Diderot would support."[13]

My own view is that nobody should put in much time dithering about which ambulance service to call in emergencies. The principle Schneewind puts in Diderot's mouth is all that we will ever get, and all we will ever need, in the way of a reconciliation of Mill with Kant. I agree with Baier when she says that we should stop telling students in freshman ethics classes that principles are terribly important, and that they are being intellectually irresponsible if they do not sign up with one ambulance service or the other.

So I read Schneewind as saying that the choice of which service to contract with is much less important than the realization that moral principles can do no more than summarize a lot of our previous deliberations – remind us of some of our previous intuitions and practices. Such thin and abstract reminders may help when thicker and more concrete considerations leave us still at odds with our neighbors. They do not provide algorithms, but they offer the only sort of guidance that abstraction has to offer.

Schneewind ended his 1968 article by saying that we should not mistake the decision that a certain moral principle sums up a lot of relevant experience "for a discovery that certain principles are basic because of their own inherent nature."[14] As a good Deweyan, Schneewind is not about to take the Kantian notion of "inherent nature" seriously. He cites Dewey as holding that "what is scientific about morality is neither some basic principle or principles on which it rests . . . but the general structure of its contents and its methods."[15] One might restate the point by saying that on a Deweyan, as opposed to a Kantian, view, what makes physics, ethics and logic rational is not that they are axiomatizable but that each is what Wilfrid Sellars called "a self-correcting enterprise which can put *any* claim in jeopardy but not *all* at once."[16]

To say that moral principles have no inherent nature is to imply that they have no distinctive source. They emerge from our encounters with our surroundings in the same way that hypotheses about planetary motion, codes of etiquette, epic poems and all our other patterns of linguistic behavior emerge. Like these other emergents, they are good insofar as they lead to good consequences, not because they stand in some special relation either to the universe or to the human mind. For Deweyans questions about sources and principles, about *das Ursprungliches* and *ta archaia*, are always a sign that the philosophers are up to their old Platonic tricks. They are trying to shortcut the ongoing calculation of consequences by appealing to something stable and permanent, something whose authority is not subject to empirical test.

Whenever Kantian reactionaries like Husserl and Russell gain the upper hand over progressive Hegelian historicists like Green and Dewey, philosophy professors once again start drawing nonempirical lines between science and the rest of culture, and also between morality and prudence. The former undertaking played a considerable role in creating what we now call "analytic philosophy." But it is now viewed skeptically by such post-Kuhnian, Hegelianized philosophers of science as Ian Hacking, Arthur Fine and Bruno Latour. These writers insist that there are only sociological distinctions between science and nonscience, distinctions revolving around such notions as expert cultures, initiation into disciplinary matrices, and the like. There are no metaphysical or methodological differences. There is nothing for philosophy of science, as opposed to the history and sociology of science, to be about.

I think this post-Kuhnian stance would have been welcomed by Dewey, for whom the term "scientific method" signified little more than Peirce's injunction to remain experimental and open-minded in one's outlook – to make sure that one was not blocking the road of inquiry. If Arthur Fine's claim that "science is not special" comes to be generally accepted, there may no longer be an overarching discipline called "philosophy of science," although there may quite well be fruitful areas of inquiry called "philosophy of quantum mechanics" or "philosophy of evolutionary biology."[17]

Something analogous might happen if we were to psychologize the morality–prudence distinction in the way that the Kuhnians have sociologized the science–common sense distinction. We could do this by saying that what distinguishes morality from prudence is not a matter of sources but simply the psychological difference between matters that touch upon what Korsgaard calls our "practical identity" – our sense of what we would rather die than do – and those that do not. The relevant difference is not one of kind, but of degree of felt importance, just as the difference between science and nonscience is a difference in degree of specialization and professionalization.

Since our sense of who we are, and of what is worth dying for, is obviously up for historical and cultural grabs, to follow out this line of thought would once again lead us away from Kant to Hegel, and eventually to Dewey's synthesis of Hegel with Darwin. In a Deweyan philosophical climate, disciplines such as the "philosophy of American constitutional law" or the "philosophy of diminished responsibility" or the "philosophy of sexual relationships" might flourish, but nobody would see much point in an overarching discipline called "moral philosophy," any more than they would see a point in one called "philosophy of science." Just as there would be nothing called "scientificity" to be studied, there would be nothing called "morality." The obsolescence of Kantian discourse would make the idea of study of the "nature of moral concepts" sound silly, and might thus lead to a remapping of the philosophical terrain. There is a reason, however, why we resist the suggestion that the morality–prudence distinction is simply a matter of individual psychology – why we think that morality is both special and mysterious, and that philosophers ought to have something to say about its intrinsic nature. We think it special because we think that "Why should I be moral?" is a good question in a way that "Why should I be scientific?" is not. This is because we interpret "moral" as meaning "having roughly the practical identity that we in fact have." We think that there ought to be people who can show us why our side is right – why we decent, tolerant, good-hearted liberals are something more than an epiphenomenon of recent socioeconomic history. Moral philosophers seem good candidates for this role. Kantians of the strict observance such as Korsgaard explicitly accept it.

Here at the beginning of the twenty-first century, we can do without philosophy of science because we have no need for reassurance about science. We can drop the idea that scientificity is an important natural kind, because science is not in danger. Philosophy of science – in its traditional form of an argument that the scientific method, and only the scientific method, could tell us how things really and truly were – seemed important back in the days when Pius IX was anathematizing modern civilization. But as the tension between religion and science gradually ceased to occupy the attention of the intellectuals, philosophy of science came to look like one more teapot in which to stir up academic tempests. Nowadays philosophy of science attracts public attention only when, for example, fundamentalist preachers decide to take another crack at Darwin, or when sociobiologists try to take over the magisterium once enjoyed by theologians.

In contrast, moral philosophy may still look indispensable. This is because there is a permanent tension between the morality of the Enlightenment and the primitive, barbaric, exclusionary moralities of cultures and populations that have not enjoyed the security and wealth we have. Those cultures have missed out on the emergence of tolerance, pluralism, miscegenation, democratic government and people like us. So nonacademics are inclined to feel that this may be one area in which philosophy professors actually earn their keep – a confidence not felt about analytic philosophers who specialize in what they call "the core areas of philosophy," metaphysics and epistemology.

This favorable predisposition may not survive Ethics 101, but students who enter that course afraid of what they call "relativism" continue to provide an appreciative audience for books that will tell them, as Kant does, that morality has a special source – a special relation to something neither contingent nor historically locatable. The best recent book of this sort – Korsgaard's *The Sources of Normativity* – attempts both to reconstruct the morality–prudence wall that Dewey tried to tear down and to *prove* that our side is right – that the European Enlightenment was not just an historical contingency, but rather a rational necessity. Replying to Schneewind and other critics of her insistence on unconditionality, Korsgaard says,

To all of the fans of the embedded, the pragmatic, the contextual, and so on, who are always insisting that justifications must come to an end somewhere, Kant would answer that justifications can come to an end only with a law you yourself will, one you'd be prepared to will for everyone, because justifications must come to an end with you – with the dictate of your own mind. And in this, I stand with Kant.[18]

For Korsgaard, one's mind has a structure that transcendental philosophy can reveal. By revealing that structure, philosophy can provide a transcendental argument for the truth of Enlightenment morality[19] – an argument that will convince even Nazis and mafiosi if they just think hard and long enough. To be reflective, for Korsgaard, is to let one's mind work freely to explore the implications of its own existence, rather than being distracted by passion and prejudice.

Dewey agreed with the later Wittgenstein that we should avoid confusing questions about sources – which should always be treated as requests for causal explanation – with questions about justification. This is the confusion that Dewey and his follower Wilfrid Sellars diagnosed in empiricist epistemology. But the confusion is, of course, common to the empiricists, the Platonists and the Kantians. It consists in the attempt to split the soul or the mind up into faculties named "reason," "the senses," "the emotions," "the will" and the like and then to legitimize a controversial claim by saying that it has the support of the only relevant faculty. Empiricists argue that since the senses are our only windows on the world, only they can tell us what the world is like. The Platonists and the Kantians say that since unleashed desire is the source of moral evil, only something utterly distinct from desire can be the source of moral righteousness.

Korsgaard revels, as happily and unself-consciously as Kant himself, in faculty psychology. She says, for example, that "the relation of the thinking self to the acting self is one of legitimate authority,"[20] and would presumably say that any authority claimed by the passionate self would be illegitimate. Again, she says that "our identity as moral beings – as people who value themselves as human beings – stands behind our more particular practical identities."[21] It stands, so to speak, in the shadows behind my identity as parent, lover, businessman, patriot, mafioso, professor or Nazi, waiting to be revealed by reflection. How powerfully it makes itself felt depends, in Korsgaard's phrase, upon "how much of the light of reflection is on."[22]

Visual metaphors of this sort are as central to Korsgaard's thinking as to Plato's, but such metaphors are anathema to those who follow Dewey in thinking of the self as a self-reweaving and self-correcting network of beliefs and desires – a homeostatic mechanism. To see all inquiry (in physics and logic as well as in ethics) as such a search for homeostasis, for temporary reflective equilibrium, is to set aside the search for legitimizing faculties and, more generally, the search for sources. "Reason" is no more a source for concepts or judgments than is "sense experience" or "physical reality." The whole idea of legitimizing a concept or a judgment by finding out where it came from is a bad one.

Readers of Wittgenstein who are accustomed to treat "our concept of X" as synonymous with "our use of the word X" will be suspicious of Korsgaard's demand that philosophers tell us the source of moral concepts. For them, the question "What is the source of our uses of the normative terms we employ in our moral deliberations?" can only be interpreted as a request for historical background. Histories of moral reflection like Schneewind's, Charles Taylor's and Alasdair MacIntyre's, rather than books like Korsgaard's own, will be thought of as providing appropriate answers to it.

Wittgenstcinians will be especially suspicious when Korsgaard goes on to ask: "Where do we get these ideas that outstrip the world we experience and seem to call into question, to render judgment on it, to say that it does not measure up, that it is not what it ought to be?" Korsgaard says that it is clear that we do not get these ideas from experience. But the notion of getting ideas from experience requires us to dredge up all the dogmas of empiricism, as well as an obsolete Lockean building-block picture of language learning. The same goes for the assumption that there is a nice, neat distinction between descriptive ideas and normative ideas, the former coming from experience and the latter from a less obvious source.

Wittgensteinians think that we get ideas that outstrip the actual from the same place we get ideas that delimit the actual – from the people who taught us how to use the words that are used to formulate those ideas. From this perspective, the question "What are the sources of normativity?" has no more appeal than "What are the sources of facticity?" For a norm is just a certain kind of fact – a fact about what people do – seen from the inside.

Suppose that, as a matter of contingent fact, a community to which I am proud to belong despises people who do A. Members of this community often say they would rather be dead than do A. My identification with that community leads me to say "We [or "People of our sort" or "People I respect"] don't do A." When I say that, using the first person, I am reporting a norm. When I stand back from my community, in my capacity as anthropologist or intellectual historian, and say "They would rather die than do A," I am reporting a fact. The source of the norm is, so to speak, my internalization of the fact. Or, if you like, the source of the fact is the externalization of the norm.

This was Sellars' account of the relation between fact and value, and of the moral point of view. For Sellars, as for Dewey, the former relation was sufficiently clarified by pointing out the relation between "Young men in Papua feel obliged to hunt heads" and "All of us young men here in Papua would be ashamed of ourselves if we did not hunt heads." It is the token-reflexive pronoun that makes the big difference, and the only difference.[23]

Korsgaard herself seems to come close to this view when she says that the answer to her question about the sources of normativity "must appeal, in a deep way, to the sense of who we are, to our sense of our identity."[24] She goes on to say that one condition on "a successful answer to the normative question" is that "it must show that sometimes doing the wrong thing is as bad or worse than death." She adds that "the only thing that could be as bad or worse than death is something that for us amounts to death – not being ourselves any more."

Dewey could agree completely with this point, but he would think that once it has been made, we know all that we shall ever know about the sources of normativity. So Deweyans will regret that Korsgaard thinks that there is more to be discovered, and that only such a discovery will enable philosophers to meet the challenge of an agent facing a difficult moral demand who asks "Why must I do it?" Korsgaard tells us that "an agent who doubts whether he must really do what morality says also doubts whether it so bad to be morally bad."

But one will take the question "Why should I be moral?" seriously only if one thinks that the answer "Because you might not be able to live with yourself if you thought yourself immoral" is not good enough. But why should it not suffice? Only, it seems to me, because the person who doubts that she should be moral is already in the process of cobbling together a new identity for herself – one that does not commit her to doing the thing that her old identity took to be obligatory.

Huck Finn, for example, fears that he may not be able to live with himself if he does not help return Jim to slavery. But he winds up giving it a try. He would not be so willing, presumably, if he were completely unable to imagine a new practical identity – the identity of one who takes loyalty to friends as releasing one from legal and conventional obligations. That, presumably, is the identity Huck will claim when explaining to St. Peter why he should not be sent to hell as a thief. Analogously, a Catholic doctor who thinks she would rather die than kill a fetus may find herself hastily weaving a new practical identity for herself when she turns out to be a desperate rape victim's only hope.

Socrates was able to make the thesis that nobody knowingly does evil sound plausible only because most of us share Huck's, or my imagined doctor's, ability to whip up a new practical identity to suit the occasion. Most of us have had experience with doing just that. We find Socrates himself explaining, in the *Apology*, that he has spent his life fashioning a new identity for himself, and that now he would rather die than be what his judges call "moral" – that is, revert to being the person whom he and they were brought up to be. This new identity may well have looked to Socrates' audience like a rationalization of neurotic perversity, just as Huck's new-found identity would have looked like a rationalization of moral weakness to the local sheriff.

Korsgaard thinks that there is an ahistorical criterion for distinguishing a rationalization of weakness from a heartening example of moral progress. Deweyans think that there is only the criterion of how well or badly we ourselves can fit Huck's or Socrates' new practical identities together with our own. There is only, if you like, the judgment of history – that particular history that leads up to us, with the practical identities we currently have. To paraphrase the old saw about treason, Huck's and Socrates' identities prospered, and none now dare call them rationalizations of weakness or perversity. By contrast, consider young Hans, a German soldier who was assigned to murder Jewish children found hiding in the hedgerows of Poland. He hastily constructed a new practical identity for himself – that of the good, obedient servant of the Fuehrer. Thanks to the might of the Allied armies, this identity did *not* prosper.

On the Deweyan view I am sketching, the pragmatic cash value of the question "Why should I be moral?" is "Should I retain the practical identity I presently have, or rather develop and cherish the new identity I shall have to assume if I do what my present practical identity forbids?" On this way of thinking of the matter, the question "Why should I be moral?" is a question that arises only when two or more alternative practical identities are under consideration. That is why the question almost never arises in traditional societies of the sort in which the jurymen who tried Socrates were raised. These jurors could make little sense of the question, and therefore little sense of Socrates' life.

But the question arises in modern pluralistic societies all the time – not to mention societies in which cruel tyrants suddenly take control. In those societies, however, it is not usually thought of as a question for philosophers to answer by giving a satisfactory theory of the sources of normativity. Rather, it is a question about which of the many available suppliers of alternative practical identities I should buy from.

On my construal, then, the question "Why should I be moral?" is typically a preliminary to asking "What morality should I have?" The latter question is itself a way of asking "Should I continue to think certain actions to be as bad as or worse than death?" This is, of course, quite different from Korsgaard's Kantian construal. She thinks it is a question to be answered by looking not at the relative attractions of various communities and identities, but at something that exists independently of the historical contingencies that create communities and identities.

To see better how this question looks from the Deweyan point of view I am recommending, consider an analogy between "Why should I be moral?" and "Why should I think this podium and these chairs to be real?" This Cartesian question, Wittgensteinians like Bouwsma have suggested, should be taken seriously only if an alternative account of the appearances is suggested: for example, that these items of furniture are actually papier-mâché imitations of the real thing, or that they are illusions produced by needles stuck in my brain. Some such concrete and detailed account of my temptation to believe in their reality has to be offered before I shall bother to consider the claim that they are unreal. Once such an account is provided, then an alternative candidate for local reality – perhaps stage setters or mad doctors – may become plausible. But to peruse the merits of these alternative candidates is not to do philosophy. No exploration of what "real" means or of the nature of reality is likely to help.

Analogously, I am suggesting that the question "Why should I be moral?" should be taken seriously only if an alternative morality is beginning to sound plausible. But to peruse the merits of these alternative candidates is not a task for the sort of philosopher who purports to tell us more about the meanings of the terms "real" and "moral" – the sort who investigates the "natures" of these concepts.

Korsgaard defines "a theory of moral concepts" as an answer to three questions: what moral concepts mean or contain, what they apply to and where they come from.[25] On the view I am suggesting, only the second of these questions is a good one. The question of what moral concepts mean is as bad as the questions of what such concepts as "real podium," "cardboard imitation podium" and "needle inserted in the podium-perceiving area of my brain" mean. Until somebody exhibits concrete puzzlement about when to use which term, the concepts do not need clarification.

A romantic and troubled adolescent who wonders whether to try to build her moral identity around the figures of Alyosha and Father Zossima, or rather around the figures of Ivan and Zarathustra, may be helped by literary critics and intellectual historians to see more clearly what these figures were committed to and how they thought of themselves. Hans, when sent to the *Einsatzkommando,* may be helped by a kindly anti-Nazi sergeant, or an equally kindly pro-Nazi chaplain, in the same way. This help can, if you like, be thought of as conceptual clarification. But it is hard to see how Kantian philosophers are going to get into the act. For their explanations of what "moral" means seem irrelevant to these adolescents' problems. Analogously, explanations of what "real" or "true" means, or accounts of the source of these normative notions, would seem irrelevant to someone who has begun to wonder whether she may not be the victim of a mad, needle-wielding brain surgeon.

Someone as impatient with Korsgaard's Kantian questions as I am finds ancient moral philosophy – focusing as it did on choosing heroes, debating which figures a youth should try to model himself upon – of more interest than the kind of thing you usually get in Ethics 101. For such debates concern alternative moral identities – and thus provide moral issues to get one's teeth into – in a way that debates about the alternative merits of the categorical imperative and the utilitarian principle do not. Discussion of the relative merits of Alyosha and Ivan seems continuous with debate concerning those of Odysseus and Achilles, or of Socrates and Pericles. Discussions of deontology versus consequentialism, or of whether our sense of moral obligation originates in reason or in sentiment, seem pedantic distractions from discussions of historical or literary personages.

In making this point, I am echoing some things that Schneewind has said. In a paper called "What Has Moral Philosophy Done for Us... Lately?"[26] he takes up some of my own doubts about moral philosophy and says that one thing that can be said for this area of culture is that "the creations of the philosopher's conceptual imagination have been as vivid and efficacious as the characters made up by the novelist or the tragedian." He cites the Epicurean and the Stoic as examples, and then goes on to say that "Philosophical portraits of the good life pick up on the pre-theoretical attitudes that we are predisposed to have about how we want to live. By showing them how to think them through, they can help us as much as fictions can to self-understanding and self-critique."

I agree with the remarks I have just quoted from Schneewind, although I should be inclined to add "yes, but no more than works of history and of fiction can, and perhaps not as efficiently." But when Schneewind goes to say that when we try to articulate resemblances between ourselves and Socrates or Mr. Casaubon we "may need to move beyond the case to something like a statement of principle," I become more dubious. Some of us, those with a taste for principles, may need to do this. But for reasons Schneewind himself adumbrated in the 1968 essay I quoted earlier, I am not sure that such needs should be encouraged.

As I see it, we almost never do what Singer thinks we ought to do: reject the moral views of the community in which we have been raised because we have found what Singer calls "a soundly based moral theory" – at least if such a theory consists in a series of inferences from some broad general principle that strikes us as intuitively plausible. Rather, when we find such a principle plausible, and realize that accepting it would lead us to change our ways, we attempt to obtain what John Rawls calls "reflective equilibrium." That is, we go back and forth between the proposed principle and our old intuitions, trying to fabricate a new practical identity that will do some justice to both. This involves imagining what our community would be like if it changed its ways, and what we would be like as a member of this reformed community. It is a detailed comparison of imagined selves, situations and communities that does the trick, not argument from principles. Formulation of general principles is sometimes useful, but only as a tool for summarizing the results of imagining such alternatives.

Singer and many other contemporary moral philosophers seem to imagine that somebody could decide to overcome her reluctance to perform abortions, or decide to help change the laws so that abortion becomes a capital crime, simply by being struck by the plausibility of some grand general principle that dictates one or the other decision. But this is not the way moral progress or moral regress occurs. It is not how people change their practical identities – their sense of what they would rather die than do.

The advantage that well-read, reflective, leisured people have when it comes to deciding about the right thing to do is that they are more imaginative, not that they are more rational. Their advantage lies in being aware of many possible practical identities, and not just one or two. Such people are able to put themselves in the shoes of many different sorts of people – Huck before he decided whether to turn Jim in and Huck afterward, Socrates and Socrates' accusers, Christ and Pilate, Kant and Dewey, Homeric heroes and Christian ascetics. Moral philosophers have provided us with some moral identities to consider, historians and biographers with others, novelists with still others.

Just as there are many imaginable individual practical identities, so there are many communal practical identities. Reflective and well-read people read history, anthropology and historical novels in order to get a sense of what it would be like to have been a loyal and unquestioning member of a community we regard as primitive. They read science fiction novels in order to get a sense of what it might be like to have grown up in communities more advanced than our own. They read moral philosophers not to find knock-down arguments, or to become more rational or more clear or more rigorous, but to find handy ways of summarizing the various reactions they have had to these various imaginings.

Let me conclude by returning to the question with which I began: the question to which I think Singer and others give bad answers. As I see it, specialists in moral philosophy should not think of themselves as people who have better arguments or clearer thoughts than most, but simply as people who have spent a lot of time talking over some of the issues that trouble people faced with hard decisions about what to do. Moral philosophers have made themselves very useful in hospitals discussing issues created by recent advances in medical technology, as well as in many other arenas in which public policy is debated. Singer himself has done admirable work of this sort. These philosophers are perfectly respectable members of the academy and of society. They no more need to be embarrassed by demands for justification of their place at the public trough than do anthropologists, historians, theologians or poets. It is only when they get up on their high Kantian horse that we should view them with suspicion.

Notes

1. Peter Singer, "Philosophers Are Back on the Job," *The New York Times Magazine*, July 7, 1974, pp. 6–7, 17–20.
2. Ibid., p. 19.
3. Ibid., p. 20.
4. Ibid., p. 20.
5. Christine Korsgaard, *Creating the Kingdom of Ends* (Cambridge University Press, 1999), p. 23.
6. John Dewey, *Outline of a Critical Theory of Ethics*, in *The Early Works of John Dewey*, vol. 3 (Southern Illinois University Press, 1971), p. 295.
7. J. B. Schneewind, "Moral Knowledge and Moral Principles," in *Revisions: Changing Perspectives in Moral Philosophy*, ed. Stanley Hauerwas and Alasdair MacIntyre (Notre Dame University Press, 1983), p. 116.
8. Ibid., p. 117.
9. J. B. Schneewind, "Korsgaard and the Unconditional in Morality," *Ethics* 109 (1998), p. 46.
10. Ibid.
11. Ibid., p. 47.
12. J. B. Schneewind, *The Invention of Autonomy: A History of Modern Moral Philosophy* (Cambridge University Press, 1998).
13. Ibid., p. 468.
14. Schneewind, "Moral Knowledge and Moral Principles," p. 126.
15. Ibid., p. 120.
16. Wilfrid Sellars, *Science, Perception and Reality* (Routledge and Kegan Paul, 1963), p. 170.
17. See Arthur Fine, "The View from Nowhere in Particular," *The Proceedings and Addresses of the American Philosophical Association* (1998); Richard Rorty, "Arthur Fine and Non-Representationalist Philosophy" in *Reverberations of the Shaky Game: Festschrift for Arthur Fine*, ed. R. Jones and P. Ehrlich (Oxford University Press, forthcoming.)
18. Christine Korsgaard, "Motivation, Metaphysics, and the Value of the Self: A Reply to Ginsburg, Guyer and Schneewind," *Ethics* 109 (1998), p. 66.
19. Cf. Christine Korsgaard, *The Sources of Normativity* (Cambridge University Press, 1996), p. 123.

20. Ibid., p. 165.
21. Ibid., p. 121.
22. Ibid., p. 257.
23. See Wilfrid Sellars, *Science and Metaphysics* (Routledge and Kegan Paul, 1963), Ch. 7.
24. Korsgaard, *The Sources of Normativity*, p. 17.
25. Ibid., p. 11.
26. J. B. Schneewind, "What Has Moral Philosophy Done for Us...Lately?" Lecture given at the University of Michigan Institute for the Humanities, February 2000; available on video at http://ethics.sandiego.edu/video/ Schneewind. Published in German as "Vom Nutzen der Moralphilosophie – Rorty zum Trotz," tr. Harald Koehl, in *Deutsche Zeitschrift für Philosophie* 48 (2000), pp. 855–66.